DESEGREGATION OF THE
UNITED STATES ARMED FORCES

DESEGREGATION
OF THE
U. S. ARMED FORCES

Fighting on Two Fronts
1939-1953

BY

Richard M. Dalfiume

UNIVERSITY OF MISSOURI PRESS
COLUMBIA • MISSOURI

Standard Book Number 8262 – 8318 – 7
Library of Congress Card Number 68 – 54897
Printed in the United States of America
Copyright © 1969 by The Curators of the University of Missouri
Second printing 1975

To
Jane and Julia Leigh

Acknowledgments

I AM INDEBTED to Professor Richard S. Kirkendall of the University of Missouri for his encouragement and constructive criticism from the beginning to the end of this study. Professor Allen F. Davis of Temple University also read the manuscript and offered valuable suggestions for revision. Two of my colleagues at The University of Wisconsin, Edward Coffman and Robert Starobin, gave of their time and wisdom to improve portions of the manuscript. For moral support and criticism from the inception of this study, my thanks go to two former graduate student colleagues, Professors Monte Poen of Northern Arizona University and Alonzo Hamby of Ohio University.

An expression of appreciation is due to the Harry S Truman Institute for a grant that in large part financed the research. Dr. Philip C. Brooks and his efficient staff at The Truman Library Institute and Dr. Elizabeth Drewry and her staff at the Franklin D. Roosevelt Library extended every courtesy to me. An equally pleasant reception awaited me at the libraries of Yale University, Princeton University, Columbia University, and the National Archives. Mrs. Susan Stege and Mrs. Jo Ann Francis of the Department of History of The University of Wisconsin did an efficient job of typing the final manuscript.

Many individuals within the Federal Government aided me in overcoming obstacles placed in my way by some in the Army who did not want to make official records available. R. A. Winnacker, Historian, Department of Defense; Robert E. Jordan, III, formerly in the office of the Assistant Secretary of Defense; and Stetson Conn, Office of the Chief of Military History, opened many doors. James C. Evans, Counselor in the Office of the Assistant Secretary of Defense, deserves my special appreciation for his hospitality, his sustained interest in my study, and for the many hours of time he gave in answering questions.

R.M.D.

The University of Wisconsin
May, 1968

Contents

Introduction

THE PURPOSE OF THIS STUDY is to describe and explain the change in the racial policy of the military services and the Negro's reaction to this policy from 1939 to 1953. In accomplishing this goal, I hope also to shed some light on American race relations during the forgotten years of the Civil Rights Revolution. During the years 1939 to 1953 the United States armed forces moved from a policy of restricting and segregating the Negro to one of equal opportunity and integration. This was truly a social revolution, the extent of which was summarized several years ago and remains accurate to this day:

Today the national armed forces are the most integrated major segment of American life. Great numbers of Americans, Negro and white, obtain their first contact with nonsegregation after they enter uniform, whether stationed North or South.[1]

This revolution was not achieved without expenditure of a great deal of time and effort. Throughout American history the black American viewed his military service in the nation's conflicts as proof of his loyalty and as a brief for his claim to full citizenship. White Americans appear to have realized this, and they continually sought to restrict or downgrade the black soldier's military service. In the Dred Scott decision, for example, Chief Justice of the Supreme Court Roger Taney cited the fact that Negroes were excluded from the state militia as part of his argument that they were not to be considered citi-

---

[1] Jack Greenberg, *Race Relations and American Law*, 355.

1

zens. In the United States it has always been assumed that citizens have the obligation to participate in the armed forces. If a group was denied the opportunity to fulfill this obligation, this restriction could provide a rationale for denying that group its full rights of citizenship. Aware of this reasoning, the Negro has sought to participate in America's wars in the hope that his sacrifices would bring the reward of increased rights.

With the World War II crisis of 1939–1945, the questions of restriction, discrimination, and segregation in the armed forces became one of two major issues for black Americans. Employment discrimination was the other, and this subject has been investigated by several authors.[2] Although employment discrimination was the main bread-and-butter issue for Negroes in World War II, discrimination and segregation in the armed forces was the more emotionally charged concern. What a hypocritical and paradoxical position for the United States — fighting with a rigidly segregated military force for the four freedoms and against an enemy preaching a master race ideology! This manifest difference between the American creed and practice provided Negroes with a powerful argument in their fight for equality. The psychological impact of the war's democratic rhetoric on the nation's largest minority has heretofore been overlooked. Ignoring these earlier years and the seeds of militancy planted in them, most writers claim that a Negro "revolution" or "revolt" occurred in 1954, 1955, 1960, or 1963.

By World War II the military had developed a racial stereotype of the Negro soldier — a military version of white supremacy — that exerted a strong influence on the use of black manpower. Military planners constantly stated that their racial policies were based upon the requirements of efficiency and that they were not concerned with social problems or social theories. The opposite was in fact the truth. Negro soldiers were restricted to certain kinds of military duty because of a widespread belief in their inherent racial inferiority. Furthermore, black service-

---

[2] Malcolm Ross, *All Manner of Men*; Louis C. Kesselman, *The Social Politics of FEPC*; Louis Ruchames, *Race, Jobs, and Politics*; Herbert Garfinkel, *When Negroes March: The March on Washington Movement in the Organizational Politics of FEPC*.

men were rigidly segregated because it was felt that most whites insisted that this be so. Segregation seemed necessary to prevent bloody racial conflict and a reduction of the armed services' effectiveness. This kind of thinking obscured the tremendous waste and inefficiency that were the actual results of segregation. Racism was not peculiar to the military; it was only a reflection of the strong thread of racism running through the general American mind. Charles E. Silberman, one of the most poignant critics of American race relations, has recently reminded us that the United States "is a racist society in a sense and to a degree that we have refused so far to admit, much less face." [3]

Segregation and discrimination in the armed forces continued into the post-World War II period and remained a grievance for black Americans. But the postwar era witnessed the emergence of several forces that made it impossible for the Federal Government and the American people to ignore the race issue any longer. The United States became, in the eyes of itself and others, the leader of the free world, and its race problem was a handicap in the Cold War battle over the destiny of the nonwhite people of the world. The American Negro came out of World War II with a determination to change his status. Coupled with this determination was a new political power, derived from the strategic location of Negro voting blocs in northern states with large electoral votes. In addition, numerous white Americans came to the conclusion that the deferred commitment of equal rights must be fulfilled at last. All of these forces converged in the Administration of Harry S Truman.

The Truman Administration's legislative proposals and actions in the field of civil rights set the pattern for a continuing involvement on the federal level that is still evident today. No longer was it the Federal Government's policy to condone or extend segregation. Of the Truman Administration's precedent-breaking actions in the civil rights field, desegregation of the armed forces was among the first. The military services were a logical place to begin adjustment of black grievances. Negroes

---

[3] Charles E. Silberman, *Crisis in Black and White*, 9–10.

had long been incensed over segregation and discrimination in this part of the government. Furthermore, the President, as Commander-in-chief, could move in this area without the consent of a reluctant Congress. Truman's Executive Order 9981 of 1948, which established the President's Committee on Equality of Treatment and Opportunity in the Armed Services, led to military integration; it was one of the first federal actions against segregation, coming six years before the 1954 school desegregation decision. This example of accomplishing integration by executive authority also provided a precedent for the Eisenhower, Kennedy, and Johnson administrations.

The success of military integration, proven in the Korean War, provided a powerful argument against the conservative position that government cannot legislate mores. Integration actually led to a decrease of racial conflict and prejudice within the military services. There is some evidence that the Supreme Court was interested in this successful experience in the period when it began to nibble away at the "separate but equal" doctrine. In 1950, for example, members of the Court gathered evidence from the President's Committee on Equality of Treatment and Opportunity in the Armed Services prior to some important decisions pointing toward a reversal of the separate but equal position. In 1954, before the epochal decision on school desegregation, members of the Court read in manuscript form journalist Lee Nichols' *Breakthrough on the Color Front* (1954), the first book-length account of military integration.[4] Desegregation of the military was indeed an important precedent for the Federal Government's new role in race relations.

---

[4] This is revealed in Lee Nichols to the United States Information Agency, January, 1963, copy in the possession of Mr. James C. Evans, Counselor, Office of the Assistant Secretary of Defense (Manpower).

CHAPTER I

Developing Traditions

Frow the beginning of a military tradition in this country, Negro manpower has been used for military purposes. Most of those who have studied the problem have discerned a desire on the part of white Americans to restrict the Negro's participation in military affairs until an emergency or crisis develops; then black manpower is utilized as a military necessity.[1] This pattern was established in the colonial militia, where each colony followed a policy of excluding Negroes as soldiers. When emergencies such as Indian threats arose and there was immediate need for manpower, however, most colonies saw fit to overlook these exclusion laws and enlisted Negroes. When the Continental Army was established at the beginning of the American Revolution, Negroes were excluded. Once again, as white volunteers became harder to enlist, this policy was reversed, and approximately five thousand Negroes served with the American revolutionary forces.[2]

---

[1] Benjamin Quarles, *The Negro in the American Revolution*, vii; Dudley Taylor Cornish, *The Sable Arm: Negro Troops in the Union Army, 1861–1865*, ix; Robert J. Dwyer, "The Negro in the United States Army: His Changing Role and Status," *Sociology and Social Research*, 38 (November, 1953), 103–12; L. D. Reddick, "The Negro Policy of the United States Army, 1775–1945," *Journal of Negro History*, 34 (January, 1949), 9–29.

[2] Benjamin Quarles, "The Colonial Militia and Negro Manpower," *Mississippi Valley Historical Review*, 45 (March, 1959), 643–52; John

With the conclusion of the Revolution, official policy barred Negroes from the militia and from the regular armed forces of the new nation. Military necessity apparently continued to override official policy, for black soldiers and sailors served in the 1798–1800 naval war with France and in the War of 1812.[3] It was not until the Civil War, however, that the Negro soldier was made a permanent part of the United States military establishment. A recent writer on this period has claimed that of all the efforts by Negroes in their own behalf, the "most important" was "the contribution of Negro soldiers [that] helped the North win the war and convinced many Northern people that the Negro deserved to be treated as a man and an equal."[4]

As in past wars, the idea of using Negroes as soldiers did not receive a sympathetic hearing in the North at the beginning of the Civil War. Most Northern whites did not at first view the war as involving the Negro; Lincoln, intent on maintaining the loyalty of the border states, refused to sanction any policy — including the use of Negro soldiers — that would support the view that this was an abolitionist war. By 1863, as the war became one for abolishment of slavery and as more military manpower was needed, Lincoln swung to the policy of utilizing Negroes as soldiers. By 1865 black soldiers were doing a good share of the fighting for the Union, comprising 9 to 10 per cent of the Army's strength. In recognition of their services, Congress made Negro units a part of the Regular Army for the

---

Hope Franklin, *From Slavery to Freedom: A History of American Negroes*, 130–36; Quarles, *The Negro in the American Revolution, passim.* Many Negro soldiers in New England were integrated into white units during the Revolution, but for an all-Negro unit, see Lorenzo J. Greene, "Some Observations on the Black Regiment of Rhode Island in the American Revolution," *Journal of Negro History*, 37 (April, 1952), 142–72. And for the not insignificant role of Negroes in the Navy, see Luther P. Jackson, "Virginia Negro Soldiers and Seamen in the American Revolution," *Journal of Negro History*, 27 (July, 1942), 247–87.

[3] Leon F. Litwack, *North of Slavery: The Free Negro in the Free States, 1790–1860*, 31, 32; Franklin, *From Slavery to Freedom*, 168–69; Horace Mann Bond, "The Negro in the Armed Forces of the United States Prior to World War I," *Journal of Negro Education*, 12 (Summer, 1943), 271–78.

[4] James M. McPherson, *The Negro's Civil War*, ix.

first time — the Ninth and Tenth U.S. Cavalry Regiments and the Twenty-fourth and Twenty-fifth Infantry Regiments were established by law.[5]

From the end of the Civil War until the Spanish-American War, the four Regular Army Negro units fought Indians and garrisoned outposts in the West. Some idea of the extent of their service can be derived from the fact that of ninety-three medals and commendations for bravery won by Army enlisted men between 1866 and 1892, twelve were won by Negroes. Black citizens were also proud of the role of their soldiers in the Spanish-American War. The Ninth and Tenth Cavalry, particularly, won fame by coming to the aid of Theodore Roosevelt's "Rough Riders" during a critical moment at San Juan Hill.[6]

By the beginning of World War I, Negro suspicions about the treatment of black soldiers were aroused by the Brownsville episode. In August, 1906, the Negro soldiers of the Twenty-fifth Infantry rioted in protest against their treatment by the white citizens of Brownsville, Texas. When the guilty men could not be found, President Theodore Roosevelt ordered the dishonorable discharge of three companies. Southerners in Congress took this opportunity to recommend that Negroes be barred completely from the Army and to attack the record of Negro troops in general. Negroes were deeply resentful toward Roosevelt, and the feeling grew among them that the South was set on discrediting their right to citizenship by discrediting the fighting ability of Negro soldiers.[7]

[5] Cornish, *The Sable Arm*, and "The Union Army as a School for Negroes," *Journal of Negro History*, 37 (October, 1952), 368–82; Bell Irvin Wiley, *Southern Negroes: 1861–1865*; Benjamin Quarles, *The Negro in the Civil War*; Fred A. Shannon, "The Federal Government and the Negro Soldier, 1861–1865," *Journal of Negro History*, 11 (October, 1926), 563–83; Herbert Aptheker, "The Negro in the Union Navy," *Journal of Negro History*, 32 (April, 1947), 169–200.

[6] "The Colored Soldier in the U.S. Army: Prepared in the Historical Section, Army War College, May, 1942" (typewritten manuscript in the Office of the Chief of Military History), 11–18; Rayford W. Logan, *The Betrayal of the Negro: From Rutherford B. Hayes to Woodrow Wilson*, 335; Franklin, *From Slavery to Freedom*, 415–16.

[7] Emma Lou Thornbrough, "The Brownsville Episode and the Negro

Before America became involved in World War I, Negroes were eager to participate in the expansion of the armed forces. In 1916 they demanded that two new artillery regiments and two new infantry regiments be specified for Negroes.[8] When Negroes were denied an opportunity to attend the peacetime officers' training camp at Plattsburg, New York, they asked for a separate Negro officers' training camp. A group headed by Dr. Joel E. Spingarn, white chairman of the executive committee of the National Association for the Advancement of Colored People (NAACP), attempted to get the War Department to agree to organizing such a camp. Spingarn was finally assured by the War Department that assistance for setting up such a camp would be provided if he could secure two hundred young college men willing to attend. There was an immediate outburst by the Negro press and public against Spingarn's proposal. He was accused of wanting to establish a "Jim Crow" camp when integrated camps should be the goal. Spingarn defended himself by saying that "the camp is intended to fight segregation" as the "south does not want the Negroes to have any kind of military training." W. E. B. DuBois, editor of the NAACP organ, *The Crisis*, defended the separate training camp by pointing out that without it, if war came soon, Negroes would be compelled to serve under white officers; the choice was one between the lesser of two evils — no segregated camp and no Negro officers, or a segregated camp and Negro officers.[9]

Soon after the United States entered the war, fourteen officers' training camps were established for whites but none for Negroes. The students and faculty of Howard University organized a protest group that became the Central Committee of Negro College Men, representing students of a number of Negro colleges. In a few days the committee obtained names of fifteen

---

Vote," *Mississippi Valley Historical Review*, 44 (December, 1957), 469–93.

[8] *The Crisis*, 12 (May, 1916), 40.

[9] Emmett J. Scott, *The American Negro in the World War*, 82–83; Franklin, *From Slavery to Freedom*, 449; "The Perpetual Dilemma," *The Crisis*, 13 (April, 1917), 270–71; "Officers," *The Crisis*, 14 (June, 1917), 60–61.

hundred young Negroes willing to take officers' training, and these were presented to the War Department together with a plea for an officers' training camp. The committee also talked to congressmen and got the endorsement of three hundred to their proposal.

Negro educators held conferences with government officials and sent messages to President Woodrow Wilson. Secretary of War Newton Baker informed Negroes in May, 1917, that a Negro officer camp would be established. The Central Committee of Negro College Men interpreted its victory as a great challenge. In a press release the Committee pointed out old charges that Negroes couldn't fight unless led by white officers. The "race is on trial":

Just think a moment how serious the situation is. Peal the tocsin; stand by the race. If we fail, our enemies will dub us COWARDS for all time; and we can never win our rightful place. But if we succeed — then eternal success.[10]

American Negroes were affected by the rhetoric of the war just as white Americans were; all were anxious "to save the world for democracy." Shortly after the United States entered the war, Negro leaders from many different organizations met in Washington and adopted resolutions to express the "attitudes and aspirations" that they thought fitting for black Americans in wartime. The *real* cause of the war was "the despising of the darker races by dominant groups of men." Despite the poor record of the United States, England, and the other Allies in dealing with colored people, "we earnestly believe that the greatest hope for ultimate democracy . . . lies on the side of the allies. . . ." All Negroes should "join heartily in the fight for world liberty . . . , [and] this despite our deep sympathy with the reasonable and deep-seated feeling of revolt among Negroes at the persistent insult and discrimination to which they are subject and will be subject even when they do their patriotic duty." Unswerving loyalty need not "lead us to abate our just complaints and just demands." These included the right to serve in the Army and receive officer training, an immediate

---

[10] Scott, *The American Negro in the World War*, 84–86, 88–89.

end to lynching, the right to vote, universal and free public education, the abolition of segregated transportation facilities, and the repeal of segregation ordinances.[11]

Black Americans responded enthusiastically to the demands of the war. Before they were allowed to enter the Army through the draft, some Negroes went to Canada and enlisted. In Mobile, Alabama, one Negro offered himself and nine hundred others for infantry service; more than six hundred Negroes in Chattanooga, Tennessee, met and pledged their services to the government; patriotic meetings were held by eight hundred Negroes in Augusta, Georgia, and by three thousand in Houston, Texas. Kelly Miller, the noted Negro educator and essayist, described how the war and its slogans of democracy aroused in the Negro "hopes and ambitions that he would enter as a full participant in the fruition of that democracy which he was called upon to sustain and perpetuate."[12] W.E.B. DuBois expressed this extreme optimism when he claimed that "the tide against the Negro in the United States has been turned, and . . . from now on we may expect to see the walls of prejudice gradually crumble before the onslaught of common sense and racial progress."[13] Prominent whites lent support to this optimistic view of the war's impact on race relations. For example, in 1918 Theodore Roosevelt was telling Negro audiences that America's war aim of securing greater international justice in the world would lead to a "juster and fairer treatment in this country of colored people."[14]

A high spirit of optimism and loyalty was not easy for Negroes to maintain in the early months of the war. As the crisis deepened, race relations seemed to worsen. On July 28, 1917, fifteen thousand Negroes paraded silently in New York, protesting lynchings and race riots against Negroes in Waco, Texas; Memphis, Tennessee; and East St. Louis, Illinois. In Houston, Texas, Negro troops of the Twenty-fourth Infantry rioted and

[11] "Resolutions of the Washington Conference," *The Crisis*, 14 (June, 1917), 59–60.
[12] *The Crisis*, 14 (June, 1917), 85; Kelly Miller, *The Everlasting Stain*, 32.
[13] "The Turning of the Tide," *The Crisis*, 15 (December, 1917), 77.
[14] Scott, *The American Negro in the World War*, 20.

killed seventeen whites in protest against their treatment by local civilians. Thirteen were hanged for murder and mutiny, forty-one were imprisoned for life, and forty others were held for further investigation.[15] To bolster Negro morale the Wilson Administration announced the appointment of a Negro adviser to the Secretary of War. The man chosen to fill this position was Booker T. Washington's former confidential secretary, Emmett J. Scott.[16]

Most Negro leaders counseled complete devotion to the war effort and the muffling of grievances, although many of the rank and file did not agree.[17] In *The Crisis* DuBois wrote an editorial that became famous:

Let us not hesitate. Let us, while the war lasts, forget our special grievances and close our ranks shoulder to shoulder with our white fellow citizens and the allied nations that are fighting for democracy. We make no ordinary sacrifice, but we make it gladly and willingly with our eyes lifted to the hills.[18]

In the following month DuBois made it more explicit that he thought the Negro should forget his own grievances for the duration of the war. The Negro's first duty was clear: "We shall not bargain with our loyalty. We shall not profiteer with our country's blood."[19]

Many militant Negroes did not appreciate DuBois' advice. The Washington, D. C., branch of the NAACP adopted a resolution scoring the "Close Ranks" editorial for being "not timely [and] inconsistent with the work and the spirit of the Association." This group saw no reason for "stultifying our consciences [or] pretending or professing to be ignorant of, or indifferent to, the acts of indignity and injustice continually heaped

---

[15] "The Negro Silent Parade," *The Crisis*, 14 (September, 1917), 241–42; Edgar A. Schuler, "The Houston Race Riot, 1917," *Journal of Negro History*, 24 (July, 1944), 301–38.

[16] Henry Blumenthal, "Woodrow Wilson and the Race Question," *Journal of Negro History*, 48 (January, 1963), 1–21; Scott, *The American Negro in the World War*, 40–48.

[17] See Scott, *The American Negro in the World War*, 411.

[18] "Close Ranks," *The Crisis*, 16 (July, 1918), 111.

[19] "A Philosophy in Time of War," *The Crisis*, 16 (August, 1918), 164.

upon us, or by admitting that they are to be excused or forgotten until they are discontinued."[20] Other individual Negroes and segments of the Negro press attacked DuBois and accused him of "selling out." The suspicion arose partly because, about the time the "Close Ranks" editorial was published, DuBois had been offered a captain's commission by the War Department. DuBois maintained that the two events were not connected, and he continued to uphold his original position. *"The Crisis says, first your Country, then your Rights,"* DuBois wrote in a later editorial. The whole event illustrates the anxiety and suspicion in the Negro community.[21]

This anxiety and suspicion fed primarily on reports and rumors of discriminatory treatment of Negro soldiers. Discrimination occurred at the beginning of the process of becoming a soldier — in the draft. In the South, Negroes who were physically unfit for service or who were entitled to exemption from the draft were railroaded into the Army by all-white draft boards. Three entire local boards had to be removed by the Secretary of War for such discrimination.

Since the opinion was prevalent in the Army that Negroes were fit only for labor duty, there was a tendency to assign Negroes to stevedore regiments and labor battalions, no matter what their education or qualifications. The white South resented the stationing of large numbers of Negro troops there, and many petitions to the War Department requested their removal. Resentment was especially strong against the stationing of Northern Negroes in the South; considerable friction was caused by the whites' determination that these "uppity" Negroes should "know their place" and keep it.[22]

A common premise in the Army was that Southern white

[20] *The Crisis*, 16 (September, 1918), 218.

[21] "A Momentous Proposal," *The Crisis*, 16 (September, 1918), 215–16; "Our Special Grievances," *The Crisis*, 16 (September, 1918), 216–17. For more on the controversy surrounding the "Close Ranks" editorial and the offer of a commission in the Army, see Elliott M. Rudwick, *W.E.B. DuBois: A Study in Minority Group Leadership*, 202–7; Francis L. Broderick, *W.E.B. DuBois: Negro Leader in a Time of Crisis*, 109.

[22] Scott, *The American Negro in the World War*, 59–62, 72, 75–81, 102–3, 428, 455.

noncommissioned and commissioned officers made the best leaders for Negro soldiers because they "understood" them. One result of this policy was resentment by black soldiers of their white leaders, who regularly called them "nigger," "coon," and "darkey." Many Negro soldiers resented what they interpreted as orders not to exercise their legitimate rights whenever a white person objected. At one post in Kansas a dispute arose when a Negro soldier protested being segregated in a local theater. The commanding officer, while admitting that the Negro soldier had the law on his side, issued an order declaring the Negro to be "guilty of the *greater* wrong in doing *anything, no matter how legally correct,* that would provoke race animosity."[23]

Emmett Scott, the Negro adviser to the Secretary of War, did what he could about these grievances. While the Secretary of War acted promptly to correct some of the most flagrant cases of discrimination, he made it clear that "there is no intention on the part of the War Department to undertake at this time to settle the so-called race question."[24] Running through the thinking of the Army during World War I, as throughout much of American society, was a firm belief in the inferiority of the Negro. Scott found that the Army did not accept Negroes for training as artillery officers because they allegedly lacked the "mentality" and "intelligence" for such technical training. It was widely assumed throughout the Army that the Negro was suited only for labor duties and that he did not possess the necessary inherent racial characteristics to make a good combat soldier. The result of this thinking was that, out of approximately 350,000 Negroes drafted, only 40,000 became combat troops. The belief in the Negro's inferiority was also reflected in the hatred and resentment felt by white officers toward their Negro counterparts.[25]

It was natural that black officers, who came from the better educated and more militant segment of the Negro population,

---

[23] Scott, *The American Negro in the World War*, 429–30, 97–98. My italics.

[24] Scott, *The American Negro in the World War*, 59.

[25] Scott, *The American Negro in the World War*, 64; "The Colored Soldier in the United States Army," 22–23.

would be most resentful toward segregation and discrimination in the Army. Furthermore, the Army had not wanted Negro officers, and it was only because of pressure that the Wilson Administration had agreed to establish a Negro officers' training camp at Fort Des Moines, Iowa. The commandant of this school explained the situation to the first class of candidates after some of them objected to being barred from local public places. Since Negroes formed only 10 per cent of the population, they could not "force social equality down the throats of the white ninety per cent." The black officer candidates should recognize the facts: "White men established this camp and gave you this great opportunity, and if members of this camp make its presence obnoxious, white men will say they don't *want* and will not *have any more* colored camps," he told them.[26]

Suspicion had long existed throughout the Negro community that "Southern Bourbons" and "Northern Copperheads" did not want Negroes to fight in America's wars and get credit for their patriotism. This suspicion was heightened at the beginning of the war by the case of Colonel Charles Young, the highest ranking black officer in the Army. Young had been retired in 1917, the official reason being physical disability because of high blood pressure. But to prove that he was fit, Young had ridden on horseback from Ohio to Washington, D.C. When the Army refused to cancel its retirement order, Negroes speculated that Young was retired mainly because his rank would have put him in line to command a regiment.[27]

The treatment of Negro officers and soldiers in Europe, which did not become generally known until after the war, led to a long-lasting bitterness among American Negroes. Most of the Negro combat officers and soldiers served with two units in France — the Ninety-second and Ninety-third Infantry Divi-

---

[26] Colonel Charles C. Ballou to General John L. Chamberlain, Inspector General, September 24, 1917, in "The Colored Soldier in the United States Army," 59.

[27] Franklin, *From Slavery to Freedom*, 448; "We Should Worry," *The Crisis*, 14 (June, 1917), 61–62; "To General H.P. McCain," *The Crisis*, 15 (February, 1918), 165.

sions. The former was a full division and the latter was composed of only four infantry regiments, which saw most of their service in attachment to French divisions. Soon after the war the white former chief of staff of the Ninety-second Division expressed his belief that Negro combat soldiers in general and Negro officers in particular were worthless. The average Negro officer's "ignorance was colossal," he announced. It is "well known to all people familiar with Negroes," that he is "naturally cowardly." Not only were the Negro officers cowardly, but they were unpatriotic, because they were in the Army "for the advancement of their racial interest." Negro troops led by Negro officers "not only . . . will fail in war, but the seed of racial ferment will be sown and we will have to reap the consequences thereafter." The average Negro soldier is fit only for service and labor troops because he is cowardly under fire. "The Negroes make excellent teamsters, better in fact than white soldiers do. They also make good chauffeurs," this officer concluded.[28]

General Robert Lee Bullard, Commander of the Second Army, to which the Ninety-second Division was assigned, recorded in his diary: "Poor Negroes! They are hopelessly inferior." In addition, General Bullard found that "the Negro is a more sensual man than the white man and at the same time he is far more offensive to white women than is a white man." The result, as Bullard saw it, was that there were many cases of rape by Negro soldiers. From his experience, Bullard concluded: "If you need combat soldiers . . . don't put your time upon Negroes." General Bullard never seems to have realized that this division had a morale problem. He felt that the white officers were a fine lot. But when talking to them before the division had ever had a real test in battle, he found that not one of them, except the commanding general, "believed that the 92nd Division would ever be worth anything as soldiers." Little wonder that when he talked to rank-and-file Negroes of the division he found that,

---

[28] Lieutenant Colonel Allen J. Greer to Assistant Commandant, General Staff College, April 13, 1920, in "The Colored Soldier in the U.S. Army," 110–12. See also 113–35 for letters written by white officers, expressing much the same opinion.

"with everyone feeling and saying that they are worthless as soldiers," they took little pride in their performance.[29]

Black morale was adversely affected by the treatment of Negro combat officers in Europe. Once overseas, Negro officers found their white commanders, who believed black officers were inherently incapable of leadership, were requesting their removal and replacement by white officers. One regimental commander made such a request even before his unit had been under fire; this unit went on to win a citation for combat efficiency, despite its leadership by Negro officers.[30]

The depth of racism in the American Army was revealed by a document sent to the French Army by the American Headquarters in August, 1918. The information was to be distributed to all French officers having any connection with American Negro troops and to French civilian officials in areas where American Negro troops were stationed. It stated that the number of Negroes in America would be a "menace of degeneracy" if it were not for segregation. Americans resented any "familiarity" with Negroes by whites and considered it "an affront to their national policy." The French were cautioned against mingling too freely with the black Americans lest they inspire "aspirations which are intolerable to whites." Americans regarded Negroes as "inferior," and "the vices of the Negro," particularly rape, "are a constant menace to the American who has to repress them sternly." French officers should never commend Negro soldiers "too highly."[31] It was such incidents that led one Negro officer to remark: "Many of the field officers seemed far more concerned with reminding their Negro subordinates that they were Negroes than they were with having an effective unit that would perform well in combat."[32]

[29] General Robert Lee Bullard, *Personalities and Reminiscences of the War*, 294, 295, 297, 298.

[30] Colonel Herschel Tupes, Commanding Officer, 372d Infantry, to Commanding General, A.E.F., August 24, 1918, in "The Colored Soldier in the U.S. Army," 64, 24.

[31] Reprinted in "Documents of the War," *The Crisis*, 18 (May, 1919), 16–21.

[32] Howard H. Long, "The Negro Soldier in the Army of the United States," *Journal of Negro Education*, 12 (Summer, 1943), 311.

While the accepted image of Negro officers and soldiers that emerged in the military after World War I was one of failure because of race inferiority, there was other, more sympathetic testimony. Displaying a mixture of racist assumptions and real insight, General Charles C. Ballou, former commanding officer of the Ninety-second Division, wrote a report after the war to appraise the service of Negroes in World War I. In his division the many good white officers at first assigned were transferred when promoted; later the division "was made the dumping ground for discards, both white and black." The Negro soldier showed little initiative, was easily stampeded if surprised, and was more dependent than the white soldier on skilled leadership. But his faults and virtues were the result of "environment and education." The Negro soldier under attack "directly reflected the qualities of the leader that he could *see* and *hear*." Colored officers were distrusted by the Negro enlisted man, who viewed them as simply "stuck-up niggers." The Negro officer was not as good as he should have been, because the Army set lower standards for Negro officer candidates than for whites. Negro officers also had a morale problem because their promotions were not made on the basis of merit; instead, the Army had provided that Negroes could fill only specified officer slots. "The colored officer could never understand this, [and] it made no end of trouble." [33]

General Ballou also gave support to the Negro view of a conspiracy within the Army to discredit the black soldier:

It was my misfortune to be handicapped by many white officers who were rabidly hostile to the idea of a colored officer, and who continually conveyed misinformation to the staff of the superior units, and generally created much trouble and discontent. Such men will never give the Negro the square deal that is his just due. [34]

Surveying the testimony on Negro soldiers, one has the suspicion that when Negro soldiers' performances did not come up to par,

---

[33] Colonel C. C. Ballou to Assistant Commandant, General Staff College, March 14, 1920, in "The Colored Soldier in the U.S. Army," 99–106.

[34] Ballou to Assistant Commandant, General Staff College, March 14, 1920, in "The Colored Soldier in the U.S. Army," 106.

the reason given was commonly race inferiority. On the other hand, when white soldiers did not measure up to standards, it was due to poor morale, or bad leadership, or some similar factor. One white officer who commanded one of the regiments of the Ninety-second Division during the war expressed a similar opinion:

The racial feeling between the white and the colored man in the United States is so strong that it is difficult to obtain a true appreciation of the worth of the colored man as a soldier. If he fails, his failure is subjected to more severe criticism, his faults are magnified to a greater extent, and his acts are more quickly criticized than in the case of a white soldier.[35]

This officer had served with the Negro Twenty-fourth Infantry in Cuba and the Philippines, and he was sure that the Negro's contribution to the Army was illustrated by the past good records of the four Regular Army regiments.

The extent to which racial attitudes generally considered as Southern had permeated the Army is seen by the charge, usually included in testimony criticizing Negro soldiers, that among them was a high incidence of rape of white women. W.E.B. DuBois wrote the mayors of twenty-one French communities where Negro soldiers were stationed and found no serious charges of misconduct. Both he and Robert R. Moton, Booker T. Washington's successor at Tuskegee Institute, examined the records of the Ninety-second Division and found that only one black soldier had been convicted of rape and two of intent to rape, a record in line with that of most white divisions.[36]

Any attempt to evaluate the service of Negro combat soldiers in World War I must take into consideration the fact that the majority of Negroes drafted came from the South and that the majority of these were illiterate or had very little education. This deficiency should have required special efforts toward improvement during the Army's training program, but the evidence in-

[35] General W. B. Jackson, to Colonel Allen J. Greer, General Staff, War Department, April 14, 1919, in "The Colored Soldier in the U.S. Army," 127–28.

[36] Franklin, *From Slavery to Freedom*, 461; *The Crisis*, 18 (May, 1919), 12–13.

dicates that little if any effort was exerted in this direction. Unlike any other division, elements of the Ninety-second were trained at seven different and widely separated camps, under different commanders. The only time the whole division trained together was after it had reached France. Once in France, American divisions were supposed to receive three phases of training before being committed to combat. The Ninety-second received only the first phase. The criticism by the commanding general of the Ninety-second, that the officers assigned to his unit seemed to be of the lowest caliber, has been mentioned above. Negro officers trained as infantrymen were transferred to artillery units without the required specialized training. Only 12 per cent of the Negroes chosen to attend officer candidate school were above average in education, while 75 per cent of those sent to white officer candidate schools were above average. These facts led one Negro to conclude that there was "a strong indication of either an intention that the Negro officer should not succeed or, at least, indifference to his success or failure."[37]

Policy makers ignored the detrimental aspects of the Army's Negro policy. The critics also overlooked the examples of the black soldiers' success. Most important were the four Negro infantry regiments — the 369th, 370th, 371st, and 372nd — attached to the French Army during the war and not so blatantly treated as inferiors. The reports on these units, by the French and their white officers, indicated that they made good fighting units. Three of these regiments were awarded the *Croix de guerre* by France.[38] Also, in the maligned Ninety-second Division there were many individual acts of bravery. Unfortunately, because of the racist assumptions prevalent in the Army, the

[37] "The Colored Soldier in the U.S. Army," 23, 50–55. Quotation from William H. Hastie, "Negro Officers in Two World Wars," *Journal of Negro Education*, 12 (Summer, 1943), 317.

[38] For accounts of the accomplishments, which do not coincide with the stereotypes of Negro soldiers that the American military derived from the war, see Scott, *The American Negro in the World War*, 197–255; Laurence Stallings, *The Doughboys: The Story of the A. E. F., 1917–1918*, 311–22; the story of one of the regiments is told by a white officer in Arthur W. Little, *From Harlem to the Rhine: The Story of New York's Colored Volunteers*.

favorable side of the picture was overlooked by those who formulated Army policy.

The contribution of Negro soldiers in labor units, to which
the majority of drafted Negroes were assigned, has not been
mentioned. Briefly, the other side of the belief in the Negro's
innate cowardice, which made him unfit for combat, was that
he was fit only for common labor. As late as 1942 a semiofficial
history of the Army considered this aspect of the Negro's history in World War I to be obvious: "The merit of the colored
man as a laborer is so well known that it is unnecessary to bring
evidence to prove it." [39]

American Negroes had hoped that in making the world safe
for democracy the United States would grant more democracy
to its largest minority. This optimism had been one of the factors behind the complete loyalty pledged by Negro leaders during the war. But the turn of race relations during and after the
war meant their hopes were unfulfilled. In 1917 thirty-eight
Negroes were lynched and fifty-eight in 1918. The Ku Klux
Klan was revived in the Southern states as early as 1915 and
began the growth that would make it a national organization in
the 1920's. More than seventy Negroes were lynched during
the first year of the postwar period, many of them soldiers still
in uniform. Racists were alarmed that the more liberal attitude
toward race in Europe had corrupted "our niggers." From June,
1919, to the end of the year approximately twenty-five race riots
occurred in urban areas. In these race riots there was a new element: no longer was the Negro a helpless victim, but he often
fought back, killing some of his white attackers. For DuBois
of the NAACP the closed ranks of the war were now broken:
"By the God of Heaven, we are cowards and jackasses if now
that the war is over, we do not marshal every ounce of our brain
and brawn to fight a sterner, longer, more unbending battle
against the forces of hell in our land." [40]

[39] "The Colored Soldier in the U.S. Army," 24. For the accomplishments of Negro labor units, see Scott, *The American Negro in the
World War*, 315–27.

[40] Franklin, *From Slavery to Freedom*, 469–76; "Returning Soldiers,"
The Crisis, 18 (May, 1919), 13–14.

The treatment accorded to Negro soldiers added insult to injury. In December, 1918, the NAACP decided to support a history of the Negro in the war; DuBois was commissioned to write it and was sent to Europe to gather materials. In articles published in *The Crisis*, beginning in March, 1919, DuBois expressed shock over what he found. He reported that "anti-Negro prejudice was rampant in the American Army." He found that the Army was "going to return to America to disparage the black officer and eliminate him from the Army despite his record." DuBois criticized Robert R. Moton who, he said, had been sent to Europe to tell the Negro soldiers "not to be arrogant" when they returned home; he challenged Emmett Scott to tell if he knew about the "astounding" state of affairs, and, if so, what had been done about it. DuBois expressed the indignation of countless Negroes when he asked how Negro soldiers, "who had offered their lives for their people and their country, could be so crucified, insulted, dègraded and maltreated while their fathers, mothers, sisters and brothers had no adequate knowledge of the real truth."[41] DuBois felt so strongly about the Negro's experience in the war that he devoted considerable time between 1918 and 1930 to the history, which, however, was never completed. Feeling within the NAACP was so strong that the organization's annual convention in 1919 passed a resolution calling for a congressional investigation of the matter.[42]

The experience of black soldiers in World War I seemed to confirm the popular belief held among the Negro community that there was a conspiracy to discredit their service. The bitterness remained for a long time, and when World War II began, those leading the protest against discrimination and segregation in the armed forces were former Negro officers and soldiers.

---

[41] See the following articles and editorials by DuBois: "The Black Man in the Revolution of 1914–1918," *The Crisis*, 17 (March, 1919), 218–23; *The Crisis*, 18 (May, 1919), 9–11; "An Essay Toward a History of the Black Man in the Great War," *The Crisis*, 18 (June, 1919), 63–87; "Success and Failure," *The Crisis*, 18 (July, 1919), 127–30.

[42] W. E. B. DuBois, "The Negro Soldier in Service Abroad During the First World War," *Journal of Negro Education*, 12 (Summer, 1943), 324–34; *The Crisis*, 18 (August, 1919), 192.

Also, many of the high-ranking officers and policy makers in the Army at the beginning of World War II had received their impressions of Negro soldiers as young officers in World War I.

Soon after World War I the Army staff began formulating a definite policy on Negro manpower. Many felt that the lack of such a policy during the war was a reason for many of the difficulties. Most of the Army officers and War Department officials in charge of policy believed that segregation was a fixed element in this planning, and many of their assumptions were based on the racism characteristic of the times. Many pointed to the practice within the Navy as the course to follow. After the war the Navy had stopped the enlistment of Negroes for general service because of the problem of "mixing the races" aboard ship, and they were now eligible only for the steward service. While exclusion might work during peacetime, the Army was aware that during a war it would need Negro troops. Because segregation, social customs, and racist assumptions were always foremost in formulating policy concerning the Negro, the goal of incorporating the Negro into a unified military team was de-emphasized.[43]

The effort to formulate a workable policy resulted in a staff study of 1922 that set forth basic guidelines. Military considerations, not "social, ethnological and psychological" theories, should determine the use of Negroes. Negro manpower should be used in proportion to its percentage of the nation's total; half of the Negro soldiers should be assigned to combat units. Past experience indicated that Negro units smaller than the division performed better and that regiments should be the largest Negro units; these could be assigned to larger white units. The report recognized that there were Negroes who were as qualified to become officers as were whites, but that during World War I a serious mistake was made in not requiring Negro officer candidates to meet the same standards as white candidates. Although this study represented a foundation, its implementation illustrated a problem that was to plague the Army for years on

[43] Ulysses G. Lee, Jr., *The United States Army in World War II: Special Studies: The Employment of Negro Troops*, 15–20.

this matter — policy did not become practice. For example, later mobilization plans, expansion plans in case of war, did not generally follow the 1922 policy as to the ratio of combat to non-combat units, and they did not provide for the utilization of Negro manpower in proportion to the general population available for military service.[44]

In 1937 the War Department Personnel Division made another study of the Army's policy regarding Negroes. It was a more detailed restatement of the 1922 policy. Negroes were to be in segregated units. It was pointed out that if Negroes were to be used according to their proportion of the population, mobilization plans would have to include an adequate number of Negro units, which had not been done in prior mobilization plans. There was one important change in comparison with plans established in 1927 and 1933. The earlier studies accepted the 1922 recommendation providing for small black combat units capable of being attached to larger white units. Now, in 1937, this feature was omitted, thus reducing the possibility for even a limited degree of integration by units in any future war.[45]

Once again, practice did not coincide with policy. Although, according to stated policy, Negroes were to be included in the Army in the same percentage as they occurred in the general population — 9 to 10 per cent — the Protective Mobilization Plan of 1940 provided units enough for only 5.81 per cent of Negroes in the total of enlisted men. Written policy also required that the ratio of Negro combat troops to service troops be the same as for white soldiers. But of the 5.81 per cent of Negro personnel provided for in mobilization plans, by far the largest number were assigned to noncombat or service units. The primary reason for this difference between policy and practice was that the chiefs of the Army branches objected to the assignment of Negroes to their commands. For example, the Chief of the Air Corps had indicated that Negroes were not suited to that branch and that their use would result in "the impossible social problem" of having Negro officers commanding white enlisted men.

[44] Lee, *The Employment of Negro Troops*, 32–37.
[45] Lee, *The Employment of Negro Troops*, 37–42.

The Signal Corps did not believe that properly qualified Negroes could be found for its branch. There was division in the War Department General Staff too. The Organization and Training Division (G-3) supported the restrictive policies of the Air Corps and the Signal Corps. The Personnel Division (G-1) felt that "the use of Negroes . . . must be predicated upon the actual availability of personnel with the required qualifications rather than upon any arbitrary elimination of the Negro as a whole on the grounds of lack of technical capacity." [46]

Racial stereotypes and a belief in the inferiority of the Negro were widespread among the high-ranking officers and officials of the military in the 1920's and 1930's. This attitude is not surprising when one remembers that the majority of the American people were racists in these same years. Many of these officers had served in World War I and had heard reports that Negroes were cowards, that they were mentally inferior to whites and could not perform technical functions — such as fly airplanes or repair radio sets. Army staff studies reflected these assumptions, and these assumptions provided the explanation for the difference between Army policy and practice in regard to the Negro. Furthermore, the Army "took the position that it was operating within a social framework which it did not create and which it did not have the power to alter in any significant manner." [47]

---

[46] Lee, *The Employment of Negro Troops*, 42–48.
[47] Lee, *The Employment of Negro Troops*, 49.

CHAPTER II

Policy and Politics

THE COVER OF THE JULY, 1940, issue of *The Crisis* depicts Air
Force planes flying over an aircraft factory turning out rows of
new planes. "For Whites Only," is the caption across the picture,
and at the bottom of the page is printed: "Negro Americans may
not help build them, repair them or fly them." The major issues
for the American Negro during World War II are graphically
illustrated on this periodical cover. The war in Europe had resulted in an expanding American defense industry; white
unemployment was being reduced while employment discrimination meant a continuation of the Depression for Negroes. Defense preparations also meant an expansion of the armed forces,
and Negroes were anxious to participate and to avoid the experience of World War I. The forthcoming presidential election of
1940 meant that Negroes would have a chance to wield some
of their new national political power to achieve their ends.[1]
Thus, war in Europe and an election at home pushed the racial
policies of the armed forces to the front as an issue in American
Negro life.

[1] For the extent of unemployment among Negroes in the 1930's and
discrimination in defense industry, see E. Franklin Frazier, *The Negro
in the United States*, 599–606; Robert C. Weaver, "Racial Employment
Trends in National Defense," *Phylon*, 2 (4th Quarter, 1941), 337–58;
Louis C. Kesselman, *The Social Politics of FEPC*, 6–7; E. Franklin
Frazier, "Ethnic and Minority Groups in Wartime," *American Journal
of Sociology*, 48 (November, 1942), 373.

At the beginning of 1940, Negroes were restricted from service in the Navy except in the messman's branch. The Marine Corps and the Army Air Corps excluded Negroes entirely. In the Army, black Americans were prevented from enlisting except in the few vacancies of the four Regular Army units, and the strength of these had been reduced drastically in the 1920's and 1930's.[2] Although the most immediate concern of Negroes was defense jobs, their position in the armed forces was an important symbol. If one could not participate fully in the defense of his country, he could not lay claim to the rights of a full-fledged citizen. *The Crisis* expressed this attitude in its demand for unrestricted participation in the armed forces: "This is no fight merely to wear a uniform. This is a struggle for status, a struggle to take democracy off of parchment and give it life."[3] One recent student of employment discrimination during this period points out that "in many respects, the discriminatory practices against Negroes which characterized the military programs . . . cut deeper into Negro feelings than did employment discrimination."[4]

By the late 1930's, there was a rapidly increasing correspondence directed to the War Department concerning Negro soldiers. This was due, in part, to the Pittsburgh *Courier*, an influential Negro newspaper, which, together with a group of World War I Negro officers, formed the Committee for Participation of Negroes in the National Defense in 1938. The reason for the formation of this group was expressed in a letter from the editor and publisher of the *Courier* to President Roosevelt:

I feel, and my people feel, that this is the psychological moment to strike for our rightful place in our National Defense. I need not tell you that we are expecting a more dignified place in our armed forces during the next war than we occupied during the World War.[5]

---

[2] For the "official" explanation of the Negro policy of the Army and the Air Corps, see memorandum, Secretary of War to the President, August 5, 1937, OF 25, Franklin D. Roosevelt Library (hereafter FDRL).

[3] "For Manhood in National Defense," *The Crisis*, 47 (December, 1940), 375.

[4] Herbert Garfinkel, *When Negroes March: The March on Washington Movement in the Organizational Politics for FEPC*, 20.

[5] Robert L. Vann to the President, January 19, 1939, OF 93A, FDRL;

Roy Wilkins, the editor of *The Crisis*, wrote Secretary of War Harry H. Woodring that he knew "of no other single issue — except possibly lynching — upon which there is a unanimity of opinion among all classes in all sections of the country." And as a reminder that a presidential election was due soon, the Secretary was told that the Administration that broke down the restrictions against the Negro serving in the armed forces "is certain to receive the gratitude of Negro voters in a substantial manner."[6]

Much of the stimulus behind the Negroes' concern over their position in the armed forces was the memory of what had happened to black soldiers in World War I. Charles H. Houston, a noted Negro civil rights lawyer, related in the Negro press his experiences as a young officer in 1917–1918. His bitter memories were recounted, he said, "so that our white fellow citizens may learn they must treat Negroes as equals, and that this generation of Negro boys may have their eyes opened to what is ahead of them."[7] Other former Negro soldiers recalled their experiences for a new generation, and the Negro press was full of general articles reopening the old wounds of World War I.[8]

Concern that the Negro soldier would be denied a combat role and confined to labor units in any future war was also widespread. There were frequent reports that the remnants of the four Regular Army regiments had been reduced to service as orderlies for white officers, gardeners, and "flunkies."[9] The Associated Negro Press brought together in September, 1939, a

see also Ulysses G. Lee, Jr., *The Employment of Negro Troops*, 51–52, and Howard H. Long, "The Negro Soldier in the Army of the United States," *Journal of Negro Education*, 12 (Summer, 1943), 314.

[6] Roy Wilkins to Harry H. Woodring, March 9, 1939, OF 93A, FDRL.

[7] Pittsburgh *Courier*, July 20, 1940. Houston's memoirs ran for a number of issues: July 27, August 10, September 7, 14, 28, October 5, 12, 1940.

[8] See the series of articles by a Negro veteran in the Baltimore *Afro-American*, December 9, 30, 1939. Examples of articles recalling abuses of World War I are Pittsburgh *Courier*, October 7, 14, 1939; Walter Wilson, "Old Jim Crow in Uniform," *The Crisis*, 46 (February, 1939), 42–44; (March, 1939), 71–73, 82, 93.

[9] Baltimore *Afro-American*, October 14, 1939; Pittsburgh *Courier*, April 13, June 8, 1940.

group of black leaders to discuss the Negro's position in national defense. The majority agreed that if the war in Europe continued the United States would be drawn into it. They were divided over whether or not Negroes should demand a segregated division in the Army and how the Negro would benefit from the war, but these Negro leaders were unanimous in their determination to resist any attempt to restrict Negroes to labor battalions.[10]

The result of this agitation was that black organizations and individuals began to ask for a more effective role in the armed forces. The National Bar Association created a committee to end the exclusion of Negroes from the National Guard of most states. The National Negro Insurance Association adopted a resolution against the restrictions on Negroes in the Army and Navy. A colored American Legion post in Memphis, Tennessee, organized a group to secure a Negro National Guard unit for that state. In Michigan, a Negro state senator proclaimed that American Negroes should refuse to fight in a future war unless admitted to the armed services in time to train properly for combat service. A Negro newspaper editorialized this line of argument: "It is better to insist on training now . . . than wait until the conflict begins and be rushed as raw recruits into a slaughter that will kill us by the thousands before we learn to protect ourselves."[11]

Negroes' efforts to broaden the opportunities available to them were first directed at legislation and focused on the Army Air Corps in particular. Since World War I, Negroes had attempted to enlist in the Air Corps, but the answer had always been that no colored units existed in this branch of the service to which they could be assigned. In 1939 Congress passed a law authorizing the use of civilian aviation schools for the basic training of military pilots. This training was to be administered by the War Department and supervised by Air Corps personnel. Negro pressure had resulted in an amendment specifying that one of

[10] Pittsburgh *Courier*, September 16, 1939.

[11] Pittsburgh *Courier*, October 28, 1939, July 6, October 19, 1940; Norfolk *Journal and Guide*, July 6, 1940; Baltimore *Afro-American*, October 21, 1939.

these schools would be designated "for the training of any Negro air pilot." Since the War Department did not want to take Negroes into the Air Corps, it took the position that this law did not direct the enlistment of Negroes in this branch of the Army. One school was designated for Negro pilot training, but, unlike those for whites, it was run by civilians instead of by the Air Corps. Furthermore, its graduates were not taken into the Air Corps as were the whites, because the War Department claimed that there were no Negro units to which they could be assigned. In short, Negro air units could never exist because Negroes were not allowed to enlist, and Negroes could not enlist because there were no Negro Air Corps units.[12]

Negroes and the congressmen who had supported the amendment construed the law as requiring the enlistment of Negroes into the Air Corps. Within the War Department General Staff, the arguments against training Negro pilots included: the lack of experience by Negroes in commercial aviation; the "lack of interest" of Negroes in aviation; the absence of Negro air units in other countries; and the testimony from World War I that colored officers were unstable and thus unsuited for flying. It was not until January, 1941, that Negroes were made a part of the Air Corps, and this occurred only because of intervention from the White House.[13]

The Air Corps was not the only branch of the military to antagonize black voters in an election year. Negro bitterness toward the Navy was especially evident in 1940. This service was the most outspoken in its racial policy; that it saw fit to allow black sailors to serve only in the menial capacity of messman insulted Negroes. In practically every issue of the Negro press during 1940 there were articles or editorials condemning the

---

[12] Lawrence J. Paszek, "Negroes and the Air Force, 1939–1949" (unpublished paper read at the Southern Historical Association meeting, November 12, 1964), 2–3; Lee, *The Employment of Negro Troops*, 55–62; W. J. Trent, Jr., Adviser on Negro Affairs in the Office of the Secretary of the Interior, to M. H. McIntyre, Secretary to the President, January 31, 1939, OF 93, FDRL; James L. H. Peck, "When Do We Fly?" *The Crisis*, 47 (December, 1940), 376–78.

[13] Lee, *The Employment of Negro Troops*, 62–63; Florence Murray, ed., *The Negro Handbook, 1942*, 78, 81–82.

Navy's racial policy, and the Navy appeared unwilling to do anything to lessen this animosity. For instance, the Naval Academy refused to allow a Negro member of Harvard University's lacrosse team to play against the Navy team. In 1940 the Navy gave "undesirable" discharges to thirteen black messmen who sent a letter to a Negro newspaper criticizing their working conditions.[14] When a member of the Committee on Participation of Negroes in the National Defense Program conferred with Navy officials in November, 1940, the Navy issued the following statement:

After many years of experience, the policy of not enlisting men of the colored race for any branch of the naval service, except the messmen's branch, was adopted to meet the best interests of general ship efficiency.[15]

Remembering the experience with the Air Corps, Negroes and their allies in Congress sought to secure more specific amendments to legislation in the summer and fall of 1940. One such piece of legislation was H.R. 9850, *An Act to Expedite the Strengthening of the National Defense*. The Committee on Participation of Negroes in the National Defense arranged to have Senators Sherman Minton of Indiana and Harry H. Schwartz of Wyoming, both Democrats, introduce an amendment providing that "no person shall be excluded from any branch of the military establishment on account of race, creed, or color." The Army General Staff objected stenuously to the amendment. Secretary of War Harry Woodring wrote congressmen that the amendment might result in the enlistment of a large number of Negroes; this would "demoralize and weaken the effect of military units by mixing colored and white soldiers in closely related units, or even in the same units." In the end an amendment that made no change in the situation was substituted: "That no Negro because of race shall be excluded from enlist-

---

[14] Pittsburgh *Courier*, October 5, November 23, 1940, May 3, 1941; Baltimore *Afro-American*, December 21, 1940, January 4, 11, 1941. "The Negro in the United States Navy," *The Crisis*, 47 (July, 1940), 200–201, 210.
[15] Pittsburgh *Courier*, November 23, 1940.

ment in the Army for service with colored military units now organized or to be organized for such service."[16]

The Selective Training and Service Act passed in September, 1940, was the occasion for the most intense Negro effort to amend legislation. Senator Robert F. Wagner, Democrat of New York, introduced an amendment that no one, on the basis of creed or color, should be denied the right to volunteer for the armed services. Although Southerners in Congress objected, this amendment was included in the bill, but with a "joker" — so Negroes thought — any person could volunteer provided that "he is acceptable to the land or naval forces for such training and service." The services were still free to refuse Negro volunteers. Representative Hamilton Fish, Republican of New York, did manage to attach another amendment to the Selective Service Act providing that draftees would be selected in "an impartial manner" and that their selection and training would be without discrimination "on account of race or color." As with other legislation, however, Negroes were to find that the intent of such amendments could be changed by their administration.[17]

The failure of Negroes to achieve a breakthrough against discrimination and segregation in the armed forces made this a major political issue for Negroes in the 1940 presidential election. As early as 1939 the Pittsburgh *Courier* was editorially "demanding" that "the color bar be abolished in the armed forces"; its readers were reminded that "there will be a hard-fought Presidential election campaign within the twelve month, and our vote will be solicited."[18] By mid-1940 Charles H. Houston, legal counsel for the NAACP, was telling Negroes to let their congressmen know that discrimination in the armed forces was an issue in the election. Walter White, Executive Secretary of the NAACP, affirmed at his organization's annual meeting that this matter was the major issue: "Any candidate for President mer-

---

[16] Pittsburgh *Courier*, June 22, 29, 1940; Lee, *The Employment of Negro Troops*, 68–69.

[17] Lee, *The Employment of Negro Troops*, 71–74; Selective Service System, *Special Groups: Special Monograph No. 10*, 3, 42–45.

[18] Pittsburgh *Courier*, October 7, 1939.

iting the colored support must stand first for elimination of the color line from the armed services." Black Democrats were supporting President Roosevelt's nomination for a third term, but they wanted him to see that Negroes were admitted to every branch of the armed services.[19]

President Roosevelt and his Administration's New Deal had had a profound influence on American Negroes. Years after Roosevelt's death the general Negro public ranked him second to President Kennedy as the President who had done most for Negro rights; Negro leaders ranked him third behind Presidents Kennedy and Truman.[20] In 1940 a Negro editor described the most important contribution of the New Deal to the black people of America as being "its doctrine that Negroes are a part of the country and must be considered in any program for the country as a whole."[21] This attention, together with the Negro's alienation from the Republican party, had led in 1936 to a majority of the Negro vote going to the Democratic party for the first time.[22] But 1940 marked the beginning of a period when Negroes would no longer be satisfied with mere recognition.

Although the Negro, as the most economically depressed group in the population, profited from New Deal relief programs, Roosevelt personally did little for the cause of civil rights. Arthur Schlesinger, Jr., has stated that Negro civil rights were not in President Roosevelt's "own first order of priorities."[23] Frank Freidel has found that Roosevelt's attitude toward segregation is "not clear," but that he "seemed ready to leave well enough alone in questions that involved white supremacy."

[19] Baltimore *Afro-American*, June 22, 29, 1940; Pittsburgh *Courier*, June 29, 1940.

[20] William Brink and Louis Harris, *The Negro Revolution in America*, 90, 214.

[21] "The Roosevelt Record," *The Crisis*, 47 (September, 1940), 343.

[22] Elbert Lee Tatum, *The Changed Political Thought of the Negro, 1915–1940*, 139, 147–61, 180–81; John Hope Franklin, *From Slavery to Freedom: A History of American Negroes*, 512–28; Walter Johnson, *1600 Pennsylvania Avenue: Presidents and the People Since 1929*, 81–82.

[23] Arthur M. Schlesinger, Jr., *The Age of Roosevelt: The Politics of Upheaval*, 431.

Roosevelt did not stand in the path of those who were endeavoring to obtain greater civil rights for Negroes, but neither would he fight in their behalf. . . . At the most his was a position of benevolent neutrality — he was disposed to capitulate when they could muster sufficient force.[24]

No doubt Roosevelt's attitude on this question was influenced by the importance of the South in his party, but he also appears to have had a conservative attitude on race relations, believing that steps on the behalf of Negroes must be slow and must be taken one at a time.[25] Perhaps this belief that efforts to aid the cause of Negro rights should go slowly was the reason for his privately expressed dislike of the NAACP.[26]

In 1940 the Republicans, anxious to get the Negro vote back into the party's fold, recognized the emotional impact upon Negroes of discrimination in the armed forces. Senator Robert Taft, a Republican hopeful, was telling Negro audiences that he stood for proportional representation of Negroes in all branches of the armed services.[27] The Republican party platform on Negro rights gave its nominee Wendell L. Willkie, known as an exponent of equal rights for Negroes, a liberal plank on which to run:

[24] Frank Freidel, *F. D. R. and the South*, 73, 81, 97.

[25] This is the impression conveyed by the memoirs of one prominent Negro New Dealer. See Mary McLeod Bethune, "My Secret Talks With F.D.R.," *Ebony*, 4 (April, 1949), 42–51.

[26] Roosevelt's private opinion of the NAACP is found in a note attached to a letter to Arthur B. Spingarn, President of the NAACP, October 1, 1943, PPF 1336, FDRL. Spingarn had written to Roosevelt asking him to write a letter recognizing the twenty-five years of service to the NAACP by Walter White. The note reads: "Miss Tully brought this in. Says the President doesn't think too much of this organization — not to be to[o] fulsome — tone it down a bit." For Roosevelt's toleration of segregation and discrimination in New Deal programs, see John A. Salmond, "The Civilian Conservation Corps and the Negro," *Journal of American History*, 52 (June, 1965), 75–88; Allen Francis Kifer, "The Negro Under the New Deal, 1933–1941" (unpublished Ph.D. dissertation, University of Wisconsin, 1961); Schlesinger, Jr., *The Age of Roosevelt: The Politics of Upheaval*, 431–32.

[27] Pittsburgh *Courier*, June 8, 1940.

We pledge that our American citizens of Negro descent shall be given a square deal in the economic and political life of the nation. Discrimination in the civil service, the Army and the Navy and all other branches of the government must cease.[28]

The Republican platform also supported legislation to guarantee the franchise to Southern Negroes and legislation against lynching, two important items that the Roosevelt Administration had indicated its reluctance to support. The Pittsburgh *Courier* gave the plank front-page treatment and called it "the strongest plank in the history" of the Republican party for the abolition of discrimination against Negroes. Underneath this story the *Courier* printed a letter from Roosevelt's secretary to Robert L. Vann, publisher of the *Courier* and prominent Roosevelt supporter in 1932 and 1936, stating that the President did not have time to meet and discuss the problem of discrimination in the armed services.[29]

Indicative of the importance of the Northern Negro vote to the Democratic coalition, as well as of the growing importance of civil rights in national politics, is the fact that the Democratic platform mentioned the Negro by name for the first time in 1940.[30] In contrast to the Republican platform, however, the Democratic platform contained a general statement of what had been done for the Negro in the past. In addition, it pledged that the party would "continue to strive for complete legislative safeguards against discrimination in government service and benefits, and in the national defense forces."[31]

By the middle of 1940 there was evidence that the 1936 Negro majorities for the Democrats were endangered by black defections. Charges of discrimination in some of the relief agencies and in defense matters became more frequent. The apparent sincerity of Willkie's stand on civil rights also played a part. In August, 1940, the Pittsburgh *Courier*, which had been one of the strongest supporters of Roosevelt in 1932 and 1936, came

---

[28] *The New York Times*, June 27, 1940.
[29] Pittsburgh *Courier*, July 6, 1940.
[30] Johnson, *1600 Pennsylvania Avenue*, 82.
[31] *The New York Times*, July 18, 1940.

out in support of Willkie for President.[32] A Gallup poll reported
that the Democrats still had a majority of the Negro vote,
but that there had been a considerable shift to the Republicans
since 1936.[33]

Negro Democrats were worried, and they voiced their concern to the White House. A Negro Democratic state senator
from Michigan wrote that black voters were very concerned
over their lack of participation in national defense. As an example, he pointed out that the Michigan legislature had appro-
priated the necessary money to form a Negro unit in the National
Guard, but that the War Department had stated it would refuse
to recognize such a unit if it were formed.[34] Mrs. Mary McLeod
Bethune, Negro adviser in the National Youth Administration,
warned the White House that "there is grave apprehension
among Negroes lest the existing inadequate representation and
training of colored persons may lead to the creation of labor
battalions and other forms of discrimination against them in
event of war." Mrs. Bethune reported that Negroes were urging
the appointment of a Negro adviser to the Secretary of War to
help in correcting this situation.[35]

As the election drew near, some Negro newspapers stepped
up their criticism of the Roosevelt Administration on civil
rights. For example, the Baltimore *Afro-American*'s editor expressed his dismay over the continued restriction of Negro
enlistments in the armed services at a time when the military
was begging for volunteers: "In this regard, President Roosevelt
not only forgot us but he neglected us, deserted and abandoned
us to our enemies." [36] The newspaper printed article after article

---

[32] Pittsburgh *Courier*, August 24, 1940.

[33] *The New York Times*, February 4, 1940; Franklin, *From Slavery to
Freedom*, 517.

[34] Charles C. Diggs to Stephen Early, July 1, 1940, OF 93, FDRL.

[35] "Memorandum on Negro Participation in the Armed Forces," n.d.
(c. August, 1940), OF 93, FDRL. This memorandum appears to have
been written by Robert C. Weaver. See Weaver, Administrative Assistant
to the Advisory Commission to the Council of National Defense, to Oscar
Chapman, July 12, 1940, Chapman Papers, Harry S Truman Library
(hereafter HSTL).

[36] Baltimore *Afro-American*, August 31, 1940.

disclosing segregation and discrimination in such New Deal agencies and departments as the Civilian Conservation Corps and the Agriculture Department. Even Roosevelt's hospital for polio patients at Warm Springs, Georgia, came under attack when a reporter found only one Negro patient there, segregated in the basement. Willkie's pledge in campaign speeches that he would do something about discrimination in the armed forces was headlined: "Willkie Says He'll End Jim Crow in Service Units." Finally, the *Afro-American*, which had not supported a Republican candidate for President since 1924, endorsed Willkie. High on its list of reasons for doing so was Roosevelt's toleration of discrimination against Negroes in the armed forces.[37]

Roosevelt was concerned over Negro criticism on this issue. On September 5, 1940, the White House directed the War Department to prepare and hold a statement to the effect that "colored men will have equal opportunity with white men in all departments of the Army."[38] In a Cabinet meeting on September 13, 1940, Roosevelt said that he was "troubled by representations of the Negroes that their race under the draft was limited to labor batallions." The Army informed the President that it planned to have 10 per cent of its strength composed of Negroes. Roosevelt then suggested that the War Department publicize this fact. After this meeting, Secretary of War Henry L. Stimson told the Army General Staff that he wanted "an exact statement of the facts in the case, and . . . how far we can go in the matter."[39] The first of a series of White House statements designed to reassure Negroes on the eve of the election was issued on September 16, 1940. This announcement stated that 36,000 out of the first 400,000 men drafted by the military under the new Selective Service Act would be Negroes

---

[37] Baltimore *Afro-American*, August 17, 24, September 7, 14, 21, October 19, 1940.

[38] Memorandum, the Office of the Chief of Staff to G-1 and G-3, September 5, 1940, quoted in Lee, *The Employment of Negro Troops*, 75.

[39] Memorandum, General George C. Marshall, Chief of Staff, to G-1, September 14, 1940, quoted in Lee, *The Employment of Negro Troops*, 75.

and that the Army was making a start in developing Negro air units.[40]

Negro criticism continued, nevertheless, to mount against discrimination in the armed forces. Walter White asked Mrs. Roosevelt to arrange a meeting between the President and a Negro delegation to discuss the matter. Mrs. Roosevelt characterized the conference as "important and immediate"; the President agreed to such a meeting on September 27, 1940, to include representatives of the Army and Navy.[41] Walter White of the NAACP, T. Arnold Hill, adviser on Negro affairs in the National Youth Administration, and A. Philip Randolph, head of the Brotherhood of Sleeping Car Porters, were the three Negro leaders to confer at the White House.

On the morning of the conference these three men put their demands concerning the Negro in national defense in the form of a memorandum to the President. The main points in this statement were directed to the demand that Negro officers and enlisted men should be used throughout the services, with the only restriction on their placement being their individual ability. One of the major demands was that "existing units of the army and units to be established should be required to accept and select officers and enlisted personnel without regard to race," which would require abandoning segregated units and integrating Negroes throughout the services as individuals. A revolution in the services' racial policies was being called for, but the chiefs of the services soon made it known that they were not revolutionaries.[42]

Present at the meeting with the three Negro leaders were the President, Secretary of the Navy Frank Knox, and Assistant Secretary of War Robert P. Patterson. The President announced that Negro units would be organized in all branches of the Army and that he would look into the ways by which discrimination in the services could be lessened. Assistant Secretary Pat-

---

[40] Pittsburgh *Courier*, September 21, 1940.

[41] Memorandum, S. T. E. [Stephen Early] to General Watson, September 19, 1940, OF 2538, FDRL; Walter White, *A Man Called White*, 186.

[42] The complete text of this memorandum is contained in an NAACP press release, October 5, 1940, OF 93, FDRL.

terson stated that the War Department planned to call Negro reserve officers to active duty, but that the date had not been decided upon. The Navy indicated that it was not willing to make any concessions in its policy; Secretary Knox stated that he felt that the problem in his service was almost impossible to resolve because of the close living conditions required on board ship. "Southern" and "Northern" ships in the Navy were not possible, Knox said. At the close of the meeting, Roosevelt promised to write or talk to the Negro leaders again after conferring with government officials, but the next word these leaders received was a White House press release announcing a decision that had been made.[43]

On October 8, 1940, the Assistant Secretary of War submitted to the President a full statement of policy already approved by the Secretary of War and the Army Chief of Staff, and Roosevelt initialed his "O.K."[44] Revealing ignorance of black feeling, the press secretary for the President, Stephen Early, quickly sent the statement to the Democratic National Committee for full publicity. "You are at liberty to use it in the colored press and to have it given the widest possible distribution among colored organizations through the country," Early said.[45]

The policy stated by the War Department and initialed by Roosevelt was not new and therefore made no concessions to Negro demands. It contained the main points of a policy adopted, but not announced, by the War Department in 1937: The Negro proportion of the Army would be the same as the Negro proportion of the country's population; Negro units would be established in each branch of the Army, combatant as well as noncombatant; Negro reserve officers would serve only in Negro units officered by colored personnel; Negroes would be given the opportunity to attend officer candidate schools

[43] NAACP press release, October 5, 1940; White, *A Man Called White*, 186–87.

[44] Stephen Early to Robert P. Patterson, Assistant Secretary of War, n.d., AG 291.21, National Archives Record Group (hereafter NARG) 319.

[45] Memorandum, Stephen Early to Charlie Michelson, teletyped to Democratic National Committee, October 9, 1940, OF 93, FDRL.

when they were established; Negro pilots were being trained, and Negro aviation units were to be formed as soon as the necessary personnel were available; Negro civilians were being given an equal opportunity for employment at Army arsenals and installations. The statement concluded:

The policy of the War Department is not to intermingle colored and white enlisted personnel in the same regimental organizations. This policy has proven satisfactory over a long period of years, and to make changes would produce situations destructive to morale and detrimental to the preparation for national defense. For similar reasons the department does not contemplate assigning colored reserve officers other than those of the Medical Corps and chaplains to existing Negro combat units of the Regular Army.[46]

Within the War Department, as long as this policy remained in effect, this statement was referred to as the President's "directive," or as Presidential "sanction" for the Army's policy, or "the President's policy of segregation of the races."[47]

In releasing this statement to the press, Early implied that it had the approval of the Negro leaders who met with the President on September 27, resulting in charges that White, Hill, and Randolph had "sold out" Negroes by agreeing to segregation in the armed forces.[48] To defend themselves, these three Negro leaders charged that the White House statement was a trick, denied they had approved of such a policy, and printed the memorandum that they had given to the President to indicate that they had opposed continued segregation in the armed services. Roosevelt's and the War Department's policy received bitter criticism in the black press. Critics pointed out that the assignment of Negro officers only to Negro units already officered by Negroes meant that they could be assigned only to two National Guard regiments. Contrary to the policy statement, not one Negro was receiving military pilot training and, as recently as October 1, The Adjutant General had written

---

[46] Early to Michelson, October 9, 1940.

[47] Lee, *The Employment of Negro Troops*, 76.

[48] Most bitter in its denunciation of the three Negro leaders was the Chicago *Defender*, October 19, 1940.

that "applications from colored persons for flying cadet appointment or for enlistment in the Air Corps are not being accepted." Finally, Negroes everywhere denied the contention that the Army's policy of segregation had proven satisfactory in the past, and they recalled the conditions during World War I.[49]

The Republicans seized the issue and used it in their appeals to Negro voters. One full-page newspaper advertisement pointed out that one hundred white colonels had been promoted over the highest ranking Negro officer in the Army, Colonel Benjamin O. Davis. Another was headed: "Roosevelt, as Commander-in-Chief, permits Jim Crow in the U.S. Navy."[50] Negro workers for the Democratic party were worried over the effect of the War Department's policy statement on the Negro vote. One worker suggested a move by the White House that Negro newspapers had advocated for several months. This party worker felt that the "greatest stroke of the year" would be the promotion of Colonel Benjamin O. Davis to the rank of general, making him the first Negro to hold this rank. Another party worker suggested that Negro voters would be soothed by the appointment of Negro assistants to the Director of Selective Service and the Secretary of War.[51]

Will Alexander, an adviser to the Administration on Negro matters, later recalled the deep concern in the White House over the black vote. Alexander received an urgent call from one of Roosevelt's chief aides, Harry Hopkins, just before the 1940 election. Hopkins told Alexander that Roosevelt had done more for Negroes than anyone since Lincoln. Now it looked as though the black voters were going to go against him in the election, and Hopkins wanted Alexander to tell him what could be done to keep the Negro vote Democratic.[52] From talks with

[49] "White House Blesses Jim Crow," *The Crisis*, 47 (November, 1940), 350–51, 357; the reaction of the Negro press to the statement is summarized in "The Problem," *Time* (October 28, 1940), 19.

[50] Baltimore *Afro-American*, October 12, 19, 26, 1940.

[51] Bishop R. R. Wright, Jr., Chairman, Colored Division, National Democratic Headquarters, Midwestern Region, to Stephen Early, October 16, 1940, OF 93, FDRL; Summary of Memorandum, James Rowe to the President, October 18, 1940, OF 2538, FDRL.

[52] Will W. Alexander, "The Reminiscences of Will W. Alexander," Oral History Research Office, Columbia University, 360.

Negroes, Alexander knew what they wanted — the promotion of Colonel Benjamin O. Davis to general, and a Negro assistant to the Secretary of War.

The White House began making a series of announcements in the last few weeks before the election in an effort to mend fences with Negro voters. To discount Negro assertions to the contrary, the War Department announced on October 16 that Negro aviation units would indeed be formed. Then there followed announcements that new Negro combat units were being formed in the Army. Walter White had complained that, since the White House release on October 9, his position as a Negro leader had "been seriously impaired" by the implication that he had agreed to segregation in the Army. Stephen Early, the White House press secretary, was reluctant to correct this impression publicly, but, apparently under pressure from Roosevelt, he did so about a week before the election. The President himself wrote White, Hill, and Randolph on October 25, 1940, expressing regret that the statement had been misinterpreted and pledging that Negroes would serve in all branches of the service. President Roosevelt pointed out that this pledge would be a "very substantial advance" over past policy, and he concluded by telling the three Negroes, "You may rest assured that further developments of policy will be forthcoming to insure that Negroes are given fair treatment on a non-discriminatory basis."[53]

The "further developments" came in the week before the election. Colonel Benjamin O. Davis was promoted to the rank of general. General Davis had served as a first lieutenant in the Eighth U.S. Volunteer Infantry during the Spanish-American War. In 1899 he enlisted as a private in the Regular Army all-Negro Ninth Cavalry and was commissioned a second lieutenant in 1901. By 1930 Davis had been promoted to colonel, and for many years served as an instructor of military science in Negro colleges. The Negro press had been hinting that, like

[53] *The New York Times*, October 16, 1940. Stephen Early to Walter White, October 18, 1940; White to Early, October 21, 1940; Early to White, October 25, 1940; Franklin D. Roosevelt to White, Randolph, and Hill, October 25, 1940; all in OF 93, FDRL.

Colonel Charles Young of World War I fame, he would be retired rather than promoted.[54]

Roosevelt also accepted the suggestion that a Negro assistant to the Secretary of War should be appointed, and he persuaded Secretary Stimson to make such an appointment. "The Negroes are taking advantage of this period just before [the] election to try to get everything they can in the way of recognition from the Army," Stimson complained in his diary.[55] The man chosen to fill this position was William H. Hastie, a graduate of Harvard Law School. He had served as an assistant solicitor in the Department of Interior; he had been the first Negro appointed to the federal bench; he had served as chairman of the National Legal Committee of the NAACP; and just prior to his appointment as Civilian Aide to the Secretary of War, he was Dean of the Howard University Law School. The NAACP persuaded Supreme Court Justice Felix Frankfurter, a former professor of Hastie's, to recommend him to Stimson; during his service as Civilian Aide to the Secretary of War, Hastie was considered within the War Department as an "NAACP man."[56]

Before the election, Roosevelt made one more significant appointment — a Negro adviser to the Director of Selective Service, Colonel Campbell C. Johnson.

In general, the Negro press praised these appointments, but their political significance did not go unnoticed. Negro Republicans charged that the appointments were a "political trick," and the Pittsburgh *Courier* warned that they "should not deceive any self-respecting Negro."[57] On the other hand, a Negro paper supporting Roosevelt looked upon these appointments as evidence of the President's "determination to bring about greater integration of colored citizens into the fundamental activities of government."[58]

Apparently the appointments and announcements by the

[54] Richard Bardolph, *The Negro Vanguard*, 449–51.
[55] Henry L. Stimson Diary, October 22, 1940, Yale University Library.
[56] Stimson Diary, October 22, 1940; Bardolph, *The Negro Vanguard*, 360–61; interview with James C. Evans, Department of Defense, July, 1964.
[57] Pittsburgh *Courier*, November 2, 1940.
[58] Norfolk *Journal and Guide*, November 2, 1940.

White House were enough, if they were needed at all, because the majority of the Negro vote went to Roosevelt again in 1940. Although some Negro leaders had begun to defect from the Administration, the masses who had received the benefits remained convinced that support for the Democratic party was in their interest. However, the Negro majority was reduced over the 1936 total.[59] The NAACP was certainly pleased with Roosevelt's actions regarding the armed forces: "We have worked night and day during recent weeks to take personally to the people the things you did and wrote, [and] I am certain tomorrow will reveal that Negroes know the truth," Walter White wrote to the President on election eve.[60] Inexperienced in wielding their new national political power and apparently feeling that half a loaf was a victory, Negro leaders felt that they had gained as much as could be expected.

But what had Negroes gained in regard to the armed forces, except the appointment of a Negro general and two Negro advisers? Most vocal Negroes, including the three leaders who had presented their demands to the President, were asking for the end of segregation in the armed forces. The Navy had refused to lift its restrictions on accepting Negroes only for the messman's branch; the Army had said there would be Negro aviation units and that Negroes would serve in all of its branches; but both of these services, and the White House policy statement of October 9, 1940, had steadfastly refused to abandon the principle of segregation. One Negro newspaper saw the point: "We asked Mr. Roosevelt to change the rules of the game and he counters by giving us some new uniforms. That is what it amounts to and we have called it appeasement."[61] The emotional impact of this issue would grow during World War II. The hypocrisy involved in fighting with a segregated military force against aggression by an enemy preaching a master race ideology would become readily apparent to black Americans.

[59] Franklin, *From Slavery to Freedom*, 517.
[60] White to the President, November 4, 1940, PPF 1336, FDRL.
[61] Baltimore *Afro-American*, November 2, 1940.

CHAPTER III

New War, Old Policy, 1940-1943

DURING THE 1920's and 1930's the strength of the Negro units in the Regular Army had been allowed to dwindle. By 1939 there were only 3,640 Negroes in the four Regular Army units and only three Negro combat officers. Between the outbreak of World War II in Europe in September, 1939, and Pearl Harbor, the Negro strength of the Army increased 25 times — from 3,640 to 97,725. By the end of the United States' first year of war, the Negro strength of the Army stood at 467,883. This rapid expansion from a small base was common to both white and Negro units of the Army and therefore led to many similar problems, but the policy of racial segregation created difficulties that were peculiar to the Negro units.[1]

For the War Department during the years from 1941 to 1943, the main focus of the "Negro problem" was the maintenance of racial balance — ensuring that Negroes represented 10 per cent of the Army, the same percentage that they composed of the general population. From this grew the problem of providing training facilities for the rapidly increasing numbers of

[1] Ulysses G. Lee, Jr., *The Employment of Negro Troops*, 88; William H. Hastie, "The Negro in the Army Today," *The Annals of the American Academy of Political and Social Science*, 223 (September, 1942), 55–59.

Negroes. New Negro units had to be formed, cadres for training had to be found, Negro officers to command the new units had to be provided, and training and replacement centers to which the new men would be assigned had to be created. Although these same problems faced the white part of the Army, there was a difference: At the beginning of the Army's expansion in 1940, white units of all types and in all of the Army's branches were already in existence, and these existing organizations provided the basis for orderly expansion of white units. On the other hand, the comparatively few Negroes in the Army at the beginning of expansion meant that Negro units were handicapped by inexperience and inadequate training facilities.[2]

The Army thought it had made a major concession to Negro opinion in 1940 when it promised that Negroes would serve in all of its branches. This expansion meant that more opportunities were available for black soldiers than ever before. Segregation was viewed as a necessity, however, a fixed element of policy that could not be changed. Segregation was part of the civilian life of the United States, and the Army believed it must conform to this fact. Furthermore, the Army adopted a separate-but-equal position that segregation did not lead to discrimination against Negro soldiers. At the same time an increasing number of Negroes were becoming convinced that segregation inevitably led to discrimination. Negroes' experiences in the armed forces confirmed their thinking.

After ten months of duty and observation as Civilian Aide to the Secretary of War, William Hastie outlined the shortcomings in the Army's Negro policy. In September, 1941, Hastie told Secretary Stimson that he felt the Army was not utilizing the Negro soldier efficiently. "The traditional mores of the South," Hastie wrote, "have been widely accepted and adopted by the Army as the basis of policy and practice affecting the Negro soldier." He had been separated "as completely as possible" from his white counterpart, and in southern training camps the Army had exerted little effort to ensure that he was properly treated by white civilians.

---

[2] Lee, *The Employment of Negro Troops*, 89.

This philosophy is not working. In civilian life in the South, the Negro is growing increasingly resentful of traditional mores. In tactical units of the Army, the Negro is taught to be a fighting man . . . in brief, a soldier. It is impossible to create a dual personality which will be on the one hand a fighting man toward the foreign enemy, and on the other, a craven who will accept treatment as less than a man at home. One hears with increasing frequency from colored soldiers the sentiment that since they have been called to fight they might just as well do their fighting here and now.[3]

Hastie pointed out to Stimson that far too large a percentage of Negro soldiers had been placed in service units and that many branches of the Army, such as the Air Corps and Signal Corps, had only a token representation of Negroes. The Army was reluctant to make 10 per cent of its strength Negro by creating more Negro units. So far, the Army's Negro policy seemed to justify the conclusion that the "Negro soldier is being approached all too often as an unwelcome requirement to be handled with a view primarily to avoiding embarrassment to prejudiced sensibilities," rather than as an opportunity to exploit a valuable military asset. Hastie recommended that small Negro units be integrated into larger white units and that Negro soldiers be assigned to all of the new types of units being formed. The policy of assigning most black soldiers to menial duties should be stopped. But, Hastie pointed out, segregation was the root of all difficulties: "Insistence upon a rigid separation of white and black soldiers is probably the most dramatic evidence of hypocrisy in our profession that we are girding ourselves for the preservation of democracy."[4]

Secretary Stimson asked General George C. Marshall, the Army Chief of Staff, to comment on Hastie's criticism. Marshall responded that it seemed to him that Hastie wanted to solve "a social problem which has perplexed the American people throughout the history of this nation [but] the Army cannot accomplish such a solution, and should not be charged with the undertaking." In dealing with the Negro problem, the Army

---

[3] This report by Hastie was reprinted in the Pittsburgh *Courier*, February 6, 1943, after he had resigned his position in protest.

[4] Quoted in Pittsburgh *Courier*, February 6, 1943.

had to recognize certain facts: Segregation was an established American custom; the educational level of Negroes was below that of whites; the Army must utilize its personnel according to their capabilities; and "experiments within the Army in the solution of social problems are fraught with danger to efficiency, discipline, and morale."[5] Through this exchange it became obvious that Hastie and the Army had reached an impasse over segregation before the United States became involved in World War II.

At the beginning of the defense build-up, there was some division among Negroes over the position they should adopt concerning military segregation. Hastie recognized this split upon first taking office and said that "as long as people who are opposed to mixed units are able to point to Negroes as also agreeing with this position our problem is extremely difficult."[6] Some of the Negroes advocating separate military units were conservatives, or "Uncle Toms" as they were labeled. Others took the view that it was unrealistic to expect the military services to end segregation, and the only way to secure broad Negro participation in the military was to push for the creation of separate Negro divisions and Negro flying units. "We have asked for a Negro division, Negro this and Negro that, without an intelligent awareness of the defeatism incurred by such a pleading," the editor of the Chicago *Defender* complained.[7]

When a conservative group of Negroes wrote the President objecting to integrated officer training schools in the Army — a significant break with the tradition of segregation — prominent Negroes reacted emotionally. Forty-one Negro leaders, a *Who's Who* of black leadership, wrote the President that segregated officer training would be a "backward step" and was not what the majority of Negroes wanted. "Segregation has always led to discrimination . . . ," their statement said.[8] When the Air Corps established a segregated aviation school at Tuskegee Institute, the editor of *The Crisis* called it "a step in the right

[5] Quoted in Lee, *The Employment of Negro Troops*, 140–41.
[6] Pittsburgh *Courier*, November 30, 1940.
[7] Chicago *Defender*, October 26, 1940.
[8] Pittsburgh *Courier*, November 1, 1941.

direction" because it opened up a branch of the Army heretofore closed to Negroes. However,

it adheres to the old Army pattern of segregation. This pattern is the
cause of most of the trouble experienced by Negroes in civilian as
well as military life. Until segregation as a procedure is overthrown,
the race will be hobbled in all of its endeavors in every field.[9]

As the war progressed, the attitude of the NAACP became the
dominant attitude of Negroes toward segregation.

When it became obvious that the Army was not going to
budge on its policy of segregated units, the NAACP began a
campaign for a volunteer integrated division. Walter White
secured the assistance of Eleanor Roosevelt to put this idea before
the President and General Marshall. White wrote Marshall that
such a division "would serve as a tremendous lift to the morale
of the Negro, which at present is at a dangerous low ebb." Since
America was now at war, White was convinced that such a
move "would also have tremendous psychological effect upon
white Americans, and it would give the lie to the attacks made
by Nazi Germany . . . to the effect that the United States talks
about democracy but practices racial segregation and discrimination."[10]

This proposal for a mixed division had considerable support
among Negroes and white liberals, and requests for its formation continued throughout the war.[11] The Negro Newspaper
Publishers Association endorsed a crusade for the establishment
of a volunteer mixed division and expressed the hope that such
a unit would provide the basis for a policy of integration
throughout the Army.[12] The War Department never seriously

[9] "Air Pilots, But Segregated," *The Crisis*, 48 (February, 1941), 39.

[10] Walter White to General George C. Marshall, December 22, 1941;
White to Justice Felix Frankfurter, January 9, 1942; both in ASW 291.2,
NARG 335.

[11] P. L. Prattis, executive editor of the Pittsburgh *Courier*, to General
George C. Marshall, December 29, 1941; memorandum to Mr. McCloy
from E. R. [Eleanor Roosevelt], May 30, 1944; both in ASW 291.2,
NARG 335; Norfolk *Journal and Guide*, January 24, 1942; Baltimore
Afro-American, January 17, 1942.

[12] Norfolk *Journal and Guide*, June 13, 1942.

considered these proposals and, indeed, thought them danger-ous to military effectiveness. White was told simply that "the War Department does not contemplate the organization of a division such as you suggested." This curt reply to what Negroes thought of as a serious proposition led to a great deal of criticism of the Army. Assistant Secretary of War John J. McCloy did not have "the slightest doubt of the unwisdom of having any such unit," but he was "inclined to think that in the future it may be advisable to handle these matters by an interview." [13]

One of the major problems for the Army was where to station the increasing number of Negro troops. Most of the Army's training camps were in the South, and this was the logical place for the Negro soldiers to be assigned. Southerners, however, were alarmed at the stationing of large groups of black troops in their areas and protested vigorously. At a Southern governors' conference in 1942 there was unanimous opposition to stationing Negro troops in the South. Governor Homer M. Adkins of Arkansas protested the use of Negro soldiers to guard an air-field in his state; it would be a "grave mistake" and would add to the agitation of Negroes by "subversive groups" and the "fiery" Negro press. The Governor of Mississippi objected to the use of Negro instructors to teach whites at military instal-lations in his state, and the entire Mississippi congressional delegation protested the assignment of Negro officers in their state. Most of the Southerners who protested pointed out that, if Negro troops must be assigned to their section, then they should be Southern Negroes.[14]

---

[13] General E. S. Adams, The Adjutant General, to White, January 8, 1942; memorandum, McCloy to General Adams, January 13, 1942; both in ASW 291.2, NARG 335.

[14] Governor Adkins to Robert P. Patterson, Under Secretary of War, April 29, 1942; Paul B. Johnson, Governor of Mississippi, to the Presi-dent, February 2, 1943; Mississippi Representatives John E. Rankin, Jamie L. Whitten, William M. Whittington, Aaron Lane Ford, Ross A. Collins, William M. Colmer, and Dan R. McGehee to Assistant Secretary of War McCloy, April 30, 1942; all in ASW 291.2, NARG 335. Letters from Governor Frank M. Dixon of Alabama and Senator John Bankhead of Alabama are reprinted in the Pittsburgh *Courier*, May 30, 1942, and August 8, 1942, respectively.

Objections to the assignment of black troops also came from other sections of the country, a fact that must have reinforced the belief within the War Department that segregation was an American custom that had to be observed by the Army. In 1943 the town of Oscoda, Michigan, demanded that the War Department remove Negro soldiers stationed there because they would "create social and racial problems in the community."[15] The citizens of Tucson, Arizona, refused an offer of fifty thousand dollars to build a U.S.O. center for Negro troops because they did not want black soldiers on leave to visit there. This was in 1942, and in 1943 the local Tucson paper and one of the state's senators requested that all Negro troops be removed from a local air base.[16] The national commander of the American Legion protested the integration of Negro soldiers in the wards of an Army hospital and in the hospital's barber shop.[17]

Objections to having Negro troops stationed in communities were so frequent that the War Department had trouble finding locations for the ever-increasing number of black soldiers. General Marshall ordered the Army General Staff to make a study of this matter in November, 1941. The results indicated that few commanders felt that more Negro troops could be accommodated in their areas without causing complaints from the civilian communities. Negro troops would be resented at five out of six northern posts and over half of the southern posts, this survey indicated. Practically all of the commanders at southern posts added that Northern Negroes would cause more resentment than would Southern.[18] The fact that these attitudes prevailed even after Pearl Harbor added to the cynicism of Negroes toward the war effort.

One of the biggest headaches for the Army during the war — and a prime example of discrimination caused by segregation — was the effect of the policy of segregation on the draft. The

[15] Pittsburgh *Courier*, April 24, 1943.

[16] Pittsburgh *Courier*, January 24, 1942; memorandum, Col. J. S. Leonard to John J. McCloy, April 24, 1943, ASW 291.2, NARG 335.

[17] Roane Waring to Robert P. Patterson, Under Secretary of War, February 22, 1943, ASW 291.2, NARG 335.

[18] Lee, *The Employment of Negro Troops*, 102–3.

Army recognized that, because of the small percentage of Negroes in the Army at the beginning of mobilization, the initial rate of increase in Negro strength would have to be proportionately higher than that for whites in order to achieve a Negro strength of 9 to 10 per cent. Once this level was reached, the Negro induction rate could continue according to the population ratio. The increase seemed simple enough on paper, but, due to a variety of factors, it proved very difficult in practice.

The first complication was that segregated Negro units required a close tabulation of men by race — the number of Negroes entering the armed services had to have available spaces in Negro units to which they could be assigned. But from the beginning of the draft in 1940 the Army indicated a reluctance to draft enough Negroes to make them 9 to 10 per cent of its strength or to create enough Negro units to which a proportionate number of Negroes could be assigned. Although the Selective Service System held conferences with the War Department over this problem, repeated promises that the Army would draft a proportionate number of draft-eligible Negroes went unfulfilled throughout 1941. This problem was highlighted when the Army failed to request a single Negro from Selective Service in the first requisition after Pearl Harbor. The Army constantly pointed to its policy of segregation and the lack of training cadres and facilities as the causes that delayed the induction of Negroes.[19]

In determining the order in which men were to be drafted, Selective Service did not at first use race as a criterion. Calls were supposed to be by order number, irrespective of race. This policy meant that Negroes should have been called at the same rate as whites, one Negro for every ten whites. Because the Army claimed that it could not induct a proportionate share of Negroes, it requested, and Selective Service complied reluctantly with, separate calls by race. Considerable problems resulted for those Negroes whose numbers had been reached by Selective Service. They were sent "notices of selection," which for white registrants

<hr>

[19] Selective Service System, *Special Groups: Special Monograph No. 10*, 89–90, 95.

were followed shortly by orders for induction but for Negroes meant only that they had been selected for induction and that they would be called at an unspecified later date. Many Negroes lost or quit their jobs after receiving these notices of selection and yet had to wait months until the Army's call actually led to their induction. By September, 1941, the total number of Negroes passed over in this manner and awaiting call was 27,986. By early 1943 it was estimated that a total of 300,000 Negroes had been passed over in favor of whites.[20]

The Army and Selective Service were subjected to considerable criticism for this situation. The Governor of Connecticut at first instructed draft boards in his state to induct men as their names came up, without regard to race.[21] All over the country, in areas with a large Negro population, local draft boards were forced to pass over Negroes and take whites who were further down the list of priority. Whites felt that Negroes were being favored, and Negroes were insulted because they were not allowed to do their share. One black editor admitted that a protest by white Southern congressmen over discrimination against white draftees caused by the racial quota brought forth a chuckle from many Negroes: "The white South made its Negrophobic bed and must continue to lie in it, even if this does result in drafting of white fathers while single Negroes remain in civil life."[22]

The Selective Service System worried throughout the war that the Army's policy of "race quotas" might be in violation of the nondiscrimination clause of the Selective Service Act. In Chicago a group of Negroes formed a group called the "Conscientious Objectors Against Jim Crow" to resist the draft because of segregation.[23] Surprisingly, the only legal case during World War II that seriously challenged separate calls was that

[20] *Special Groups*, 46–47, 94–95; Lee, *The Employment of Negro Troops*, 89–91; Lewis B. Hershey, Director of Selective Service, to the President, October 4, 1941, OF 93, FDRL.
[21] Pittsburgh *Courier*, November 23, December 21, 1940, February 22, 1941.
[22] *The New York Times*, January 22, 24, 1941; Pittsburgh *Courier*, October 9, 1943.
[23] Chicago *Defender*, January 18, 1941.

NEW WAR, OLD POLICY | 53

of Winfred W. Lynn of New York City. Lynn had failed to report for induction, giving as his reason the belief that the racial quota violated the nondiscrimination clause of the Selective Service Act. Various federal courts, including the Supreme Court, refused to rule on the real issue that Lynn was attempting to determine, and racial quotas, together with the resulting discrimination, were allowed to continue throughout the war.[24]

The problem of passing over Negroes in the draft was compounded because until 1943 the Army was the only branch of the service utilizing Selective Service. The Navy relied on volunteers, and since it allowed only a limited number of Negro enlistments in the messman's branch, and the Marine Corps did not take Negroes at all, the Army was left to utilize the great bulk of Negro manpower. Furthermore, the Navy, even after Pearl Harbor, showed no inclination to broaden opportunities for Negroes on its own. The bitter criticism of the Navy by Negroes had prompted Secretary Frank Knox to create a committee in July, 1941, to determine if changes in the Negro policy of the Navy and the Marine Corps were needed. Two weeks after Pearl Harbor a majority of this committee reported that "the enlistment of Negroes (other than as mess attendants) leads to disruptive and undermining conditions." This report claimed that there was no discrimination against Negroes in the Navy, because Negroes' "characteristics" made them fit only for messman's duty.[25]

The Army added pressure to that of Negroes for a change in Navy policy. Secretary of War Stimson complained to President Roosevelt in early 1942:

---

[24] *Special Groups*, 49–50; Dwight MacDonald, "The Novel Case of Winfred Lynn," *The Nation*, 156 (February 20, 1943), 268–70, and "The Supreme Court's New Moot Suit," *The Nation*, 159 (July 1, 1944), 13–14; S. P. Breckinridge, "The Winfred Lynn Case Again: Segregation in the Armed Forces," *Social Service Review*, 18 (September, 1944), 369–71.

[25] "United States Naval Administration in World War II, Bureau of Naval Personnel: The Negro in the Navy" (typewritten manuscript in the Bureau of Naval Personnel, n.d.), 3–4. This work is cited hereafter as "The Negro in the Navy."

By voluntary recruiting the Navy has been able to avoid acceptance of any considerable number of Negroes. As a result, while the Army has absorbed its proper proportion of Negro manpower [this was not true], it is now faced with the possibility of having to accept an even greater proportion in the future. This it cannot absorb without adverse affect on its combat efficiency.[26]

The solution to the problem, as Stimson saw it, was for the President to order the Navy to take its recruits from Selective Service as did the Army.

Roosevelt sent Stimson's memorandum to Secretary Knox, and the Navy Secretary suggested that the President refuse the Army's request. Roosevelt sided with the Navy and refused to order that service to take its men from Selective Service. "If the Navy living conditions on board ship were similar to the Army living conditions on land," Roosevelt wrote Stimson, "the problem would be easier but the circumstances . . . being such as they are, I feel that it is best to continue the present system at this time."[27] Roosevelt had accepted the Navy's argument that segregation was difficult to maintain on board ship.

Although the President was not willing to force the Navy to rely on the draft for its manpower, he did take note of Negro criticism and pressure for the Navy to open ratings other than messman for Negroes. "I think that with all the Navy activities," Roosevelt wrote Knox in January, 1942, the Navy "might invent something that colored enlistees could do in addition to the rating of messman." Knox had a board of officers consider the President's suggestion. They concluded that the Navy's Negro policy was no more discriminatory than the general policy toward Negroes throughout the United States; therefore, no change in policy was needed. This board's reasoning is a good example of the kind of thinking predominant among the military at the time:

---

[26] Memorandum, Stimson to the President, February 16, 1942, OF 18, FDRL. Also see Henry L. Stimson Diary, January 17, 1942.

[27] Memorandum, Knox to the President, n.d. (probably February, 1942); memorandum, Roosevelt to Stimson, February 24, 1942; both in OF 18, FDRL.

The reasons for discrimination in the United States are rather generally that: (a) the white man will not accept the negro in a position of authority over him; (b) the white man considers that he is of a superior race and will not admit the negro as an equal; and (c) the white man refuses to admit the negro to intimate family relationships leading to marriage. These concepts may not be truly democratic, but it is doubtful if the most ardent lovers of democracy will dispute them, particularly in regard to intermarriage.[28]

Secretary Knox transmitted the officers' report to the President, suggesting that the only service that could be opened to Negroes and still maintain segregation was the Marine Corps. Roosevelt replied that he did not think that the choice lay only between messman duty and full utilization of Negroes throughout the Navy. "To go the whole way at one fell swoop would seriously impair the general average efficiency of the Navy," wrote Roosevelt. Nevertheless, there were jobs other than messman that could be opened to Negroes, and the President suggested that the matter be returned to the board of officers "for further study and report." The board of Navy officers stubbornly maintained that service for Negroes other than the messman's branch was undesirable, but, if it was necessary, a number of labor duties were suggested that might be performed by black sailors. After Roosevelt had conferred with Secretary Knox, the Navy finally announced in April, 1942, that Negroes might enlist for general service as well as for the messman's branch.[29]

Negroes were not particularly happy about the more liberal assignment policy of the Navy. For them the proper goal was an end to segregation. The Pittsburgh *Courier* characterized the Navy's new policy as a "setback" because "it strengthens the vicious institution of segregation, the root cause of all the ills the Negro suffers in this country." *The Crisis* said that "the old system of segregation which has fathered inequalities and humiliations in the Army and in civilian life is now transferred to the Navy."[30] The Army's problem of having to take "too

---

[28] "The Negro in the Navy," 5–6.

[29] "The Negro in the Navy," 7–8.

[30] Pittsburgh *Courier*, April 18, 1942; "The Navy Makes a Gesture," *The Crisis*, 49 (May, 1942), 51.

many" Negroes was not eased either. The Navy planned to enlist only fourteen thousand Negroes the first year under the new plan.[31]

One of the main reasons that the armed services were reluctant to have Negroes was their low educational achievement as a group. The Army graded its manpower by tests designed to indicate the ability to absorb training. This Army General Classification Test (AGCT) was designed so that scores fell into the following grades, highest to lowest: Grade I, 7 per cent; Grade II, 24 per cent; Grade III, 38 per cent; Grade IV, 24 per cent; Grade V, 7 per cent. Grades I, II, and III were supposed to produce Army leadership classes and enlisted specialists and technicians; Grades IV and V were expected to produce the semiskilled soldiers and laborers. The scores of the white soldiers generally matched the curve above, but over 80 per cent of the black soldiers scored within Grades IV and V.[32]

While Negroes generally ranked lower on the AGCT than whites, Negroes and whites of comparable educational backgrounds made comparable scores, but because of the policy of segregation, Negro units received a much higher percentage of low-scoring men than white units. For example, the 351,951 white AGCT Grade V men, or 8.5 per cent of the total, drafted between March, 1941, and December, 1942, could be distributed among a total of 4,129,259 whites. On the other hand, the 216,664, or 49.2 per cent of the Negro total inducted in the same period could be distributed only among the total of 440,162 Negroes. Negro units were not only handicapped from the beginning by inexperienced or inadequate cadres, but they were also handicapped by inadequate education of the bulk of their personnel.[33]

The overwhelming majority of the low-scoring black personnel, as well as the majority of low-scoring whites, came from the South. This section spent comparatively less on education than other areas of the country, and there was a striking correlation between education expenditures and rejection as unfit for

[31] "The Negro in the Navy," 8.
[32] Lee, *The Employment of Negro Troops*, 239–43.
[33] Lee, *The Employment of Negro Troops*, 243–44.

the services due to "mental deficiency."[34] Such distinctions were generally not made within the Army in regard to these scores. For example, it was common within the Army to refer to AGCT scores as indices of intelligence although they actually measured a man's educational achievement. From the first false assumption was derived the postulate that *all* Negroes were innately inferior in intelligence, and this allowed Army planners to use the unfavorable scores to justify restrictive practices in the use of Negro manpower. For example, in late 1941 the Army had adopted more rigid literacy standards "mainly" to reduce the number of Negroes that the Army had to induct. But Secretary Stimson saw this as "reacting badly in preventing us from getting in some very good and illiterate [white] recruits from the southern mountain states."[35] White illiterates, it was somehow reasoned, were superior to Negro illiterates.

The example of Secretary of War Stimson indicates to what extent racist assumptions existed within the Army and dictated its Negro policy. From the beginning of his tenure as Secretary of War, Stimson warned President Roosevelt against placing "too much responsibility on a race which was not showing initiative in battle."[36] Stimson drew upon what he thought were World War I experiences; according to him, Woodrow Wilson had yielded to political pressure, appointed some Negro officers, "and the poor fellows made perfect fools of themselves."

Leadership is not imbedded in the negro race yet and to try to make commissioned officers to lead men into battle — colored men — is only to work disaster to both. Colored troops do very well under white officers but every time we try to lift them a little bit beyond where they can go, disaster and confusion follows. In the draft we are preparing to give the negroes a fair shot in every service . . . , even to aviation where I doubt very much if they will not produce disaster there. Nevertheless they are going to have a try but I hope for heaven's sake they won't mix the white and colored troops together in the same units for then we shall certainly have trouble.[37]

[34] Eli Ginzberg and Douglas W. Bray, *The Uneducated*, 48–55.
[35] Lee, *The Employment of Negro Troops*, 244–46; Stimson Diary, May 12, 1942.
[36] Stimson Diary, October 25, 1940.
[37] Stimson Diary, September 30, 1940.

In discussing the racial policy of the Army, Stimson frequently pointed out his abolitionist background, his long experience with the race problem, and his contention that he was not prejudiced. In the same breath, he would complain that those "foolish leaders of the colored race" who objected to segregation in the Army were really seeking "social equality"; this was impossible to achieve "because of the impossibility of race mixture by marriage."[38] The ambiguity of Stimson's thought on the race problem sometimes showed itself in a burst of anger at the South and the institution of slavery as the roots of the problem. "We are suffering from the persistent legacy of the original crime of slavery," Stimson wrote in his diary after receiving protests from the South against stationing Negro troops there. And "the south which foisted that crime upon us," he continued, "is the part of the country which now protests most loudly against being subject to any of the risks which have followed the wrong-doings of their ancestors."[39] Stimson's thinking on the Negro was not unique within the War Department.

This view of the black soldier as a problem, rather than as a manpower asset to be fully utilized, pervaded the armed services in the first years of the war. In turn, this view led to many of the difficulties in regard to Negroes that plagued the War Department. The passing over of Negro draftees by Selective Service was due to the Army's failure to provide enough units and housing for Negro troops. Adequate units and housing were not furnished because Army planners and commanders viewed Negroes as undesirable soldier material, and they wanted to induct as few as possible. Stereotypes of the black soldier were based on the 80 per cent of the Negroes who were in Grades IV and V on the AGCT; this led to a situation whereby the other 20 per cent were not utilized according to their skills or education. These AGCT scores were also viewed as an index of intelligence and reinforced the idea that Negroes were inherently inferior, fit only for labor duties.[40] Often the concentration of so many low AGCT men became an excuse for inadequate

---

[38] Stimson Diary, January 24, 1942.
[39] Stimson Diary, January 17, 1942.
[40] Lee, *The Employment of Negro Troops*, 93–100.

training progress and discipline. But low scores did not provide the answer to all of the problems of Negro units.[41]

The War Department policy announcement of October, 1940, had stated that Negro units were to be provided in all branches of the Army. According to the Army's mobilization regulations, Negroes were to be assigned to the combat branches in the same ratio as whites. In early 1942 Civilian Aide Hastie noted that this policy was not being put into practice. Hastie found that there was a tendency to assign Negroes to small scattered units. Furthermore, the vast majority of black soldiers were assigned to general labor units. An example of this phenomenon was the Medical Corps, which had 11 per cent of its strength Negro practically all of whom were assigned to sanitation companies. There were no white sanitation companies. "Generally," Hastie found, "plans for utilization of Negro soldiers still reflect a prevailing view in the Army that as small a number of Negroes as possible be given combat training." [42]

Hastie's point was true. The Army General Staff was formulating plans to place the bulk of the colored soldiers in the noncombatant units to "release" white troops for combat units. The necessity for a token number of Negro combat units — "due to unavoidable reasons" — was recognized, but they were to be kept to a minimum. This was the Army's answer to pressure from Selective Service to draft a proportionate share, by this time determined to be 10.6 per cent, of Negroes. Mobilization plans for the rest of the war provided for the "exclusive use of colored troops" in labor units — port battalions, water supply battalions, gasoline supply battalions, ammunition battalions, and the like. To provide more units to which Negroes could be assigned, the creation of new types of units was suggested. These included "station maintenance companies" for fighting fires and for landscaping and grading, and "metropolitan service companies" for moving office furniture, fixtures, and supplies around cities. The type of thinking that resulted in such planning is contained in an Army staff memorandum: "There is

[41] Lee, *The Employment of Negro Troops*, 273–74.
[42] Memorandum, Hastie to Under Secretary of War Patterson, February 5, 1942, ASW 291.2, NARG 335.

[a] general consensus of opinion that colored units are inferior to the performance of white troops, except for service duties," and this weakness was "due to the inherent psychology of the colored race and their need for leadership."[43]

The Army's burst of concern over the types of units to which Negroes could be assigned resulted from the necessity to induct more Negroes in order to have 10.6 per cent of its strength black. As the number of Negroes passed over in the draft became greater, Selective Service increased its pressure on the Army and threatened to abandon calls on the basis of race for selection by order number alone. The Army was reluctant to draft a proportionate number of Negroes because of the objection of the various branches to including Negroes. At the end of 1941, most of the Negroes in the Army were concentrated in the Infantry, Engineers, and Quartermaster Corps, and in the Infantry only 5 per cent of the personnel were black. In the Air Corps and Signal Corps less than 2 per cent of all enlisted men were Negro. Of all men who were unassigned or were in miscellaneous detachments throughout the Army, 27 per cent were Negro. As the black strength of the Army doubled in the next seven months, this imbalance was increased. For example, the Air Corps increased its size faster than any other branch, yet its Negro strength declined to less than 1 per cent of its total.[44]

Under pressure from Selective Service to induct more black soldiers, the Army General Staff was compelled to order the various branches to provide sufficient units to make 10.6 per cent of their strength Negro. Under these conditions, the provision of segregated units to which Negroes could be assigned became a major goal. "In some cases," Ulysses G. Lee, the authority on the Army and the Negro during World War II, has written, "careful examination of the usefulness of the types of units provided was subordinated to the need to create units which could receive Negroes."[45] The general assumption within

---

[43] Memorandum, General Dwight D. Eisenhower, Assistant Chief of Staff to the Chief of Staff, March, 1942; memorandum, General R. W. Crawford to Eisenhower, April 2, 1942; both in OPD; RTF; CWL, NARG 319.

[44] Lee, *The Employment of Negro Troops*, 111–12.

[45] Lee, *The Employment of Negro Troops*, 113.

the armed forces that Negroes could perform only unskilled jobs and that they were particularly suited for labor units, dictated the types of units each branch would provide for its share of colored manpower. The Air Corps is a good example. This branch formed such units as "aviation squadrons," which despite their name performed only housekeeping chores around air bases. "Aviation quartermaster truck companies" and "air base transportation platoons" were invented to perform general service duties. "Airdrome defense units" and "airbase security battalions" were supposed to protect air bases against riots, parachute attacks, and air raids.[46]

The concentration of Negroes into service or labor units, resulting in inadequate representation of Negroes in combat units, was encouraged by other factors. Army commanders in the field objected to having Negro combat units assigned to their command, and the General Staff had adopted the policy of not forcing unwanted units on a commander. In May, 1942, Stimson described the Negro problem as "very explosive and serious." Negroes were protesting the fact that black units that had completed their training were not being sent to the war zones. When it was suggested to General Marshall that some Negro combat units be sent to North Africa, he quickly replied that commanders there would object.[47] In the spring of 1942 the all-Negro Ninth Cavalry was alerted for overseas shipment, but when the commander of the theater to which it was to be assigned objected, the unit was sent back to its home station.[48] These incidents reflected the belief that the Negro was inferior as a combat soldier, a fact many thought had been proven in World War I.

By the fall of 1942 the waste of Negro manpower became so obvious that a planning group of the Army General Staff suggested that Negroes and whites be integrated in the same units. Colonel E. W. Chamberlain felt that if Negroes were placed in white units at a ratio of one Negro to nine whites, there would

---

[46] Lee, *The Employment of Negro Troops*, 113–16; Lawrence J. Paszek, "Negroes and the Air Force, 1939–1949," 7–8.

[47] Stimson Diary, May 12, 1942.

[48] Major Bell Irvin Wiley, *The Training of Negro Troops*, 3.

be "no more integration of the white and colored races than is the employment of Negroes as servants in a white household." Integration at this rate would enable the Army to absorb more black soldiers without placing them in useless units. The suggestion was opposed, on the grounds that it would impair the general quality of white combat units.[49]

The policy of segregation and the necessity to provide Negro units quickly also brought about a change in the Army's thinking as to the size of Negro units. After World War I, Army planners insisted that large all-Negro units, such as a division, were undesirable, and they suggested that no Negro unit larger than a regiment be created in the future. This was the general policy at the beginning of mobilization in 1940. The White House informed Negroes that no Negro division was planned in the Regular Army or National Guard; instead, black units such as a regiment were to be combined with white units to form division and corps-size units.[50]

The pressure from Selective Service for the Army to take more Negroes, the complaints by Negroes that they were utilized only in small miscellaneous units, and the demand for a volunteer integrated division all made the advantages of large all-Negro units look more attractive. A division could absorb over fifteen thousand men and the supporting units of a division would afford the Negro representation in almost every branch of the service. Following this line of reasoning, the War Department decided in early 1942 to activate four Negro Infantry divisions in the near future. Once again segregation was the primary reason for a policy, and military efficiency was a subordinate consideration. This decision, and the policy of segregation, meant that Negro divisions would be handicapped from the beginning, with 80 to 90 per cent of their personnel in AGCT Grades IV and V, as compared to 30 to 40 per cent in white divisions.[51]

[49] Lee, *The Employment of Negro Troops*, 152–57.

[50] Lee, *The Employment of Negro Troops*, 122–28; Baltimore *Afro-American*, September 7, 1940.

[51] Stimson Diary, January 17, 1942; Lee, *The Employment of Negro Troops*, 127–28.

Separate-but-equal was not achieved in the armed forces during the first years of the war. There is some doubt that it ever could have been achieved, because the thinking behind military policy was focused on the *separate* to such an extent that efficiency, supposedly the major goal of the military, was always subordinated to the goal of segregation. The effect of racist assumptions upon the utilization of Negro manpower seems obvious today. But those who made policy in the early 1940's identified their thinking with that of American society — white American society to be sure, but what American Negroes thought did not seem so important at the time.

CHAPTER IV

Frustration and Violence, 1940-1943

ALTHOUGH THE POLICIES of the War Department required segregation, the men who formulated these policies did not always realize the impact they would have on the individual soldier — particularly the Negro soldier. The Army's proclaimed goal was maximum military efficiency, yet its policy makers failed to realize that policies that led to underutilization and demoralization of 10 per cent of the nation's manpower were grossly inefficient.

The reluctance of the Army to call the few colored reserve officers to active duty at the beginning of mobilization was a cause for discontent among Negroes. In January, 1940, there were only five Negro officers in the Regular Army — three chaplains and two combat officers.[1] Resistance to Negro officers was based on what was thought to be the experience of World War I. Negroes were supposed to be inherently deficient in leadership ability, and thus they did not make good officers and should be kept to a minimum. A corollary to this thinking was that white officers who had some experience with Negroes, particularly Southerners, were best for black units.[2]

Despite the prevalence of World War I thinking about black

[1] Pittsburgh *Courier*, October 5, 12, 1940, February 8, 1941. Baltimore *Afro-American*, November 4, 1939.

[2] Ulysses G. Lee, Jr., *The Employment of Negro Troops*, 180; Henry L.

officers' abilities, there was a significant change in the training of Negro officers in World War II. With the exception of the Air Corps, officer candidate schools in the Army were integrated from the beginning in World War II, because of the expense and inefficiency that a separate officers' training program would have entailed. White and Negro slept, ate, and trained together in these camps without any serious incidents. Although Army policy makers failed to see any lesson in this important break with segregation, it put on record, for others to point to, evidence that integration could work in the Army without drastic consequences.[3]

The Army's Negro policy statement of October, 1940, stated that black officers would be assigned only to units of the National Guard. This meant that Negro officers were to be restricted from Negro Regular Army units, and thus only a few would be needed. Consequently, as the Army's black strength expanded, most of the new Negro units were staffed with white officers. In January, 1942, Hastie complained to Secretary Stimson that only twelve Negroes had been selected to attend Officer Candidate School in the preceding three months.[4] By the spring of 1942 Negro protests had grown so loud on this point that President Roosevelt intervened, and, in turn, Secretary Stimson ordered that more Negro officers must be provided for the Army. Forcing the Army to utilize colored officers led to a situation in which "the provision of position vacancies for Negro officers and not the provision of leadership for Negro troops became the criterion for policy decisions."[5]

Stimson Diary, January 17, May 12, 1942; Major Bell Irvin Wiley, *The Training of Negro Troops*, 28–29. The old charges against Negro officers were also revived in the white press: see "Problems," *Time*, 36 (August 12, 1940), 15–16.

[3] Charles Dollard and Donald Young, "In the Armed Forces," *Survey Graphic*, 36 (January, 1947), 68. This is an important source not only because the authors are sociologists, but also because both were affiliated with the Army's Information and Education Division during World War II.

[4] Memorandum, Robert P. Patterson to Secretary Stimson, January 10, 1942, ASW 291.2, NARG 335.

[5] Lee, *The Employment of Negro Troops*, 191–98; Jean Byers, *A Study*

Under pressure to designate units to which Negro officers could be assigned, most branches of the Army subordinated the consideration of ability to that of the numbers of Negro officers they thought they could accommodate. In this manner the Army duplicated the process followed in providing Negro units — "numbers and quotas and not potential leadership ability became the criterion for the acceptance of Negro [officer] candidates."[6] By the end of 1942 the number of Negro officers was beginning to exceed the number of possible assignments, due to several factors: the preference of white commanders for white officers for their Negro units; the belief that black officers did not possess leadership ability, together with the widespread conviction that Negro troops preferred service with white officers; and the objection by many communities around Southern training camps to Negro officers.[7]

The black officer knew that he was not wanted, and, under the circumstances, it is difficult to see how he could have maintained high morale. Army policy required that the Negro officer serve in designated units and grades only and that no black officer was to outrank or command a white officer in the same unit. This policy not only limited the Negro officers' opportunities and was a constant reminder of discrimination, but it also barred promotions. Since no black officer could hold a rank higher than that held by the lowest-ranking white officer, only the few Negroes in units with all-Negro officers could advance above the rank of first lieutenant. One post commander even went so far as to claim that a white first lieutenant would be considered superior to a Negro captain. This policy also meant that, whenever a new white officer was assigned to a unit having black officers, a shift among the officers occurred to ensure that no Negro commanded a white. Because Negro officers were considered to be a class somewhere between enlisted men and white officers, the black officer was often downgraded in the

of the Negro in Military Service (Washington, D.C.: mimeographed study for Department of Defense, 1950), 39–40. This study by Byers is polemical and incomplete.

[6] Lee, *The Employment of Negro Troops*, 205–12.
[7] Lee, *The Employment of Negro Troops*, 212–16.

eyes of his men, and this served to reduce further the morale and leadership effectiveness of the Negro officer.[8]

At the beginning of the war, segregation was rigidly maintained for Negro officers. At Fort Huachuca, Arizona, a primarily black post where an all-Negro division was in training, separate officers' clubs were established, even though there were only a few white officers.[9] Sometimes segregation was carried to ridiculous extremes. At Camp Wheeler, Georgia, the lone Negro officer on the post was provided two-story bachelor officer's quarters in which he lived alone; in the officers' mess a corner was fenced off for his eating area.[10] When a touring group of Latin American officers passed through Montgomery, Alabama, staff officers of Maxwell Field, Alabama, arranged a party at a white hotel and secured girls from a local white college to help entertain. The most popular group with the girls were the dark Haitian officers who spoke with French accents. At the time that the Maxwell Field authorities were arranging interracial entertainment for "foreign" Negroes, they were prohibiting American black officers stationed at the nearby Negro Air Corps pilot training center at Tuskegee from staying in town overnight.[11]

The most frequent complaint against Negro officers was "a chip-on-the-shoulder attitude concerning race." One white officer recalled that "Negro officers were often judged by whether they had the 'right attitude' toward race problems, so that obsequious and bootlicking individuals were favored far more than in white units."[12] The extreme race consciousness was not peculiar to Negro officers during the war but was in evidence throughout black communities, and it should not have been surprising, since the black officer was confronted on all sides by the fact that his race subjected him to different rules. Never-

[8] Byers, *A Study of the Negro*, 40–41.

[9] Pittsburgh *Courier*, July 4, 1942.

[10] Baltimore *Afro-American*, August 23, 1941.

[11] Colonel Noel F. Parrish, "The Segregation of Negroes in the Army Air Forces," (unpublished Air University Thesis, Maxwell Field, Alabama, 1947), 43–44. This is an important source because Col. Parrish, white, was stationed at the Air Corps' Tuskegee Flying School and actually commanded it for a period.

[12] Parrish, "The Segregation of Negroes," 34.

theless, white officers pointed to this race consciousness as causing Negro officers to see routine administrative acts and discipline as discriminatory. Although not generally recognized
in the Army at this time, the tendency for black soldiers to
blame everything that they did not like on racial discrimination
was a natural product of segregation.[13]

Furthermore, because of the high educational qualifications
for officer candidates, most Negroes who qualified to become
officers were from the North. They were therefore more likely
to resent the discrimination and segregation found in the Army
and were more prone to fight the system of segregation. At Camp
Stewart, Georgia, black officers would periodically ride up to
the white officers' club to seek admission, leaving their drivers
waiting in anticipation of refusal. In the officers' mess of a Negro
division, white officers arrived one time to find a black lieutenant
sitting at each of the tables usually occupied by whites. Such acts
of defiance by Negro officers were not infrequent, and they
added to the stereotype among most white officers of the black
officer as a nuisance, an incompetent, and an undesirable.[14]

The restricted opportunities for promotion, the strict segregation, and the animosity they encountered were frequently more
than black officers could take. They would request relief, or, in
more extreme cases, resignation from their commission. "I am
unable to adjust myself," one young officer wrote in requesting
that he be allowed to resign his commission,

to the handicap of being a Negro officer in the United States Army.
Realizing that minorities are always at odds for consideration commensurate with the privileges enjoyed by the greater number, I have
tried earnestly to find this expected lack of equality, and nothing
more, in the relationships and situations around me here. Prolonged
observation reveals that inconsistencies over and above a reasonable
amount are rampant. Sins of omission, sins of commission, humiliations, insults — injustices, all, are mounted one upon another until
one's zest is chilled and spirit broken.[15]

[13] Wiley, *The Training of Negro Troops*, 29.
[14] Wiley, *The Training of Negro Troops*, 30–31.
[15] Quoted in Lee, *The Employment of Negro Troops*, 235.

The attitude adopted by the Army toward Negro officers hindered the development of leadership qualities and, in this way, became a self-proving proposition.

The reluctance to have black officers and the belief that black troops preferred white officers, particularly those from the South, meant that most of the officers of Negro units were white. Actually, the Army's assumption that Negroes preferred white officers was false from the beginning: Surveys among black soldiers indicated that they overwhelmingly preferred Negro officers to white officers and preferred Northern white officers to Southern white officers.[16] Negro civilians were concerned about the officers their sons had for commanders. Columnist P. L. Prattis was convinced that at least 50 per cent of the Southern white officers assigned to Negro units should be transferred out:

Down the line somewhere somebody seems to have sold the idea to somebody else in the War Department that southern whites are the men to command Negro troops. Southern whites themselves have probably helped to sell the notion. They have been so used to bullying Negroes around in civilian life that they think the only difference in the Army is the uniform.[17]

Unfortunately, there were incidents enough to indict Southern white officers in the eyes of Negroes. One that caused a great outcry, for example, occurred when the white officers, mostly Southern, of a Negro unit stationed in Pennsylvania issued the order: "Any association between the colored soldiers and white women, whether voluntary or not, would be considered rape." And the penalty would be death.[18]

The white officer of black units had to face all of the problems of the officer of white units, but his job was made more difficult by additional problems peculiar to being an officer of a Negro unit. The white officer had to be on constant guard against any action on his part that might be construed as the result of prejudice. The result was a dilemma, for if he attempted to right an injustice against his troops, or if he tried to be proud of them,

[16] Samuel A. Stouffer and others, *The American Soldier*, Vol. I, 580–86.
[17] Pittsburgh *Courier*, July 19, 1941.
[18] Pittsburgh *Courier*, January 10, 1942.

he was often defamed by his white colleagues and labeled "pro-Negro." On the other hand, if the white officer indicated a reluctance to stick his neck out for his Negro troops, he was no longer an effective commander.[19]

The white officer of a Negro unit also found that he had extra duties to perform, as compared with his counterpart in a white unit. One white officer recalled that fear of outbreaks of violence led the post commander to require every unit to assign a white officer and three enlisted men to patrol the street along which the black troops were housed. Daily, from 6:00 P.M. to 11:00 P.M. six jeeps roamed up and down three-quarters of a mile of road. "The officers felt the duty ridiculous and unnecessary . . . ," he recalled. At some posts with both white and Negro officers, the belief in the incompetence of black officers led to assignment of white officers only to such extra duties as officer of the day, town patrol officer, and officer of the guard.[20]

In addition, the white officer of a Negro unit had a unique leadership problem because 70 to 90 per cent of the personnel under his command were in the low AGCT category, as compared to 20 to 40 per cent in white units. The training of his men thus required more time, effort, and patience. Under the circumstances it was not uncommon for men to break under the strain and to adopt the attitude that no amount of effort on their part would produce an efficient unit.[21] Added to the difficulty of more work was the fact that in the South, where most of the black troops were stationed, the usual prejudice against Negroes was applied by civilians to white officers serving with black units. White officers were treated as though they were "tainted." One of the first questions a civilian asked on meeting an Army officer was, "What type of troops do you have?"[22]

---

[19] Lee, *The Employment of Negro Troops*, 182; Parrish, "The Segregation of Negroes," 51.

[20] E. T. Hall, Jr., "Prejudice and Negro-White Relations in the Army," *American Journal of Sociology*, 52 (March, 1947), 402; Lee, *The Employment of Negro Troops*, 185–86, 221. Hall was a white officer who served with Negro units in the U.S., Europe, and the Pacific during World War II.

[21] Lee, *The Employment of Negro Troops*, 186–87.

[22] Hall, "Prejudice in the Army," 401–2.

There was a general belief within the Army that white officers assigned to Negro units had done something to incur the disfavor of former superiors and were thus being punished. Many times a new white officer reporting to a black unit was greeted with: "Well, what did you do to get sent here?" As a result a widespread belief developed among white officers that they were regarded at large as inferiors, as men who had failed to meet the requirements necessary to serve with white troops. There was also a general belief that once successful service with black troops was entered on a man's record he was stuck with service in Negro units for the duration. It is not surprising, then, that "loathing of service with colored troops was almost universal among white officers of Negro combat units and common among those in service organizations."[23]

A situation was created whereby most of the white officers of Negro units were desperate to get out of their assignments. "For God's sake can't you do something to get me out of here — anything but this," was the constant refrain from white officers whenever an officer from higher headquarters visited Negro units. The most popular way of seeking relief from a black unit was to feign illness and go to a hospital when the unit was about to be moved, hoping not to be returned.[24] The desperation reached by some white officers is shown by a letter written by a general in a Negro division, asking for a transfer:

General, I am asking the first favor I have asked in the Army. Please relieve me from this assignment; reduce me to my permanent grade; and send me to a combat unit on the European front. . . . I could be . . . of more use there as a lieutenant colonel than I am in this division. As a matter of fact, I am a pretty poor general, whereas I was a pretty good battalion commander.[25]

An important result of this reluctance to serve with Negro units was that requests to be transferred were numerous and the turn-

[23] Wiley, *The Training of Negro Troops*, 37–40. Also see Hall, "Prejudice in the Army," 407–8.

[24] Wiley, *The Training of Negro Troops*, 40; Hall, "Prejudice in the Army," 409.

[25] Quoted in Wiley, *The Training of Negro Troops*, 40.

over of officers in these units was rapid, an undesirable condition as far as leadership was concerned.

Added to the handicaps of inexperience and a high percentage of low-scoring AGCT personnel, Negro units were saddled with a situation destructive to the morale of the leaders — both black and white. Certainly segregation and the Army's racial policy did not favor military efficiency in the case of officers for Negro units. More important, because the numbers involved were far larger, was the effect of the Army's racial policies on the black enlisted men.

From the beginning of his military career, the Negro soldier was rigidly segregated. At induction centers he was placed in "special" companies and tested and classified separately. When black soldiers arrived at their assigned training camps, they found that a separate area within the camp had been set aside for them. The Negro area of an Army camp was usually on the fringe of the main post area, and the recreational facilities and living facilities in general were not as good as those for whites. At the beginning of the war the usual policy of posts where Negroes were stationed was for segregation in theaters, post exchanges, service clubs, and buses operating on the post.[26] Many Negroes were demoralized because they believed that maintaining racial separation was a more important goal for the Army than creating a fighting force to preserve the four freedoms. Many believed that segregation was inconsistent with the national goals in the war and should be challenged.

Since most of the Army's training camps were in the South, the majority of Negro soldiers were sent there for training. This meant that the black soldier found himself in an area where the white civilian population was hostile to his presence. A Negro in military uniform evoked hostility, fear, and suspicion on the part of many Southern whites. I remember these fears in a small Louisiana town during the war: It was felt that a Negro in the Army had been "spoiled"; he had forgotten his "place" and had

---

[26] Dollard and Young, "In the Armed Forces," 67.

become "uppity." Added to this anxiety was the belief that Northern whites and Negroes were taking advantage of the war to push for equal rights for Negroes.[27]

The situation was ripe for conflict and violence, and between 1941 and 1945 numerous outbreaks occurred. Southern white police shot and killed Negro soldiers on leave in communities nearby the camps. Negro soldiers traveling off post were expected to conform to the local mores, such as sitting in the back of the bus, or risk being clubbed and thrown into jail, maybe even shot. There was frequent conflict between white and Negro soldiers on and off military posts, many of these incidents involving skirmishes with weapons.[28] This race conflict within the military was paralleled by race conflict in civilian communities. Lynchings increased, and a peak was reached with a series of race riots in several large urban communities in 1943.

The Negro press protested vigorously over every incident. Especially outrageous to Negroes were numerous incidents involving the shooting or beating of black soldiers by white military police. After touring several Army camps, a Negro reporter charged that the military policemen's attitude was "challenging and repulsive": "Backed by the city police they do not hesitate to beat up and kill Negroes in the streets and in the jails." [29] When a Negro soldier was shot and killed by a white military policeman at Fort Bragg, North Carolina, the dead soldier was made a hero and memorialized in a poem. One stanza read:

> They say this is a war
> For Freedom Over There.
> Say, Mr. F D R

---

[27] Wiley, *The Training of Negro Troops*, 52–55.

[28] Nearly every issue of the Negro press during this period contains stories of violence between Negro soldiers and white civilians, or between white and Negro soldiers. For specific examples of conflict, see Byers, *A Study of the Negro*, 62–69; "The Pattern of Race Riots Involving Negro Soldiers," *A Monthly Summary of Events and Trends in Race Relations*, 2 (August–September, 1944), 15–18, cited hereafter as *Race Relations*; Lee, *The Employment of Negro Troops*, 348–79.

[29] Pittsburgh *Courier*, June 14, 1941.

How 'bout some Freedom Here?
'T was a Fort Bragg M.P. shot him down
One Evening when he was leaving town.[30]

The NAACP suggested that a civilian or civilian-military board be appointed by the President to investigate military police activities in the Army. The Army thought this "most unwise" and assured Negroes that "the War Department can and will maintain the dignity of the uniform."[31] The Army did create Negro military police units and improved its police training program, which eased the situation somewhat.

Negro reporters visiting Southern Army camps continuously reported low morale among black soldiers. Many Northern Negroes stationed in the South found it hard to adjust to the strict segregation and became convinced that there was no protection for them in the South.[32] Many Negro soldiers wrote letters home or to the press detailing their experiences. A young soldier at Fort Sill, Oklahoma, wrote that "the cross-section of the Negro soldiers' opinions here is that we had just as soon fight and die here for our rights as to do it on some foreign battlefield."[33] "How can we be trained to protect America, which is called a *free* nation, when all around us rears the ugly head of segregation?" wrote another.[34]

The paradox of building a segregated Army to fight an enemy dedicated to conquering the world in the name of a racist ideology was too obvious for black Americans to ignore. In an editorial entitled "Hitlerism at Home," the Pittsburgh *Courier* charged that "the War Department has bowed from the begin-

[30] "Ballad of Ned Turman," Pittsburgh *Courier*, January 31, 1942.

[31] Under Secretary of War Patterson to Walter White, September 18, 1941, ASW 291.2, NARG 335.

[32] Pittsburgh *Courier*, June 21, 1941; Baltimore *Afro-American*, September 7, 14, 1940.

[33] Pittsburgh *Courier*, August 30, 1941.

[34] A Negro Enlisted Man, "Jim Crow in the Army Camps," *The Crisis*, 47 (December, 1940), 385. For other examples, see Chicago *Defender*, July 19, 1941; Sergeant Warren T. Brunson, "What a Negro Soldier Thinks About," *Social Service Review*, 18 (December, 1944), 534–35; Lucille B. Milner, "Jim Crow in the Army," *New Republic*, 110 (March 13, 1944), 339–42.

ning of the national emergency to the doctrine of white supremacy and racial separatism with a zeal that Dr. Joseph Goebbels would regard as commendable."[35] *The Crisis* was convinced that segregation must be rooted out whether it "resides in the Mein Kampf of a Hitler, or in a memorandum in the adjutant general's office of the American Army."[36]

Negro soldiers found that many white Americans packed their prejudices as well as their clothes in their duffle bags when they went overseas. The first major concentration of American troops abroad occurred in Great Britain, and, unfortunately, America's race problem followed them there. Prejudiced whites resented the liberal treatment accorded black soldiers by British civilians, particularly the freedom with which British girls associated with Negro soldiers. Many white officers sought to discourage this challenge to American racial mores by placing English towns and pubs off limits to Negroes. Individual white soldiers spread stories among the English civilians that American Negroes were beasts with tails and that they raped white women. Resentful of the slander and discrimination, black soldiers frequently rioted, and many clashes between small groups of white and Negro soldiers occurred.[37]

This situation caused considerable embarrassment to the United States, and many solutions were offered. Arthur Sulzberger, publisher of *The New York Times*, told Secretary Stimson of his concern about the effect equal treatment of American Negroes by the English would have when these black soldiers returned home. Stimson proposed to President Roosevelt that Negro soldiers be concentrated in English cities where the populace would be less likely to associate so freely with them. General Benjamin O. Davis, after surveying the situation for the

[35] Pittsburgh *Courier*, August 23, 1941.

[36] "The Negro in the United States Army," *The Crisis*, 49 (February, 1942), 47.

[37] Byers, *A Study of the Negro*, 71–76; Nichols, *Breakthrough on the Color Front*, 66; Joseph Julian, "Jim Crow Goes Abroad," *The Nation*, 155 (December 5, 1942), 610–12; Lee, *The Employment of Negro Troops*, 440–41; "Colored Troops in Britain," *New Statesman and Nation*, 24 (August 22, 1942), 121; George W. Goodman, "The Englishman Meets the Negro," *Common Ground*, 5 (Autumn, 1944), 3–11.

Army Inspector General, found that much of the violence was due to poor leadership by white officers of Negro units and to the prejudiced attitudes of many white soldiers. General Davis found Negro soldiers asking, "Who are we over here to fight, the Germans or our own white soldiers?" The General recommended that the Army introduce the subject of race relations to soldiers in their basic training.[38]

Mrs. Roosevelt also was concerned about the situation in England. "I have heard . . . ," she wrote Secretary Stimson, "that the young Southerners were very indignant to find that Negro soldiers were not looked upon with terror by the girls in England and Ireland and Scotland." Her solution was to do "a little educating among our Southern white men and officers"; they should be told that "normal relationships with groups of people who do not have the same feeling that they have about the Negro cannot be prevented and that it is important for them to recognize that in different parts of the world certain situations differ and have to be treated differently."[39]

The racial situation in Great Britain was eased somewhat by vigorous command action on the part of General Dwight D. Eisenhower, Supreme Allied Commander. Eisenhower issued an order that was distributed to every officer in England, emphasizing that the British population held a different attitude toward race than did Americans. Any attempt to curtail association "by official order or restriction," the order said, "is unjustified and must not be attempted." Although racial friction was not eliminated entirely, the number of incidents was reduced.[40]

The violence directed against the black soldier and the segregation to which he was subjected led Negroes, civilian as well as military, to talk about their soldiers fighting on two fronts. "Here we are at war," derided a Negro editor, "and the blood

---

[38] Stimson Diary, September 24, 1942; Memorandum, General Benjamin O. Davis to the Inspector General, December 24, 1942, ASW 291.2, NARG 335.

[39] Eleanor Roosevelt to Secretary Stimson, September 22, 1942, ASW 291.2, NARG 335; Stimson Diary, November 20, 1942.

[40] Nichols, *Breakthrough on the Color Front*, 66–67; Lee, *The Employment of Negro Troops*, 623–26.

of Negro soldiers is being spilled not on the battlefield where America is engaged . . . with a powerful enemy, but on the field of racial antagonism and prejudice."[41] The Negro soldier, another editor claimed, is beginning "to realize that his real enemy is right here, and not far from the compound of his training camp."[42] The Norfolk *Journal and Guide* stated that it was "too much to expect" for Negroes "to fight on two fronts."[43] The militant *Crisis* was acrid:

Negro Americans might as well discover at the beginning whether they are to fight and die for democracy for the Lithuanians, the Greeks, and the Brazilians, or whether they had better fight and die for a little democracy for themselves.[44]

Unfortunately, there was little that the Federal Government or the Army could do about the acts of violence by white civilians against Negro soldiers. Then, as now, convictions in such cases were hard to achieve. There were steps that the Army could have taken, however, and its failure to do so in the early stages of the conflict must have been due to ignorance of the damage being done to Negro morale. After an incident in 1941 involving the shooting of two black soldiers by white military policemen, Civilian Aide Hastie recommended that the War Department issue a strong statement condemning racial violence in this and other cases. Assistant Secretary of War John J. McCloy discussed this proposal with the Army Staff. The timid consensus reached was that Hastie's statement "places too much emphasis upon white soldiers and civilians, in which case the War Department would be exposed to criticism." Also, "it might further aggravate the feeling of certain groups against colored soldiers and thus lead to more serious disturbances."[45]

---

[41] Chicago *Defender*, January 4, 1942.

[42] Chicago *Defender*, August 30, 1941.

[43] Norfolk *Journal and Guide*, April 19, 1941.

[44] "The Army Must Act," *The Crisis*, 48 (September, 1941), 279. Other examples of this cynical attitude are found in editorials of the Chicago *Defender*, September 6, 20, 1941, April 4, 1942; and the Norfolk *Journal and Guide*, September 20, 1944.

[45] McCloy to Under Secretary of War Patterson, September 19, 1941, ASW 291.2, NARG 335.

The War Department sought to blame the Negro press for the low morale of Negro soldiers. The Adjutant General of the Army charged the Negro press with "distorting" incidents of violence and discrimination against black soldiers. "Such distorted publicity has not only contributed to the lowering of morale of soldiers . . . , but the morale of the people at home," he complained.[46] This idea seeped down to individual post commanders, some of whom went so far as to ban Negro newspapers. Incidents such as these only proved to Negroes that their complaints and exposures had some substance.[47] Seeking to find the cause of low Negro morale outside of its own segregation policies, the Army failed to realize that the Negro press only mirrored what most Negroes were thinking.

The Research Branch of the Army made opinion surveys among soldiers during the war, from which it is possible to determine something about morale. Black soldier opinion was evenly divided over the desirability of having segregated Negro units, with the majority of those approving separation coming mainly from the South. The majority of black soldiers were opposed to segregation as a principle, however, although many accepted segregation as a practical necessity to prevent racial friction. In contrast, almost 90 per cent of the white soldiers, from the North as well as the South, expressed agreement with segregated units. Under these circumstances a certain amount of conflict and low morale appeared to be inevitable.[48]

These surveys appeared to confirm the Army's basic defense of segregation: that it was necessary for efficiency because practically all of its white personnel favored separation. If segregation was abandoned, the Army reasoned, it would certainly be a blow to the morale of 90 per cent of its strength, and it might

[46] Pittsburgh *Courier*, September 6, 1941.

[47] Lee, *The Employment of Negro Troops*, 384.

[48] Research Branch, Special Service Division, Services of Supply, War Department, "Attitudes of Enlisted Men Toward Negroes for Air Force Duty, November 30, 1942," and "Attitudes of White Enlisted Men Toward Sharing Facilities with Negro Troops, July 30, 1942"; both in ASW 291.2, NARG 335; Stouffer and others, *The American Soldier*, Vol. I, 568–69, 572–73.

result in bloody conflict. Many high-ranking Army officers also argued that segregation suited most Negroes because they were accustomed to it in civilian life. On the surface, the opinion surveys tended to confirm the beliefs of Army officials about the necessity of maintaining segregation, and they in turn interpreted them in this way.[49]

The social scientists in charge of the Army's opinion surveys cautioned that it was a mistake to assume that these surveys represented a "definitive" vote on the issue of segregation. Analysis of white attitudes indicated that, like some Negroes who accepted segregated units, many did not accept segregation as a basic principle, but as an expedient measure. The white soldiers were aware also that by expressing an opinion favorable to segregation they were voting for things as they were, as the Army's official policy was one of segregation. Furthermore, it was pointed out that a verbal response does not predict a person's actual behavior in a hypothetical situation that he has never experienced. In short, a slackening of the degree of segregation in the Army would not necessarily have been followed by violent resistance on the part of whites. Few questions of Army policy were decided on the basis of soldier preference, but the War Department overlooked the social scientists' qualifications of their findings, preferring to see them as confirming their predilections about the necessity of segregation.[50]

Negro soldiers reacted to their situation as members of a mi-

---

[49] Dollard and Young, "In the Armed Forces," 68.

[50] Dollard and Young, "In the Armed Forces," 68; Stouffer and others, *The American Soldier*, Vol. I, 571, 579-80; "Military Policy Implications of Report by Research Branch . . . on 'Attitudes of the Negro Soldier,'" cited hereafter as "Attitudes of the Negro Soldier," July 31, 1943, ASW 291.2, NARG 335. The warning of the Army's social scientists that behavior cannot be predicted from expressed opinions was proved when desegregation finally came to the Army. This insight has also proven to be important in desegregation situations of more recent years. For more on this, see Melvin M. Tumin, *Desegregation: Resistance and Readiness*; Joseph D. Lohman and Dietrich C. Reitzes, "Note on Race Relations in a Mass Society," *American Journal of Sociology*, 63 (November, 1957), 240-46; Dietrich C. Reitzes, "Institutional Structure and Race Relations," *Phylon*, 20 (1st Quarter, 1959), 48-66.

nority group rather than as individuals. Unlike white soldiers, they were prone to define events in racial terms. Thus, many complaints common to soldiers of both races — poor recreational facilities and poor food, for example — became racial discrimination in the eyes of black troops. This tendency was due to the system of segregation that made it easier to claim racial discrimination and to the Negro's general position as a disadvantaged minority in civilian life. It was obvious from opinion surveys that the black soldier was not satisfied with his status in American society. This dissatisfaction was probably increased by the fact that whites seemed to be ignorant of Negroes' opinions; over two thirds of Southern white soldiers and over half of Northern white soldiers expressed the opinion that most Negroes were satisfied with their status.[51]

Compared to white soldier morale, the morale of Negro soldiers was low. One commander of a Negro unit wrote in 1943: "The most difficult thing in all our work here is trying to instill a desire or determination in these soldiers' minds that they must and will fight. Approximately 95 per cent 'just don't want to.' "[52] While this was probably an exaggeration, black soldiers often displayed an ambivalent attitude toward the war. As Americans, Negro soldiers tended to respond to the appeals of patriotism and loyalty; furthermore, many Negroes saw the war as an opportunity to prove their loyalty, in the hope that their efforts would be rewarded. Struggling with the patriotic motivation for dominance in the black soldier's mind, however, was the bitterness over his treatment in and out of the armed services. Comparison of his treatment with the idealistic war aims often bred cynicism. One result of this conflict was that Negro soldiers were less likely than white soldiers to identify with the war or to endorse idealistic views of the war.[53]

Black soldiers also had more doubt than white soldiers concerning the importance of their role in the Army. When an opinion survey asked, "Do you think that most Negroes are being given a fair chance to do as much as they want to do to

[51] Stouffer and others, *The American Soldier*, Vol. I, 502–7.
[52] Quoted in Wiley, *The Training of Negro Troops*, 12.
[53] Stouffer and others, *The American Soldier*, Vol. I, 507.

help win the war?" 54 per cent of the Negro soldiers said "No," and 76 per cent of the white soldiers said "Yes." This feeling of unimportance was due in large part to the idea that the services had not really wanted Negroes and to the belief, not without foundation, that Negro soldiers were used primarily for labor duties. Paradoxically, black soldiers who claimed that they were denied full participation in the war tended to be both more cynical about the war and to claim that Negroes were doing more than their share to win it. The reasoning behind this complaint was that whites had denied equal Negro participation; under the circumstances, Negroes were doing more than whites had a right to expect. Black soldiers who thought in this vein felt that their contribution to the war effort provided a moral claim for improved postwar conditions. One paradox led to another: The profound cynicism of Negro soldiers toward the war was accompanied by a widespread belief that conditions for their race would be vastly improved after the war.[54]

It is not surprising that a study of opinion among black soldiers found that "the Negro was somewhat less likely than others to think that he had had a square deal from the Army."[55] The Army's policy statement of October, 1940, had claimed that segregation "had proven satisfactory over a long period of years." By the beginning of 1943 this position became increasingly difficult to believe, if one knew the extent of the trouble caused by the Army's "Negro problem."

---

[54] Stouffer and others, *The American Soldier*, Vol. I, 511–15, 529, 535; "Attitudes of Negro Soldiers," ASW 291.2, NARG 335. An excellent summary of Negro soldier morale by a Negro reporter who visited twenty-six Army camps and talked with the soldiers is, P. L. Prattis, "The Morale of the Negro in the Armed Services of the United States," *Journal of Negro Education*, 12 (Summer, 1943), 355–63.

[55] Stouffer and others, *The American Soldier*, Vol. I, 535.

CHAPTER V

Problems and Progress, 1943-1945

By 1943 the Army's "Negro problem" had become so serious that changes in policy were necessary. It became obvious that Negro manpower was being wasted at a time that the armed forces were suffering from an acute manpower shortage. Furthermore, race conflict between white and Negro soldiers was increasing. Because of the delicate posture the race problem had assumed in the Army, actual changes in policy came slowly after the need for change had been recognized. A series of crises was needed to push the policy makers along. One of the first crises was the resignation of the Civilian Aide to the Secretary of War, William Hastie, in early 1943.

Hastie's office had originally been conceived as being an advisory body on all matters pertaining to Army racial policy. To perform this function it was necessary that the Civilian Aide's office be kept informed of all matters relating to the Negro. In the beginning this was the rule, but by late 1941 and throughout 1942 the exceptions to the rule grew increasingly frequent. As the Army's Negro problem grew, many within the War Department became more irritated with it. The feeling grew that Hastie was an NAACP man and therefore a troublemaker. Many believed that Hastie was unrealistic in opposing segregation and that he really wanted to start a social revolution. The change in attitude can be traced in Secretary Stimson's impressions of Hastie. In early 1941 Stimson was impressed with the "temperateness" of a Hastie memorandum. By early 1942 some of his Civilian Aide's complaints "were of the impossible class to solve," representing "the hopeless side of the insoluble problem of the black race in this country." By late 1942 Stimson was no longer urging a frustrated Hastie not to resign; instead, Hastie's attitude was "not realistic," and Stimson felt that his usefulness was now limited. That Stimson's attitude was shared by others was obvious, as notes began appearing on correspondence: "Not to be coordinated with the office of the Civilian Aide."[1]

The failure of the Army's Negro policy was so apparent by August, 1942, that the War Department found it necessary to establish the Advisory Committee on Negro Troop Policies (McCloy Committee). Hastie had not even been informed that an advisory committee was to be formed, and when it was established, he was not made one of its members. The chairman of the new committee, Assistant Secretary of War John J. McCloy, had already made it known that he considered Hastie's attack on military segregation unrealistic. The Civilian Aide had written McCloy that he was disturbed over McCloy's attitude that Negroes should not agitate for an end to discrimination at home because of the war.[2] In replying, McCloy illustrated a common attitude and common ignorance of the black American's view of the war:

Frankly, I do not think that the basic issues of this war are involved in the question of whether colored troops serve in segregated units or in mixed units, and I doubt whether you can convince the people of the United States that the basic issues of freedom are involved in such a question.

---

[1] Ulysses G. Lee, Jr., *The Employment of Negro Troops*, 80–82, 139–41, 144–48; Stimson Diary, March 5, 1941, January 13, October 19, 1942.

[2] Memorandum, Hastie to McCloy, June 30, 1942, ASW 291.2, NARG 335. The McCloy Committee was composed of representatives from the General Staff and the major Army commands. It did not begin to affect the Army's Negro policy substantially until the later years of the war.

The Negro press and Negro leaders urging protest were "misleading" their people.[3] The appointment of a man to head a committee on Negro policy who showed so little understanding of black feelings about the war must have added to Hastie's frustrations.

Hastie had threatened to resign several times, but the immediate cause of his resignation in January, 1943, was the Army Air Force's racial policy.[4] From the beginning the Air Force had been one of the most reluctant of the Army branches to take Negroes. With the establishment of a Negro flying school at Tuskegee, Alabama, in 1941 the Air Force sought to concentrate all Negro training there, unlike the other branches, which utilized existing schools. By late 1942 the morale among Negro pilots at Tuskegee was very low because of the rigid segregation enforced by the commander. Orders were issued forbidding social contact between white and Negro officers; "white" and "colored" signs were posted over toilets despite War Department regulations that such would not be the case; black officers in staff positions were replaced by white officers. Originally it had been announced that Negro officers would take over administrative positions at Tuskegee as trained men became available. But the Air Force justified its failure to carry out this policy by deciding that Negroes "are definitely lacking in the qualifications essential for leadership and the urgency of the war situation does not justify experimentation."[5]

The last straw, as far as Hastie was concerned, was the Air Force's decision to set up a segregated Negro Officer Candidate School. The other Army branches had conducted integrated officer training from the beginning; Hastie saw no reason why the Air Force should not follow this example of integration.

---

[3] Memorandum, Hastie to McCloy, June 30, 1942; McCloy to Hastie, July 2, 1942, both in ASW 291.2, NARG 335.

[4] Accurate press reports of Hastie's threatened resignations appeared in the Pittsburgh *Courier*, January 31, October 3, 1942. For their accuracy, see Henry L. Stimson Diary, January 13, October 19, 1942.

[5] Quoted in Lee, *The Employment of Negro Troops*, 164. The Pittsburgh *Courier*, January 2, 1943, published an exposé of conditions at Tuskegee.

Perhaps even more galling to Hastie was that the Air Force had attempted to keep him in the dark on this step and had even lied to him that no such move was contemplated.[6] Hastie wrote Secretary Stimson on January 5, 1943, that the action by the Air Force was "so objectionable and inexcusable that I have no alternative but to resign in protest and to give public expression to my views." While admitting that the Army had made some progress on racial matters, Hastie believed that other changes were needed:

I believe that some of these changes involve questions of the sincerity and depth of our devotion to the basic issues of this war and thus have an important bearing, both on the fighting spirit of our own people and upon our ability as a nation to maintain leadership in the struggle for a free world.[7]

The whole issue of rigidly segregating Negroes in the armed services was the most important of these questions.

Hastie went out of office at the end of January, still fighting. In a parting memorandum he pointed out some of the immediate problems involving Negroes. Provisions for the promotion of Negro officers should be made; in most units Negroes could serve only as lieutenants. Pointing to a problem that would grow increasingly embarrassing throughout 1943, Hastie indicated that Negro service units were being sent overseas in large numbers, but Negro combat units were not. Negro combat units that had finished their training over three years earlier were still stationed in this country. The all-Negro Ninety-second Division was not even being trained as a unit, but was divided between four widely scattered posts.[8]

Hastie kept his word about informing the public of conditions in the Army: "It is difficult to see how a Negro in this position with all his superiors maintaining or inaugurating racial segregation can accomplish anything of value," he told a press conference in despair.[9] By February Hastie began a series of articles

---

[6] Lee, *The Employment of Negro Troops*, 166–74.

[7] Hastie to Stimson, January 5, 1943, ASW 291.2, NARG 335.

[8] Memorandum, Hastie to McCloy, January 30, 1943, ASW 291.2, NARG 335.

[9] Pittsburgh *Courier*, January 30, 1943.

in the black press telling why he had resigned.[10] Hastie's resignation was praised in the Negro press; he was pictured as a man who had fought segregation and had resigned his position to draw the public spotlight on a deplorable situation.[11] He was awarded the NAACP's Spingarn Medal as a man who "refused to temporize with racial bigotry, segregation or discrimination."[12]

The Chief of the Air Staff denied Hastie's indictment of his service's treatment of the Negro problem, but he admitted Hastie's charge that the all-Negro aviation squadrons had no reason for existence except to provide a place for Negroes was "bluntly true."[13] Despite the denials, Hastie's resignation appeared to have some impact on policy. The plan for a separate Air Force officer school was dropped; Negro doctors were given training in aviation medicine; technical training for Negro troops in the Air Force was expanded generally; and the barriers to the promotion of Negro officers were removed.[14] Assistant Secretary of War McCloy saw that Hastie's successor, Truman K. Gibson, Jr., was invited to attend the McCloy Committee's meetings regularly.

Throughout 1943 the McCloy Committee proved relatively ineffective in charting a new course for race relations in the Army. It did serve, however, to acquaint the Army General Staff and the War Department with the extent of the race problem within the military services. But here as elsewhere the depth of the Negroes' discontent apparently was not realized. McCloy himself had early expressed the belief, common throughout the Army, that the black press was the cause for discontent: "This discrimination now has gotten such momentum in the Negro press that one demand granted leads only to an-

[10] Pittsburgh *Courier*, February 6, 20, 27, March 6, 1943.

[11] Baltimore *Afro-American*, February 6, 1943; "Hastie Resigns," *The Crisis*, 50 (February, 1943), 41.

[12] Pittsburgh *Courier*, March 20, 1943.

[13] Memorandum, Major General George E. Stratemeyer to McCloy, January 12, 1943, ASW 291.2, NARG 335.

[14] Pittsburgh *Courier*, March 6, 1943; Lee, *The Employment of Negro Troops*, 175.

other, and you do not bury any issue permanently by concession."[15] Answering one of the numerous inquiries on behalf of
Negro soldiers from Eleanor Roosevelt, McCloy said: "The Negro soldier has been so sensitized by references to his abused
position that he is prepared to believe anything and does," and
the Negro press was blamed for playing up "alleged mistreatment."[16]

Making the black press a scapegoat diverted attention from
the shortcomings of the Army's Negro policy. Reports coming
in to the committee disclosed that Army policies to ensure equal
treatment of Negroes were not generally known or followed
by commanders in the field.[17] Yet McCloy continued to be convinced that "there is an over-sensitivity on the part of the negroes, largely induced by the articles carried in the negro press."
Emphasis should be placed upon being a good soldier; this

will do more to improve the position of the negro in the country
than the constant harping on alleged discrimination which in many
cases do not exist at all or, if they do, are largely based upon fundamental segregation instincts of the people generally that it is too
much to ask the Army to change overnight. The fact is that the
Army has largely eliminated discrimination against the negroes
within its ranks and has gone further in this direction than the
country itself."[18]

The paucity of achievements by the McCloy Committee
prompted one committee member, General Benjamin O. Davis,
to ask pointedly what the committee had achieved since its inception. "The War Department is making no appreciable efforts to lessen the Jim-Crow practices, which are by far the great-

---

[15] McCloy to Attorney General Francis Biddle, March 24, 1942, ASW
291.2, NARG 335.
[16] McCloy to Mrs. Roosevelt, July 26, 1943, ASW 291.2, NARG 335.
See the ASW 291.2 alphabetical files for Mrs. Roosevelt's notes.
[17] Memorandum from Colonel J. S. Leonard, Secretary to McCloy
Committee, to McCloy, May 25, 1943; Memorandum, Lieutenant Colonel
H. A. Gerhardt, Assistant to the Assistant Secretary of War, to McCloy,
August 15, 1944; both in ASW 291.2, NARG 335.
[18] McCloy to Herbert B. Elliston, editor of the *Washington Post*, August 5, 1943, ASW 291.2, NARG 335.

est factor in the morale of the colored soldiers," Davis wrote, answering his own question.[19]

The McCloy Committee did encourage a few steps to ease the race problem in late 1943 and 1944. Good relations between the War Department and the Negro press were established.[20] Equitable transportation for Negro troops on and off military posts, the lack of which was a cause for much friction, was encouraged.[21] Publicizing the black soldier's contributions to the war was achieved by the release of a film, "The Negro Soldier," which was very favorably received by the Negro press.[22] The Research Branch and the McCloy Committee cooperated in producing a pamphlet to inform officers of the official War Department position on Negro soldiers.[23] Written by two social scientists, this pamphlet was later expanded into the Army's *Leadership and the Negro Soldier* (1944) and the Navy's *Guide to Command of Negro Personnel* (1944). Although not grappling with the problem of segregation, these works did put forth a common theme that the Negro should be judged as an individual and utilized according to his abilities. Unfortunately, like much of the Army's Negro policy, these attempts had little effect on the practices at lower levels.[24]

The boldest step taken by the McCloy Committee was a directive issued in July, 1944, that all facilities on military posts would be utilized without restriction because of race. Post exchanges, transportation, and movie theaters were supposedly desegregated. The order was widely publicized, but it had little effect. By the time the order was issued, each military post had its separate Negro section with its own recreational facilities. The device of assigning recreational facilities by units served the purpose of maintaining segregation. Segregated officers' clubs re-

---

[19] Memorandum, General Davis to McCloy, November 10, 1943, ASW 291.2, NARG 335.

[20] Memorandum, Truman K. Gibson to McCloy, May 14, 1943, ASW 291.2, NARG 335; Lee, *The Employment of Negro Troops*, 382–87.

[21] Stimson Diary, July 5, 1943.

[22] For the reaction to this film, see ASW 291.2 Negro Troops — Publicity File, NARG 335.

[23] *Command of Negro Troops* (Washington, 1944).

[24] Lee, *The Employment of Negro Troops*, 390–92.

mained at most posts. In short, most post commanders continued segregation as usual. Attempts by Negroes to test the validity of the new directive led to a great deal of conflict.[25]

Many of the minor changes in the armed forces' Negro policy in 1944 were undoubtedly influenced by the fact that another presidential election was due. Late in 1943 Truman Gibson, the Negro Civilian Aide, pointed this out to McCloy and suggested early releases of the Army's pamphlets and the film on the Negro soldier so they might have a greater political effect.[26] Twenty-five national Negro organizations joined together and made the Negro in the armed services one of their main issues:

No injustice embitters Negroes more. . . . The national policy of segregating Negroes in the armed forces violates every principle of democracy. Any party or candidate that hopes to win the support and respect of Negroes . . . must prove their belief in democracy by adopting a democratic program for the integration of all Americans into unsegregated military forces.[27]

The Republicans seized upon the issue of discrimination in the armed forces by pledging a congressional investigation of the matter.[28]

There was once again some concern in the White House about the black vote. Attorney General Francis Biddle supplied ammunition that would appeal to Negro voters for some of Roosevelt's campaign speeches. "The situation among the Negro voters," Biddle wrote, "is still very serious. The greatest resentment comes from Negroes in the armed forces, particularly those who have been in southern camps, and they are writing home about it."[29] Although the Administration took no dramatic action, several

[25] Charles Dollard and Donald Young, "In the Armed Forces," *Survey Graphic*, 36 (January, 1947), 67; Florence Murray, ed., *The Negro Handbook, 1946-1947*, 364-65.

[26] Memorandum, Gibson to McCloy, November 3, 1943, ASW 291.2, NARG 335.

[27] Quoted in Walter White, *A Man Called White*, 264.

[28] *The New York Times*, June 28, 1944.

[29] Memorandum, Biddle to the President, October 20, 1944, PPF 1820, FDRL. Also see memorandum, Roosevelt to S.I.R. [Samuel Rosenman], October 24, 1944, and memorandum, Biddle to Roosevelt, October 23, 1944, all in the same file.

sweeteners were released in this election year. In addition to the pamphlets, film, and desegregation of recreational facilities already mentioned, the Navy announced in February, 1944, that it was accepting its first Negro officers.[30] In September Roosevelt intervened to correct War Department plans for segregated rest centers for returning combat veterans.[31] In October it was announced that the President had approved a plan for the acceptance of the first Negro women in the Navy.[32]

Another problem with political consequences in 1944 had its origin in earlier years. In 1943 the Army experienced a threat to its system of requesting men from Selective Service through racial quotas. President Roosevelt had issued an executive order in December, 1942, requiring all of the services to secure their men from the draft and placing Selective Service under the War Manpower Commission. The Chairman of the War Manpower Commission, Paul V. McNutt, was moved to action by the waste of manpower. The problem was "acute." At a time that a general shortage of manpower was developing, Negroes made up only 6 per cent of the armed forces, a little over half of their percentage of the population. Shocking was the fact that 300,000 eligible Negroes had been passed over in the draft to fill white calls, a situation created by the general reluctance of the armed services to make 10.6 per cent of their strength Negro. "This condition has been the cause of continuous and mounting criticism," McNutt wrote to the Secretaries of War and the Navy:

It possesses grave implications should the issue be taken into the courts, especially by a white registrant. The probability of this action increases as the single white registrants disappear and husbands and fathers become the current white inductees, while single Negro registrants who are physically fit remain uninducted.[33]

McNutt had recommended that, beginning in April, 1943, Selective Service call registrants without regard to race.

Roosevelt pressed the Navy, the Marine Corps, and the Coast

---

[30] Pittsburgh *Courier*, February 5, 1944.
[31] Murray, ed., *The Negro Handbook, 1946–1947*, 336–37.
[32] *The New York Times*, October 20, 1944.
[33] McNutt to Stimson and Knox, February 17, 1943, OF 93 FDRL.

Guard into expanding their number of Negroes.[34] The War Department feared that abandoning racial quotas would force the Army to integrate whites and Negroes in the same units. When the War Manpower Commission refused to back down, the Army was saved from what it viewed as an uncontrollable situation by a general shortage of Negro manpower. Beginning in April, 1943, Selective Service began to fall behind in its deliveries of Negroes requested by the Army. The shortages were due to the high rejection rates of Negroes eligible for the draft — over 50 per cent from 1943 to 1945 as compared to 30 per cent for whites. By the end of 1943 the Army was short approximately 88,000 Negroes for Negro units already planned. The earlier reluctance of the Army to take a fair share of Negroes, together with the developing shortages in 1943, meant that throughout World War II it never achieved the goal of having 10.6 per cent of its strength Negro.[35]

The Army had earlier adopted rigid literacy standards, primarily to reduce the number of black soldiers it would have to accept. Now, in 1943, a general shortage of manpower, both black and white, led to a reversal of this policy. In June, 1943, Special Training Units were established to give illiterates basic education in reading and writing. As soon as the trainees reached the equivalent of the fourth grade they were sent on to regular basic training. Due to their lower average education, five times more Negroes than whites benefited from this special training. Of the Negroes who were assigned to Special Training Units, 85 per cent successfully finished the course. The program was started so late that only 136,000 Negroes received training, but for those willing to see, the results indicated that the low AGCT scores of Negroes were due to educational deficiency rather than mental deficiency.[36]

The growing general shortage of manpower in 1943 led to a change in the Army's policy toward black units. In 1940 the Army had announced that Negroes would be proportionately

[34] Knox to the President, February 25, April 14, 1943, both in OF 18, FDRL; "The Negro in the Navy" (Bureau of Naval Personnel), 11–14.
[35] Lee, *The Employment of Negro Troops*, 408–13.
[36] Jean Byers, *A Study of the Negro in Military Service*, 36–38.

represented in combat units. The general belief that the black soldier was racially inferior in a combat role, but especially suited for service or labor duties, had kept this policy from becoming a reality. But the existence of the policy meant that there were more Negro combat units than if it had not existed. Now the Army was presented with the embarrassing situation of keeping Negro combat units stationed in the United States while the war zones were suffering from a manpower shortage. Even Negro service units, to which the vast majority of Negroes were assigned, were still in this country. In the spring of 1943 only 79,000 out of 504,000 Negro troops were overseas.[37]

Commanders considered Negro units undesirable and less efficient than similar white units, and therefore they were not utilized overseas. Many foreign governments also objected to having American Negroes sent to their countries. Governors of the British West Indian Islands and the Belgian Congo, for example, objected to having American Negroes because their higher standard of living might cause unrest among the natives. The problem of having trained black units waiting in the United States had first appeared in May, 1942. At this time the War Department adopted a policy that the three main divisions of the Army — the Army Air Forces, the Army Ground Forces, and the Services of Supply — would see that Negro troops were ordered overseas in proportion to their percentage of these commands. Overseas commanders were not to be allowed to reject Negro units. Like many of the Army's Negro policies, however, this one did not work. Commanders were asked if they desired black troops, and the answer was usually "No."[38]

Since Negro troops were more acceptable to overseas commanders as service units, and since the continuing shortage of manpower resulted in a need for more service units, the Army adopted the course of converting Negro combat units to service units in 1943. All pretense of proportionate assignment of Negroes to combat units was ended. The gap between policy and practice on this matter widened at a rapid pace in 1943. Although conversion resulted in a rapid increase in the number

[37] Lee, *The Employment of Negro Troops*, 450.
[38] Lee, *The Employment of Negro Troops*, 428–34.

of black soldiers overseas, old fears were aroused among Negroes that they were being denied a role in winning the war.[39]

Complaints that no Negro combat units were in action and that combat units were being converted to labor units became frequent in the Negro press. "The tactics appear to disclose a determination to prohibit Negroes . . . from reaching any of the front lines where they might gain glory and prestige for themselves and their race . . . ," the Pittsburgh *Courier* claimed.[40] Fuel was added to the fire of suspicion by reports that black soldiers were being used to shovel snow in Seattle and that serious consideration was being given to having Negro soldiers pick cotton in Arizona.[41] Mrs. Roosevelt wrote the War Department that Negroes "should be given a chance to prove their mettle. I feel they have something to gain in the war."[42]

Pressure to commit some Negro combat units began to build within the War Department itself. In July, 1943, the McCloy Committee had recommended that "Negro combat troops be dispatched to an active theater of operations at an early date. In the opinion of the Committee, such action would be the most effective means of reducing tension among Negro troops."[43] When no action was taken on this recommendation, General Benjamin O. Davis pointed out the low morale resulting from continuing conversions of Negro combat units to service units. "The colored soldier," General Davis told the McCloy Committee, "has lost confidence in the fairness of the Army to Negro troops." A white officer with experience in black units told the committee that commanders in the field did not know what the War Department's policy was toward Negroes. The field commanders needed to be reassured that Negroes could be made

---

[39] Lee, *The Employment of Negro Troops*, 414–21, 468–74.

[40] Pittsburgh *Courier*, October 30, 1943. See similar complaints in the *Courier*, October 9, 16, November 27, and December 4, 18, 1943.

[41] Pittsburgh *Courier*, February 13, 1943; "Snow Cleaners, Cotton Pickers," *The Crisis*, 50 (March, 1943), 72.

[42] Eleanor Roosevelt to McCloy, November 23, 1943, ASW 291.2, NARG 335.

[43] Memorandum, McCloy to the Chief of Staff, July 3, 1943, ASW 291.2, NARG 335.

into soldiers; when they saw black combat troops continuously converted to service duties their doubts were substantiated.[44]

By January, 1944, Secretary Stimson recognized that the War Department was leaving itself open to serious criticism by not committing Negro units to combat. He agreed reluctantly to the General Staff's request that the all-Negro Second Cavalry Division, a unit that had trained for its combat role for two years, be converted into a service corps. But he told the staff that he "had come to the conclusion that we must face the situation more seriously. . . . We have got to use the colored race to help us in this fight."[45]

The dam burst when Secretary Stimson put his signature on a letter to Representative Hamilton Fish, Republican of New York. Fish had written Stimson asking for an explanation for the conversion of Negro combat units and the failure to commit black combat units to battle. In his widely publicized reply, Stimson admitted such conversions had taken place; in converting units, however, the sole criterion had been the efficiency of the unit concerned. In the most controversial passage of the letter, Stimson claimed:

It so happens that a relatively large percentage of the Negroes inducted in the Army have fallen within the lower educational classifications, and many of the Negro units accordingly have been unable to master efficiently the techniques of modern weapons.

In what was at best a half truth, Stimson concluded that "any implication that the War Department is deliberately attempting to avoid sending overseas, or to keep out of combat, troops of the Negro or any other race, is entirely without foundation."[46]

Representative Fish raised a pertinent question in responding to Stimson's letter: Why was it possible for the French Senegalese, the British troops from India, and the illiterate Russian peasants to be good combat soldiers, when a large percentage

---

[44] Memorandum, General Davis to McCloy, November 10, 1943; Minutes of the Advisory Committee on Negro Troop Policies, January 4, 1944, both in ASW 291.2, NARG 335.

[45] Stimson Diary, January 27, 1944.

[46] This letter was inserted in U.S., *Congressional Record*, 78th Cong., 2d Sess. (1944), 2007–8.

of American Negroes exceeded these groups in educational qualifications?[47] What about the thousands of Negroes with a more than adequate educational background to master modern weapons? The Negro press angrily charged that Stimson was saying black soldiers were "too dumb to fight."[48] Roy Wilkins of the NAACP wrote the President that there was fear among Negroes that a conspiracy existed in the armed services to prevent Negroes from getting into combat; the only solution was for the President to end segregation in the military services, the root of all problems.[49] Congressman William L. Dawson, Negro Democrat of Illinois, wrote that these conversions seemed to be the result of an Army attitude "all too familar to Negroes"; he was well acquainted with the attitude, having been a Negro officer in World War I.[50]

The strong public and political reaction forced the War Department to face the fact that it had been evading its Negro policy. McCloy now told Stimson and Chief of Staff Marshall that Negro combat troops must be used. When they raised the question of dictating to the theater commanders on how they should use their troops, McCloy told them that "we have to dictate" in this case: "It is a vital national policy to make a military asset out of that part of the population."[51] The McCloy Committee unanimously adopted a resolution, which it sent to the Secretary of War:

It is the feeling of the Committee that colored units should be introduced in combat at the earliest practicable moment. There has been a tendency to allow the situation to develop where selections are

---

[47] *Congressional Record*, 78th Cong., 2d Sess. (1944), 2008.

[48] Norfolk *Journal and Guide*, April 8, 1944; Baltimore *Afro-American*, March 4, 1944; Pittsburgh *Courier*, March 4, 11, 18, 1944. Ira F. Lewis, President of the Pittsburgh Courier Publishing Co., to McCloy, March 13, 1944, ASW 291.2, NARG 335, discusses the heavy volume of mail Stimson's letter provoked. Congressman William L. Dawson to McCloy, February 28, 1944, same file, tells of the protests he had received from Negroes all over the country.

[49] Wilkins to the President, March 9, 1944, ASW 291.2, NARG 335.

[50] Dawson to McCloy, February 19, 1944, ASW 291.2, NARG 335.

[51] Minutes of Meeting of Advisory Committee on Negro Troop Policies, February 29, 1944, ASW 291.2, NARG 335.

made on the basis of efficiency with the result that the colored units are discarded for combat service, but little is done by way of studying new means to put them in shape for combat service.[52]

In explaining the meaning of this resolution, McCloy made it known that he and his committee had experienced a change in thinking on the Negro problem. With 10 per cent of the population Negro, with the example of effective use of poorly educated soldiers by other nations, "we must, I think, be more affirmative about the use of our Negro troops. If present methods do not bring them to combat efficiency, we should change those methods," McCloy informed Stimson.[53] Stimson concurred with the committee's resolution; in a meeting with the Army General Staff he said, "The Army has been drifting in regard to putting the colored troops into combat action." Stimson told the Army commanders that he and McCloy had decided "We must settle on a policy which will use this great asset of the colored men of the nation in a more effective way." At this meeting it was decided to put elements of the all-Negro Ninety-third Division in combat, as well as the entire Negro Ninety-second Division.[54]

The news of the commitment of black troops to battle was spread to soothe Negro feelings. Stimson announced to a press conference that elements of the Ninety-third Division were in combat in the Pacific. Walter White was invited to the McCloy Committee meeting at which it was disclosed that the Ninety-second Division had been ordered to Italy.[55] The long-delayed commitment of large Negro units to combat proceeded under the direction of the War Department. The haphazard way in which this came about was characteristic of much of the Army's Negro policy during World War II; like the drafting and assignment to units, the commitment of Negroes to combat was

[52] Memorandum, McCloy to the Secretary of War, March 2, 1944, ASW 291.2, NARG 335.

[53] McCloy to the Secretary of War, March 2, 1944.

[54] Stimson Diary, March 6, 1944.

[55] Pittsburgh *Courier*, April 8, 1944; Minutes of Meeting of Advisory Committee on Negro Troops Policies, April 26, 1944, ASW 291.2, NARG 335.

a reaction to pressure rather than the planned fulfillment of a need.[56]

The main effort to get black soldiers into combat was focused on the Ninety-second Division in Italy. Arriving in Italy in June, 1944, this unit experienced several successes. While there were over seven thousand awards to individuals of the Division, there were also reports that units melted away from panic in the face of the enemy. Reports from high-ranking officers to the War Department placed the responsibility for the failures completely on the shoulders of the black officers and men and requested that the Ninety-second never be used for offensive action again. Civilian Aide Gibson was sent to Italy to investigate these reports, and he quickly concluded that the underlying causes for the poor performances had not been recognized. Gibson found that many white officers blamed inherent racial qualities that made the Negro unfit for combat, but this analysis was contradicted by the many acts of bravery and the number of casualties suffered by Negroes of the Division.

Gibson also found that morale was very low among the Division's Negroes. Negro officers were not promoted on the same basis as white officers; white-only officers' clubs were common throughout the Division. Negro company commanders had been removed from their commands and replaced by white officers without any explanation. Many of the Negro enlisted men felt that the Division's white officers were not interested in the success of the unit and that they really wanted to discredit the black officers and men. Added to this situation was the fact that the overwhelming majority of the Negro enlisted men were AGCT Grade IV and V. This situation existed in spite of the fact that military authorities had determined that no unit could operate efficiently with more than 10 per cent Grade V men. Segregation produced unsound military results, Gibson concluded. In March, 1945, Gibson made much the same explanation to a press conference in Rome, but the press reports emphasized the admission that some Negro units had "melted away" in battle and the low literacy rating of the bulk of Negro

---

[56] Lee, *The Employment of Negro Troops*, 474-85.

men. A public controversy was evoked over Gibson's press conference, with those who argued that Negro soldiers could not fight finding support in Gibson's statements and the Negro press arguing over the merits and faults of Gibson's analysis.[57]

The whole controversy was reminiscent of arguments over the success or failure of Negro combat troops in World War I. If one believed that Negroes were racially unsuitable as combat soldiers, he found support in the failures of the Ninety-second; on the other hand, if one believed that military segregation led to poor fighting units, he also found support in the experience of the Ninety-second. Many military men found support for their belief that black soldiers were suited only for labor units in the experience of this Division.[58] One cannot help but wonder to what extent the failure of the Ninety-second was a self-fulfilling proposition. *The New York Times* reporter on the scene said that the notion that "Negro troops can't fight" was widely held when the Negro Division arrived in Italy.[59] A former white officer of the Division recalled that most of the white officers believed and said that "colored troops cannot fight; . . . they are all or almost all cowards, or inept, or both." Furthermore, they had no hope that the situation could be improved.[60]

The War Department's willingness to see Negroes committed to combat resulted in an experiment much more successful than

[57] Detailed accounts of the Ninety-second Division controversy in military terms are found in Lee, *The Employment of Negro Troops*, 575–79; Lee Nichols, *Breakthrough on the Color Front*, 12–18; Byers, *A Study of the Negro*, 129–47. Gibson's charges of low morale and discrimination were substantiated by reports of Negro war correspondents both before and after Gibson's press conference; Norfolk *Journal and Guide*, March 10, 24, April 21, 1945; Pittsburgh *Courier*, March 10, 24, April 7, November 10, 17, 1945.

[58] General Mark W. Clark, Commander of the Fifth Army, of which the Ninety-second was a part, appears to take a moderate stand on the experience of this division in *Calculated Risk*, 414–15. He repeats the old charges, however, and emphasizes that "it would be a grave error now for the Army to attempt the indiscriminate mixing of white and Negro soldiers."

[59] *The New York Times*, March 15, 1945.

[60] Warman Welliver, "Report on the Negro Soldier," *Harper's Magazine*, 192 (April, 1946), 334.

the experience of the Ninety-second Division. The Army experienced a drastic shortage of infantry replacements as a result of the Battle of the Bulge in the winter of 1944–1945. A crash program to retrain soldiers from service units was begun. Lieutenant General John C. H. Lee, Commander of the Communications Zone of the European Theater, persuaded General Eisenhower that black service troops should be given the opportunity to volunteer as infantry replacements. General Lee's appeal for volunteers proposed complete integration: "It is planned to assign you without regard to color or race to the units where assistance is most needed, and give you the opportunity of fighting shoulder to shoulder to bring about victory."[61] Before the plan could be carried out, however, Eisenhower's Chief of Staff, General Walter B. Smith, questioned the advisability of completely integrating the Negro volunteers; he felt that this was contrary to War Department policy and might cause trouble. General Eisenhower agreed with Smith and decided that individual integration was not workable, but General Lee persuaded him to form the black volunteers into platoons that could be assigned to white companies. The arrangement ensured that the volunteers would be in close association with white troops.[62]

Negro volunteers responded enthusiastically. Sergeants gave up their rank; as high as 80 per cent of some Negro service units volunteered. The number of Negro volunteers was so great that a limit of twenty-five hundred was set. This quota resulted in the turning away of three thousand volunteers. After six weeks of intensive training, the volunteers were assigned to various white units pushing across Germany in 1945.[63]

All of the evidence indicates that these troops fought well. General Eisenhower praised the volunteers and reported that all of their commanders were pleased with their performance. General George S. Patton approved of the mixed units under his command and told a Negro correspondent that he was thinking about recommending a continuation of mixed units in the

---

[61] Lee, *The Employment of Negro Troops*, 689.
[62] Lee, *The Employment of Negro Troops*, 689–95.
[63] Byers, *A Study of the Negro*, 165–67; Nichols, *Breakthrough on the Color Front*, 68–69.

Army.[64] Most important, opinion surveys conducted by the Army's Research Branch indicated that the white men of the integrated units had experienced a profound change of opinion toward Negroes. Whereas only a third of the white soldiers had expressed a favorable opinion of having Negroes in their companies before this experiment, afterward 77 per cent said they had become more favorable, and none said they were less favorable. Of the white officers 84 per cent and of the white sergeants 81 per cent said that the Negro soldiers in their companies performed well in combat. Only 1 per cent of the sergeants and none of the officers said they did not do well. When these results are compared with the fact that 62 per cent of the men in divisions that had no mixed companies said that they would dislike having Negro platoons in their units, it appears that the experience of serving with Negro troops markedly reduced the prejudice against them.[65]

Those within the Army, like General Benjamin O. Davis, who desired integration wanted this survey made public. Here was an example of the successful integration of white and Negro troops, and the widespread fear within the Army that violence and disorder would result had proved to be unfounded. Those within the Army who held to the old ideas about black soldiers, however, looked upon this experience as only an experiment that proved little. They feared publication of the survey results would lose support for the peacetime draft proposal among powerful Southern senators in Congress and would encourage agitation for further experiments by Negro organizations.[66] Those who preferred the *status quo* won. As soon as the war in Europe came to an end, the Negro platoons were unceremoniously detached from their white units and either returned to all-Negro service units or discharged.[67] Although

---

[64] *The New York Times*, June 16, 1945; Pittsburgh *Courier*, June 23, 1945.

[65] Samuel A. Stouffer and others, *The American Soldier*, Vol. I, 587–99; Byers, *A Study of the Negro*, 171–76.

[66] Nichols, *Breakthrough on the Color Front*, 70.

[67] Byers, *A Study of the Negro*, 179–82. The Pittsburgh *Courier*, September 29, 1945, describes the bitterness felt by the Negro volunteers after being dropped from their units.

the Negro platoons appeared to be forgotten by the War Department, the few who believed that integration was the solution to efficient utilization of manpower continued to remember this experience as proof that they were right.

Surprisingly, the Navy, which began the war with the most restrictive practices, had moved toward the end of the war to a policy of integration. The Navy had experienced all of the waste of manpower and conflict that the Army had under a policy of segregation. The result of this experience, however, was different in the Navy. An official Navy study states that this service approached the end of the war "believing that all its experience demonstrated that integration rather than segregation was the road to efficient, harmonious working relations of the races."[68]

The great change in the Navy's policy was brought about by individuals within the Department of the Navy who desired equal opportunity for the Negro and efficient utilization of this part of the nation's manpower. Adlai E. Stevenson, a special assistant to Secretary of the Navy Knox, sought to encourage these trends.[69] The Navy was first forced by President Roosevelt in 1942 to use Negroes for duties other than messmen. Then a Special Programs Unit was set up within the Bureau of Naval Personnel to oversee the Navy's Negro policy. By the first of 1944 Secretary Knox had been persuaded to allow two ships of the fleet to be manned by all-Negro crews, the first of their kind. The liberalization of the Navy's Negro policy was speeded up, considerably by the new Secretary of the Navy, James V. Forrestal, who succeeded to this post in early 1944 after the death of Knox. Almost immediately upon assuming his new position, Forrestal approved a plan for integrating the crews of twenty-five auxiliary ships of the fleet.[70]

[68] "The Negro in the Navy," 84 and *passim*.

[69] Stevenson's role in this matter is briefly mentioned by most works about him, but no detailed account of his role has appeared. For examples, see Noel F. Bush, *Adlai E. Stevenson of Illinois: A Portrait*, 71; Nichols, *Breakthrough on the Color Front*, 56.

[70] Nichols, *Breakthrough on the Color Front*, 58–59. Lieutenant Dennis D. Nelson, *The Integration of the Negro into the United States Navy, 1776–1947* (M.A. thesis, Howard University; reproduced by the Navy as

While the Navy's experiment of integrating ships' crews was proving successful, riots and mutinies were breaking out among some of the many labor units that had been the Navy's earlier solution to the Negro problem. Forrestal was convinced that the only answer to the disturbances was integration; although no crusader, his sense of fair play told him that the Navy had been seriously remiss in its treatment of black sailors. After getting the highest Navy leadership to agree with him, Forrestal sent for Lester Granger, head of the National Urban League, to act as his adviser on Negro policy.[71] For six months in 1945, Granger traveled fifty thousand miles and visited sixty-seven naval facilities throughout the world as the special representative of the Secretary of the Navy. Forrestal saw that action was taken on practically every one of the suggestions made by Granger for better treatment of Negro sailors.[72]

With the encouragement of Forrestal and Navy officers who recognized that a change in the Navy's Negro policy was in order, restrictions on the assignment of Negro sailors were dropped. Integrated training and assignment increased. On February 27, 1947, the following order went out to all Navy commands:

Effective immediately, all restrictions governing the types of assignments for which Negro naval personnel are eligible are hereby lifted.

NAVEXOS–P–526, 1948), 43–62, reproduces the policy statements that indicate the steady liberalization of the Navy's Negro policy. William R. Mueller, "The Negro in the Navy," *Social Forces*, 24 (October, 1945), 110–15, is a convenient short summary.

[71] Forrestal to Granger, February 1, 1945, Correspondence, Box 63, 1945, G-O, James V. Forrestal Papers, Princeton University Library; Forrestal described his motivation and actions in a speech to the National Urban League, February 12, 1948, Box 31, Forrestal Papers; Lester Granger, "The Reminiscences of Lester B. Granger" (Columbia University Oral History Collection, 1963), 145–46, 159–60, recalls the first meeting with Forrestal and his thinking on the race problem.

[72] Granger's experiences as special adviser are described in his "Racial Democracy — The Navy Way," *Common Ground*, 7 (Winter, 1947), 61–68; the support of Forrestal for Granger's recommendations is evident in Forrestal to Granger, July 14, 1945, and September 11, 1945, both in Correspondence, Box 63, 1945, G-O; and memorandum, Forrestal to Mr. Gates, Admiral Jacobs, and Admiral Miller, July 16, 1945, Day Files, Box 89, all in Forrestal Papers.

Henceforth, they shall be eligible for all types of assignments in all ratings in all activities and all ships of the Naval Service. . . . In the utilization of housing, messing and other facilities, no special or unusual provisions will be made for the accommodation of Negroes.[73]

The Navy ended the war with the most progressive Negro policy of all of the armed services. The Navy shared a common defect with all of the armed services, however: the difference between policy and practice. During the postwar years the bulk of the Navy's Negro personnel continued to be in the messman's branch, and Negro Navy officers were very few in number.

The opportunities for Negroes in the armed services were certainly much greater in World War II than World War I. Although many judgments were made about black troops on the basis of the poor performance of the large all-Negro combat units, many smaller Negro units made an indisputable contribution to the war effort. The first Negro military pilots of the Ninety-ninth Pursuit Squadron had a fine record. There were many small Negro artillery and armored units that established good combat records. The smaller Negro service units, particularly engineer and quartermaster units, performed vital functions for the war effort.[74] Yet most Negroes were not content with a continuation of the segregation policy, and the number of individuals questioning the policy within the War Department itself was growing as the war closed.

Negro bitterness over segregation in the armed forces showed itself in the opposition to a proposed peacetime draft bill. The Fraternal Council of Negro Churches was opposed to a continuation of the draft if segregation remained in effect.[75] If segregation was part of a new draft law, "thousands of Negro lads who have not been segregated from their fellows in civilian life will be embittered annually by their government's training program," the NAACP wrote Roosevelt.[76] President Roosevelt held out some hope for these critics. The Army's peacetime

---

[73] Quoted in Nelson, *The Integration of the Negro*, 59.

[74] The generally good record of these units, although all were hobbled in some way by the policy of segregation, is discussed at length in Lee, *The Employment of Negro Troops*, Chaps. 18, 20, 21.

[75] Pittsburgh *Courier*, February 10, 1945.

[76] Roy Wilkins to the President, January 5, 1945, OF 109, FDRL.

policies had not been decided, he said, and there was actually a study under way to determine the future utilization of black soldiers.[77]

The study Roosevelt referred to was the result of a realization by some within the War Department that the Army's traditional Negro policy had been far from successful. As early as February, 1944, Assistant Secretary of War McCloy had recommended that a history of the Negro soldier in World War II should be written.[78] Civilian Aide Gibson recommended in July, 1944, that the Army General Staff initiate a study of the Negro's role in the postwar Army. McCloy agreed with this suggestion, and the McCloy Committee adopted a resolution that such a study be made.[79] In May, 1945, the War Department finally dispatched a letter to commanders throughout the world requesting a report on the performance of Negro units and recommendations on postwar Negro policy.

It remained to be seen if this high-level review of Army Negro policy would produce a change in that policy. A change in thinking had occurred, however, for some of those who had been intimately concerned with the Army's Negro problem during the war. From seeing nothing wrong with the Army's policy and blaming most of the problems on the Negro press in 1943, Assistant Secretary of War McCloy could admit in 1945 that "it has always seemed to me that we never put enough thought into the matter of making a real military asset out of the very large cadres of Negro personnel we receive from the country."[80] From viewing the Negro as a "problem," some had come to a recognition that Negro manpower was an asset that had not been fully realized. The same re-evaluation had occurred in past crises, however, only to be forgotten when the emergency passed. Would this be repeated?

[77] Roosevelt to Wilkins, January 22, 1945, OF 109, FDRL.
[78] Memorandum, McCloy to the Assistant Chief of Staff, G-2, February 23, 1944, ASW 291.2, NARG 335.
[79] Memorandum, Gibson to McCloy, July 20, 1944; memorandum, McCloy to the Advisory Committee on Special Troop Policy, September 1, 1944, ASW 291.2, NARG 335.
[80] McCloy to Forrestal, August 22, 1945, ASW 291.2, NARG 335.

CHAPTER VI

The Negro's Mind and Morale

A RECENT PRESIDENT of the American Sociological Society addressed himself to a puzzling question about what we know as the Negro Revolution: "Why did social scientists — and sociologists in particular — not foresee the explosion of collective action of Negro Americans toward full integration into American society?" He pointed out that "it is the vigor and urgency of the Negro demand that is new, not its direction or supporting ideas."[1] Without arguing the point further, we can place the blame for this situation on two groups — the ahistorical social scientists and the historians who, until recently, have neglected modern Negro history.

Anyone studying American race relations for the years 1939–1945 will find it difficult not to conclude that this period marks a watershed in recent Negro history. James Baldwin has written of these years:[2] "The treatment accorded the Negro during the Second World War marks, for me, a turning point in the Negro's relation to America: to put it briefly, and somewhat too simply, a certain hope died, a certain respect for white

---

[1] Everett C. Hughes, "Race Relations and the Sociological Imagination," *American Sociological Review*, 28 (December, 1963), 879.

[2] Quoted in J. Milton Yinger, *A Minority Group in American Society*, 52. In a public opinion poll years later, many Negroes agreed with Baldwin in recalling the bitterness they experienced. William Brink and Louis Harris, *The Negro Revolution in America*, 50.

Americans faded." Writing during World War II, Gunnar Myrdal predicted that the war would act as a stimulant to Negro protest, and he felt that "there is bound to be a redefinition of the Negro's status in America as a result of this War."[3] The Negro sociologist E. Franklin Frazier stated that World War II marked the point where "the Negro was no longer willing to accept discrimination . . . without protest."[4] Charles E. Silberman wrote that World War II was a "turning point" in American race relations, in which "the seeds of the protest movements of the 1950's and 1960's were sown."[5] While a few writers have indicated the importance of the World War II years in the recent Negro protest movement, the majority have failed to do so. Overlooking what went before, most recent books on the subject claim that a Negro "revolution" or "revolt" occurred in 1954, 1955, 1960, or 1963.[6] Because of neglect of the World War II period, these years of transition in American race relations comprise the "forgotten years" of the Negro Revolution.

To understand how the American Negro reacted to World War II, some idea of the discrimination he faced is necessary. The defense build-up begun by the United States in 1940 was welcomed by Negroes, who were disproportionately represented among the unemployed. Employment discrimination in the revived industries, however, was rampant. When Negroes sought jobs at aircraft factories begging for workers, they were informed that "the Negro will be considered only as janitors and in other similar capacities."[7] Government-financed training programs to overcome the shortages of skilled workers discriminated against Negro trainees. When government agencies issued orders against such discrimination, they were ignored.[8]

---

[3] Gunnar Myrdal, *An American Dilemma: The Negro Problem and Modern Democracy*, 756, 997.

[4] E. Franklin Frazier, *The Negro in the United States*, 682.

[5] Charles E. Silberman, *Crisis in Black and White*, 60, 65.

[6] See, for example, Lewis M. Killian and Charles Grigg, *Racial Crisis in America: Leadership in Conflict*; Louis E. Lomax, *The Negro Revolt*; Leonard Broom and Norval D. Glenn, *Transformation of the Negro American*; Brink and Harris, *The Negro Revolution in America*.

[7] Quoted in Louis C. Kesselman, *The Social Politics of FEPC*, 7.

[8] Charles H. Thompson, "The American Negro and National De-

The armed forces of democracy discriminated against and segregated its black soldiers; the factories of the "arsenal of democracy" discriminated against Negroes. Added to the rebuffs from industry and the armed services were a hundred others. Negroes eager to contribute to the Red Cross blood program were turned away. Despite the fact that white and Negro blood is the same biologically, the Army decided that "it is not deemed advisable to collect and mix caucasian and negro blood indiscriminately for later administration to members of the armed forces."[9] When black citizens called upon the Governor of Tennessee to appoint Negro members to the state's draft boards, he told them: "This is a white man's country. . . . The Negro had nothing to do with settling America."[10] At a time when the United States was claiming to be the last bulwark of democracy in a war-torn world, the legislature of Mississippi passed a law requiring different textbooks for black schools than for white schools: All references to voting, elections, and democracy were to be excluded from the Negroes' textbooks.[11] After Pearl Harbor the white citizens of Washington, D.C., talked a great deal about building air raid shelters — but there would be separate shelters for whites and for Negroes.[12]

The Negro's morale at the beginning of World War II is partly explained by his experience in World War I. Black America had gone into World War I with high morale, generated by the belief that the democratic slogans literally meant what they said and would result in democracy at home for Negroes. Most Negroes succumbed to the "close ranks" strategy announced by the crusading NAACP editor W. E. B. DuBois, of subduing racial grievances in order to give full support to winning the war. But the image of a new democratic order was

fense," *Journal of Negro Education*, 9 (October, 1940), 547–52; Frazier, *The Negro in the United States*, 599–606; Robert C. Weaver, "Racial Employment Trends in National Defense," *Phylon*, 2 (4th Quarter, 1941), 337–58.

9 General James C. Magee, Surgeon General, to Assistant Secretary of War McCloy, September 3, 1941, ASW 291.2, NARG 335; Pittsburgh *Courier*, January 3, 1942.

10 Pittsburgh *Courier*, November 2, 1940.

11 "Text Books in Mississippi," *Opportunity*, 18 (April, 1940), 99.

12 "Jim Crow Air Raid Shelters?" *The Crisis*, 49 (January, 1942), 7.

smashed by the race riots, lynchings, and continued rigid discrimination that followed the war. The result was a mass trauma and a series of movements among Negroes in the 1920's that were characterized by a desire to withdraw from a white society that wanted little to do with them. When the war crisis of the 1940's developed, the bitter memories of World War I were recalled, with the result that from the beginning there was a built-in cynicism among Negroes toward the democratic slogans of the new war.[13]

In spite of the natural cynicism toward the slogans of democracy in 1940, Negroes were part of the general population being stimulated to come to the defense of democracy in the world. Negroes, like other Americans, responded and attempted to do their share, but black Americans were turned away. The result was that, at the beginning of World War II, American Negroes were frustrated and cynical toward the aims of the war. The Negro's morale toward the war effort was low, as compared with the rest of American society. But paradoxically, the Negro's general morale was both low and high.

While the black American's morale, as an American, was ambivalent toward the war effort, the Negro, as a member of a minority group, had high morale in his heightened race consciousness and determination to fight for a better position in American society. The same democratic slogans that caused the Negro to react with cynicism also served to emphasize the disparity between creed and practice as far as the Negro in America was concerned. Because of their position in American society, Negroes reacted to the war both as Americans and Negroes. Discrimination against the Negro had given rise to "a sickly negative attitude toward national goals, but at the same time a vibrantly positive attitude toward racial aims and aspirations."[14]

---

[13] Kenneth B. Clark, "Morale of the Negro on the Home Front: World Wars I and II," *Journal of Negro Education*, 12 (Summer, 1943), 417–28; Walter White, "It's Our Country, Too: The Negro Demands the Right to be Allowed to Fight for It," *The Saturday Evening Post*, 213 (December 14, 1940), 27, 61, 63, 66, 68; Metz T. P. Lockard, "Negroes and Defense," *The Nation*, 152 (January 4, 1941), 14–16.

[14] Cornelius L. Golightly, "Negro Higher Education and Democratic Negro Morale," *Journal of Negro Education*, 11 (July, 1942), 324. This paragraph and the previous one are also based on Horace R. Cayton,

When war broke out in Europe in 1939, many Black Americans tended to adopt an isolationist attitude. Those who took this position viewed the conflict as a "white man's war." George Schuyler, iconoclastic columnist, was a typical spokesman for this view: "So far as the colored peoples of the earth are concerned," Schuyler wrote, "it is a toss up between the 'democracies' and the 'dictatorships.' There is no difference between British rule in Africa and German rule in Austria."[15] Another Negro columnist claimed that it was a blessing to have war so that whites could "mow one another down" rather than "have them quietly murder hundreds of thousands of Africans, West Indians and Chinese."[16] This kind of isolationism took the form of anticolonialism, particularly against the British. There was some sympathy for France, however, because of its more liberal treatment of black citizens.[17]

Another spur to isolationist sentiment was the obvious hypocrisy of calling for defense of democracy abroad while, for many, it was not a reality at home. The NAACP bitterly expressed this point:

The Crisis is sorry for brutality, blood, and death among the peoples of Europe, just as we were sorry for China and Ethiopia. But the hysterical cries of the preachers of democracy in Europe leave us cold. We want democracy in Alabama and Arkansas, in Mississippi and Michigan, in the District of Columbia — *in the Senate of the United States.*[18]

The editor of the Pittsburgh *Courier* proclaimed that Negroes had their "own war" at home "against oppression and exploitation from without and against disorganization and lack of con-

"Negro Morale," *Opportunity*, 19 (December, 1941), 371–75; Louis Wirth, "Morale and Minority Groups," *American Journal of Sociology*, 47 (November, 1941), 415–33; Kenneth B. Clark, "Morale Among Negroes," in Goodwin Watson, ed., *Civilian Morale*, 228–48; Arnold M. Rose, *The Negro's Morale: Group Identification and Protest*, 5–7, 54–55, 122–24, 141–44.

[15] Pittsburgh *Courier*, September 9, 1939.

[16] P. L. Prattis in the Pittsburgh *Courier*, September 2, 1939. Similar sentiments were also expressed by Chicago *Defender* editorials, May 25, June 15, 1940.

[17] See, for example, Pittsburgh *Courier*, September 9, 16, 1939.

[18] "Lynching and Liberty," *The Crisis*, 67 (July, 1940), 209.

fidence within"; and the Chicago *Defender* thought that "peace at home" should be the main concern of Negroes.[19]

Many Negroes agreed with columnist George Schuyler that "our war is not against Hitler in Europe, but against the Hitlers in America."[20] The isolationist attitude toward the war in Europe and the antagonism toward Great Britain led to an attitude that was rather neutral toward the Nazis and the Japanese or, in some extreme cases, pro-Axis. Appealing to this latent isolationism, isolationist periodicals tried to gain Negro support in their struggle against America's entrance into the war.[21] By 1940 there were also Negro cults, such as the Ethiopian Pacific Movement, the World Wide Friends of Africa, the Brotherhood of Liberty for the Black People of America, and many others, which preached unity among the world's non-white people, including the Japanese. Many of these groups exploited the latent anti-Semitism common among Negroes in the urban ghettos by claiming that the racial policies of Germany were correct.[22]

Reports reached the public that some black Americans were expressing a vicarious pleasure over successes by the "yellow" Japanese and by Germany. In a quarrel with her employer in North Carolina, a Negro woman retorted: "I hope Hitler does come, because if he does he will get you first." A Negro truck driver in Philadelphia was held on charges of treason after he was accused of telling a black soldier that he shouldn't be in uniform and that "this is a white man's government and war and it's no damned good." After Pearl Harbor, a Negro sharecropper told his plantation owner: "By the way, Captain, I hear

---

[19] Pittsburgh *Courier*, September 9, 1939; Chicago *Defender*, May 25, 1940.

[20] Pittsburgh *Courier*, December 21, 1940.

[21] Ulysses G. Lee, Jr., *The Employment of Negro Troops*, 65–67; Horace Mann Bond, "Should the Negro Care Who Wins the War," *The Annals*, 223 (September, 1942), 81–84; Adam Clayton Powell, Jr., "Is This a White Man's War?" *Common Sense*, 11 (April, 1942), 111–13.

[22] Roi Ottley, "A White Folks's War," *Common Ground*, 2 (Spring, 1942), 28–31, and *New World A-Coming*, 322–42; Lunnabelle Wedlock, *The Reaction of Negro Publications and Organizations to German Anti-Semitism*, 116–93; Alfred M. Lee, "Subversive Individuals of Minority Status," *The Annals*, 223 (September, 1942), 167–68.

the Japs done declared war on you white folks." Another Negro announced that he was going to get his eyes slanted so that the next time a white man shoved him around he could fight back.[23]

It is impossible to determine the extent of latent pro-Axis sentiment among Negroes, but it was widespread enough for the Negro press to make rather frequent mention of it.[24] In 1942 and 1943 the Federal Government arrested the members of several pro-Japanese Negro cults in Chicago, New York, Newark, and in East St. Louis, Illinois. Although the numbers involved were small, the evidence was clear that Japanese agents had been at work among these groups, capitalizing on Negro grievances.[25]

By the time of the attack on Pearl Harbor, certain fundamental changes were obviously taking place among American Negroes. Nowhere is this fact more evident than in a comparison of Negroes' reactions to World War I and to World War II. The dominant opinion among Negroes toward World War I was expressed in W. E. B. DuBois' "Close Ranks" editorial — the Negro should forego his racial grievances for the duration of the war. Now, in World War II, most Negroes looked upon the earlier stand as a great mistake. The dominant attitude was that during World War II the Negro must fight for democracy on two fronts — at home as well as abroad. This attitude had first appeared in reaction to the discriminatory treatment of Negro soldiers,[26] but with the attack on Pearl Harbor, this idea,

---

[23] These and similar incidents are recorded in St. Clair Drake and Horace R. Cayton, *Black Metropolis*, 744–45; Ottley, *New World A-Coming*, 306–10; Horace R. Cayton, "Fighting for White Folks?" *The Nation*, 155 (September 26, 1942), 267–70.

[24] "The Negro and Nazism," *Opportunity*, 18 (July, 1940), 194–95; columns by Horace R. Cayton, Pittsburgh *Courier*, December 20, 1941, and J. A. Rodgers, the *Courier*, December 27, 1941; article by Chandler Owen in the Norfolk *Journal and Guide*, December 13, 1941; report of a correspondent who infiltrated one of the pro-Nazi Negro cults, in the Baltimore *Afro-American*, November 21, 1942.

[25] *The New York Times*, September 15, 22, 1942, January 14, 28, 1943.

[26] See Chapter 4; "Conference Resolutions," *The Crisis*, 47 (September, 1940), 296; "Where the Negro Stands," *Opportunity*, 19 (April, 1941), 98; Lester M. Jones, "The Editorial Policy of the Negro News-

stated in many different ways, became the slogan of Negro America.[27]

American Negroes took advantage of the war to tie their racial demands to the ideology for which the war was being fought. Before Pearl Harbor the Negro press frequently pointed out the similarity of American treatment of Negroes and Nazi Germany's treatment of minorities. In 1940 the Chicago *Defender* featured a mock invasion of the United States by Germany in which the Nazis were victorious because a fifth column of Southern senators and other racists aided them.[28] Later, *The Crisis* printed an editorial that compared the white-supremacy doctrine in America to the Nazi plan for Negroes, a comparison that indicated a marked similarity.[29] Even the periodical of the conservative Urban League made such comparisons.[30]

Many Negroes adopted a paradoxical stand on the meaning of the war. At the same time that it was labeled a "white man's war," Negroes often stated that they were bound to benefit from it. For example, George Schuyler could argue that the

papers of 1917–1918 as Compared with That of 1941–42," *Journal of Negro History*, 29 (January, 1944), 24–31.

[27] For examples of the fighting-on-two-fronts attitude, see editorials in the Baltimore *Afro-American*, December 20, 1941, February 7, 1942; Norfolk *Journal and Guide*, March 21, 1942; "Now is the Time Not to be Silent," *The Crisis*, 49 (January, 1942), 7; "The Fate of Democracy," *Opportunity*, 20 (January, 1942), 2. Two Negro newspapers adopted this theme for their war slogans. The Pittsburgh *Courier*, February 14, 1942, initiated a "Double V" campaign — "victory over our enemies at home and victory over our enemies on the battlefields abroad." When a Negro was brutally lynched in Sikeston, Missouri, a few weeks after Pearl Harbor, the Chicago *Defender*, March 14, 1942, adopted as its war slogan: "Remember Pearl Harbor and Sikeston too." Ralph N. Davis, "The Negro Newspapers and the War," *Sociology and Social Research*, 27 (May, 1943), 373–80, notes the extent of this idea in the Negro press.

[28] Chicago *Defender*, September 25, 1940.

[29] "Nazi Plan for Negroes Copies Southern U.S.A.," *The Crisis*, 48 (March, 1941), 71.

[30] "American Nazism," *Opportunity*, 19 (February, 1941), 35. For examples of other comparisons in the Negro press, see the following editorials: Pittsburgh *Courier*, March 15, April 19, 26, 1941, May 30, 1942; Chicago *Defender*, September 7, 1940; Norfolk *Journal and Guide*, April 19, 1941; Baltimore *Afro-American*, February 17, 1940, September 6, 1941.

war was not for democracy, but "peace means . . . a continuation of the status quo which must be ended if the Negro is to be free." According to Schuyler, the longer the war the better: "Perhaps in the shuffle we who have been on the bottom of the deck for so long will find ourselves at the top."[31]

Cynicism and hope existed side by side in the Negro mind. Cynicism was often the attitude expressed after some outrageous example of discrimination became known. After Pearl Harbor, however, a mixture of hope and certainty that great changes favorable to the Negro would result from the war, that things would never be the same again, became the dominant attitude. Hope was evident in the growing realization that the war provided the Negro an excellent opportunity to prick the conscience of white America: "What an opportunity the crisis has been . . . for one to persuade, embarrass, compel and shame our government and our nation . . . into a more enlightened attitude toward a tenth of its people!" the Pittsburgh *Courier* proclaimed.[32] Certainty that a better life would result from the war was based on the belief that revolutionary forces had been released throughout the world. It was no longer a "white man's world," and the "myth of white invincibility" had been shattered for good.[33]

There was a growing protest against the racial *status quo* by

[31] Pittsburgh *Courier*, October 5, 1940; also see George S. Schuyler, "A Long War Will Aid the Negro," *The Crisis*, 50 (November, 1943), 328–29, 344. Other columnists and editorials expressing the advantages of war to the Negro before the United States became a participant were J. A. Rodgers, Pittsburgh *Courier*, June 28, 1941; Horace R. Cayton, Pittsburgh *Courier*, March 22, 1941; Baltimore *Afro-American*, September 12, 16, 1939. For a historical assessment of the benefits of war for the Negro, see Guion Griffis Johnson, "The Impact of War Upon the Negro," *Journal of Negro Education*, 10 (July, 1941), 596–611.

[32] January 10, 1942. Also see the *Courier* editorial of August 8, 1942. Charles S. Johnson, "The Negro and the Present Crisis," *Journal of Negro Education*, 10 (July, 1941), 585–95. Opinion surveys indicated that most Negro soldiers expressed support for this kind of opportunism. Samuel A. Stouffer and others, *The American Soldier*, Vol. I, 516–17.

[33] Baltimore *Afro-American*, June 12, October 31, 1942; Walter White's remarks in the Pittsburgh *Courier*, May 23, 1942. The impact of world affairs on the American Negro is detailed in Harold R. Isaacs, *The New World of Negro Americans*.

black Americans, evidenced by the re-evaluation of segregation in all sections of the country. In the North there was self-criticism of past acceptance of certain forms of segregation.[34] Southern Negroes became bolder in openly questioning the sacredness of segregation. In October, 1942, a group of Southern Negro leaders met in Durham, North Carolina, and issued a statement on race relations. In addition to pledging their support for the idea that the Negro should fight for democracy at home as well as abroad, these leaders called for complete equality for the Negro in American life. While recognizing the strength and age of the South's race customs, the leaders declared themselves "fundamentally opposed to the principle and practice of compulsory segregation in our American society." In addition there were reports of deep discontent among young Southern Negro college students, and evidence that political activity among the blacks of the South, particularly on the local level, was increasing.[35]

The American Negro, stimulated by the democratic ideology of the war, was re-examining his position in American society. "It cannot be doubted that the spirit of American Negroes in all classes is different today from what it was a generation ago,"

[34] For example, see the following editorials: Pittsburgh *Courier*, December 28, 1940, February 1, June 28, 1941, May 30, 1942; Baltimore *Afro-American*, May 23, 1942.

[35] The Durham statement is reprinted in Charles S. Johnson, *To Stem This Tide*, 131–39. Malcolm S. MacLean, president of Hampton Institute, to Marvin H. McIntyre, November 20, 1942, OF 93, FDRL. George B. Tindall, "The Significance of Howard W. Odum to Southern History: A Preliminary Estimate," *Journal of Southern History*, 24 (August, 1958), 302, indicates that Odum, as Chairman of the Commission on Interracial Cooperation, noted a marked shift in the attitude of Southern Negro leaders during the war — a growing reluctance to accept the principle of segregation. Anthropologist Hortense Powdermaker, in *After Freedom: A Cultural Study of the Deep South*, 331–33, 353, supports the observations of a tendency to rebel among the younger Negroes of the South. For increased political activity among Southern Negroes, see Ralph J. Bunche, "The Negro in the Political Life of the United States," *Journal of Negro Education*, 10 (July, 1941), 567–84; Myrdal, *An American Dilemma*, 499; Henry Lee Moon, *Balance of Power: The Negro Vote*, 178–79.

Gunnar Myrdal observed during the war.[36] Part of this new spirit was an increased militancy, a readiness to protest loudly and vigorously against grievances. The crisis gave Negroes more reason and opportunity to protest. Representative of all the trends of black thought and action — the cynicism, the hope, the heightened race consciousness, the militancy — was the March on Washington Movement (MOWM).

The general idea of exerting mass pressure upon the Administration to end defense discrimination did not originate with A. Philip Randolph's call for a march on Washington in early 1941.[37] Agitation for mass pressure had been growing since the failure of black leaders to gain any major concessions from Roosevelt in September, 1940. The continued flagrant discrimination in the defense industries also served to intensify Negro agitation for change. In September, 1940, Negroes and whites in the Conference on the Negro in the National Defense called for government action to ensure equal participation for black Americans in the armed forces and defense industries. In December, 1940, the Committee for Participation of Negroes in the National Defense called upon Negro groups to band together and "hold huge defense mass meetings in their cities and towns to which their congressmen and senators would be invited."[38] Apparently unconnected with this plea was "a mass demonstration that has never been equaled in Kansas City" in early December, 1940. More than fifty Negro organizations had cooperated in organizing the protest, which brought out a crowd of five thousand persons to hear denunciations of local defense plants that refused to hire Negroes.[39] Negro leaders appealed for more of these local protests.[40]

By January, 1941, the plea for a nationwide network of committees by the Committee for Participation of Negroes in the National Defense had resulted in the organization of Allied

[36] Myrdal, *An American Dilemma*, 744.
[37] Herbert Garfinkel, *When Negroes March*, fails to emphasize this point.
[38] Pittsburgh *Courier*, December 7, 1940.
[39] Pittsburgh *Courier*, December 14, 1940.
[40] Pittsburgh *Courier*, December 21, 1940.

Committees on National Defense. The purpose of this group was to organize defense committees on the local and state level, and February 9, 1941, was designated as National Negro Defense Sunday.[41] Illustrating the rivalry among Negro organizations, the NAACP announced that its own "National Defense Day" would be held on January 26, 1941. On this day mass protest meetings were held in twenty-four states.[42]

The weeks passed and these efforts did not seem to have any effect on the government; Walter White, A. Philip Randolph, and other Negro leaders could not even secure an appointment to see the President. "Bitterness grew at [an] alarming pace throughout the country," Walter White recalled.[43] The first week of January George Schuyler wrote that it was time to stop "pussy footing": "We should publicly announce a policy of non-violent non-cooperation unless immediate steps are taken."[44] The extent of the sentiment for this kind of action is unknown, but Randolph publicized it later in the month, in an article written for the Negro press. He pointed out that all of the committees and pleas by Negro leaders had not succeeded in achieving any action against defense discrimination. Negotiations should continue, but alone they could not do the job: "Only power can affect the enforcement and adoption of a given policy," and "power is the active principle of only the organized masses, the masses united for a definite purpose." To focus the weight of the Negro masses, Randolph suggested that ten thousand Negroes march on Washington, D.C., with the slogan: "We loyal Negro American citizens demand the right to work and fight for our country."[45]

Randolph's suggestion was received enthusiastically by the Negro masses.[46] Herbert Garfinkel, the major historian of the

[41] Pittsburgh *Courier*, December 14, 21, 1940, January 25, February 8, 1941. By the first of March, 1941, this group had organized ten state units, four of which were in southern states. *Courier*, March 8, 1941.

[42] Pittsburgh *Courier*, January 4, 1941; Florence Murray, ed., *The Negro Handbook, 1942*, 72.

[43] Walter White, *A Man Called White*, 189–90.

[44] Pittsburgh *Courier*, January 4, 1941.

[45] Pittsburgh *Courier*, January 25, 1941.

[46] The Chicago *Defender*, February 8, 1941, considered it "timely." The Baltimore *Afro-American*, March 15, June 14, 1941, enthusiastically

MOWM, has pointed out the apparent reluctance with which the NAACP and the Urban League supported this new mass movement, but he maintains that the reason for this hesitation was the historical conservatism of these groups. He has overlooked the militancy already displayed by these two groups before Randolph made his proposal. Lester Granger of the Urban League and Walter White of the NAACP had encouraged mass protests before Randolph proposed his march.[47] The most likely explanation for the reluctance displayed by the two groups is that they did not want a new organization undercutting their efforts and sharing in the glory.

Regardless of how reluctant the old protest organizations were in bolstering it, the MOWM experienced mushrooming support from the Negro masses. Randolph increased the number to march on Washington to fifty thousand; with this threat of a mass march on the capital on July 1, 1941, drawing nearer, a reluctant President was forced to issue an executive order establishing the President's Committee on Fair Employment Practices (FEPC). This is the familiar story told by both contemporary accounts and later studies. Unfortunately, not one of the scholarly accounts has made use of the materials in the Franklin D. Roosevelt Library.[48] Although not conclusive, the evidence in the library suggests another story. Rather than a great victory by a Negro pressure group over a reluctant President, FEPC might have been a shrewd victory by a politically wise President over the demands of a militant minority.

---

supported it. The Norfolk *Journal and Guide*, June 14, 1941, viewed the MOWM as necessary under the circumstances. The Pittsburgh *Courier*, June 14, 1941, called it a "crackpot" proposal, but it appeared to be bitter because the MOWM had undercut the Allied Committees on National Defense, which it sponsored.

[47] Garfinkel, *When Negroes March*, 41; Pittsburgh *Courier*, December 21, 1940, January 4, 1941. Before Randolph's proposal had achieved much momentum, the NAACP had planned mass protests and picketing of defense plants against defense discrimination. Pittsburgh *Courier*, February 8, 15, April 19, 1941.

[48] The scholarly studies touching upon the MOWM or the FEPC are: Garfinkel, *When Negroes March*, written by a sociologist; Louis C. Kesselman, *The Social Politics of FEPC*, written by a political scientist; and Louis Ruchames, *Race, Jobs, and Politics*, written by a sociologist.

The size of the Negro victory represented by FEPC is diminished when one examines the extent of the original MOWM demands. These demands were: an executive order forbidding government contracts to be awarded to a firm with a discriminatory hiring policy; an executive order ending segregation in the armed forces; an executive order abolishing discrimination in government defense training courses; a request from the President to Congress to pass a law forbidding benefits of the National Labor Relations Act to unions denying Negroes membership; an executive order requiring the United States Employment Service to supply workers without regard to race; and an executive order abolishing discrimination and segregation on account of race, creed, or color in all departments of the Federal Government.[49] These specific demands were never made public. Articles and statements about the march defined the aims in general terms as an end to discrimination in the defense industries and an end to segregation in the military forces.[50]

There is no doubt that President Roosevelt did not want the march to occur, and in this sense Negroes exerted pressure on him.[51] The President had submitted the proposals of MOWM to the military departments for their reaction in early June, 1941. While amenable to some action against employment discrimination, there was a different attitude toward the demand for an end to military segregation. It was recognized that Negroes were demanding integration, but "such a mingling was not part of the President's policy, and for practical reasons it would be impossible to put into operation."[52]

[49] "Proposals of the Negro March-On-Washington Committee to President Roosevelt for Urgent Consideration," June 21, 1941, OF 391, FDRL.

[50] For example, see articles by Randolph in the Norfolk *Journal and Guide*, March 15, April 12, 1941.

[51] Memorandum, Edwin M. Watson [Secretary to the President] to the President, June 14, 1941, OF 391, FDRL, describes a conversation with Fiorello La Guardia who had met with White and Randolph along with Mrs. Roosevelt in New York in an effort to get the march called off.

[52] Memorandum, Robert P. Patterson, Under Secretary of War, to General Watson, June 3, 1941, OF 391, FDRL. This was an answer to a request for comment on a letter to the President from Randolph setting

The much-heralded meeting between Roosevelt, White, and Randolph did not take place until June 18, 1941. Before this meeting the military had let the President know that integration of the armed services was "impossible." They agreed, however, that the state of Negro discontent called for some action.[53] By June 12, before there was any meeting between MOWM officials and representatives of the Administration, Roosevelt had already decided what concessions he was willing to make, although the precise nature of his decision is not definitely known.[54] The next day, June 13, Fiorello La Guardia, representing Roosevelt, met with White and Randolph in New York and told them that provisions carrying penalties for nonobservance of fair employment ought to be placed in government contracts with defense industries.[55] Apparently this is what Roosevelt had decided upon the day before the meeting, but the Negro leaders demanded an executive order and refused to call off the march.

On June 12 Roosevelt had also sent a memorandum to the Office of Production Management (OPM) giving a generalized statement of support to an earlier letter from this agency to defense contractors asking that they not discriminate in employment. This letter by the President was not made public until June 15.[56] It is possible that this was the decision the President had made on June 12. However, the nature of the suggestion made by La Guardia to the Negro leaders on June 13 was much

forth the general demands of the MOWM. Randolph to the President May 20, 1941, OF 391, FDRL.

[53] Secretary of War Stimson believed that the leaders of the MOWM were conservatives who feared a Communist takeover of Negro leadership if the Administration did not take some action. If this was a general attitude within the Administration, it could have acted as a spur to Roosevelt's recognition that he had to do something to salve the feelings of Negroes. See Henry L. Stimson Diary, June 18, 1941.

[54] Memorandum, Edwin M. Watson, Secretary to the President, to Captain Beardall, June 12, 1941, OF 391, FDRL, indicates that the President had decided what his answer to White and Randolph was to be before there had ever been a meeting. This memorandum was originally a covering note for the President's proposed answer; unfortunately the answer itself cannot be found.

[55] Ruchames, *Race, Jobs, and Politics*, 18.

[56] Ruchames, *Race, Jobs, and Politics*, 18–19.

more specific and far-reaching than Roosevelt's letter to OPM. The general interpretation of the letter to OPM made public on June 15, before the President met with the MOWM leaders, is that it was an attempt to stop the march with less than an executive order.[57] Overlooked, however, is the overwhelmingly favorable response this letter received from Negroes around the country, a fact that must have indicated to the President how little was required of him to satisfy black opinion.[58]

When the march was not canceled, Roosevelt agreed to meet with White and Randolph on June 18.[59] At this meeting Roosevelt told the Negro leaders that he was opposed to the march but that he was considering the creation of a board to investigate complaints of discrimination in defense industry,[60] an extension of the proposal made by La Guardia on June 13. Representatives of the Navy and Army clearly refused to meet the demand for desegregation. Negotiations continued until June 24, with reports that "little or no satisfaction had been obtained" by the Negro leaders.[61] Faced with the possibility of accepting an executive order substantially as written by the White House or of proceeding with a march on Washington that no one was sure would occur, Randolph and White accepted the President's proposed order and canceled the march.[62]

From La Guardia's proposal of June 13, which was made part of the executive order, and the President's suggestion of June 18, the course of action decided upon by Roosevelt on June 12, appears to have been for some form of fair employment practices committee. Although the MOWM had pressed this from Roose-

---

[57] Ruchames, *Race, Jobs, and Politics*, 18; Garfinkel, *When Negroes March*, 60.

[58] OF 93, FDRL, contains numerous letters from Negroes praising the President's general statement to OPM. For an example of this reaction, see the Pittsburgh *Courier*, June 21, 1941.

[59] Memorandum, Roosevelt to General Watson, June 14, 1941, OF 391, FDRL. A. Philip Randolph to the President, June 16, 1941, OF 391, FDRL, agrees to the meeting, but refuses to call off the march.

[60] Ruchames, *Race, Jobs, and Politics*, 20.

[61] Ruchames, *Race, Jobs, and Politics*, 50.

[62] For the stubbornness of Administration negotiators, see Ruchames, *Race, Jobs, and Politics*, 20–21; White, *A Man Called White*, 192–93.

velt, it was only a part of what had been demanded. By refusing to consider desegregation of the armed forces or some of the other demands, the President managed to focus attention on that area in which he had apparently already decided to take action — discrimination in defense industry employment. The leaders of the MOWM had to accept this situation or risk possible embarrassment by having their bluff called. Once the executive order establishing the FEPC was issued, it was trumpeted as a great victory for Negroes, which served to distract attention away from what had been demanded but not conceded. The perpetuation of the story that American Negroes had forced the President to make a big concession also served Roosevelt by soothing the feelings of Southern Democrats: He had been *forced* to establish the FEPC. Interpreted in this way, the postponing of the March on Washington was a definite victory for Roosevelt.[63]

There was an undercurrent of discontent among Negroes who thought that the march should not have been called off and that Executive Order 8802 gave far less than had been demanded.[64] There were objections that the order did not provide for penalties; many claimed the postponement of the march was a "sellout" by the black leaders. Many of the dissatisfied objected that the demand for desegregation of the armed forces had been ignored, and Randolph did avoid a frank statement on this point.[65]

---

[63] Garfinkel, *When Negroes March*, 65, admits that "a good case can be made that the White House conferees had not obtained all that the march was originally organized to attain," but he does not support this line of reasoning.

[64] Kesselman, *The Social Politics of FEPC*, 15–24, adequately describes the shortcomings of the first FEPC. It is obvious that Roosevelt was not going to let the FEPC embarrass his Administration. When the committee in 1942 found that the United States Office of Education was condoning discrimination in defense training programs, in violation of the executive order establishing FEPC, Roosevelt forbade the publication of these hearings as had been the usual procedure. See Lawrence W. Cramer, Executive Secretary of FEPC, to the President, July 3, 1942, and memorandum, F.D.R. to Mac (Marvin McIntyre), Assistant to the President, July 17, 1942; both in OF 4245-G, FDRL.

[65] The discontent over cancellation of the march is discussed in Garfinkel, *When Negroes March*, 65–70; Chicago *Defender*, July 5, 1941; Pittsburgh *Courier*, July 12, 1941.

His only defense of why this demand was not met was that jobs in defense industries were more vital to Negroes than openings in the armed services.[66] Apparently Randolph did not want to say publicly that the Administration had absolutely refused to discuss this matter. Perhaps this criticism over the failure to achieve integration of the armed forces spurred Randolph on in his later demands for military integration, culminating in a threat to lead a boycott against the draft in the postwar years.

Regardless of the extent of the success of the MOWM, however, it did represent something different in black protest. Unlike the older Negro organizations, the MOWM had captured the imagination of the masses.[67] The MOWM pioneered what has become the common denominator of today's Negro revolt — "the spontaneous involvement of large masses of Negroes in a political protest."[68] Furthermore, as August Meier and Elliott Rudwick have recently pointed out, the MOWM clearly foreshadowed "the goals, tactics, and strategy of the mid-twentieth-century civil rights movement." White individuals were excluded purposely to make it an all-Negro movement; its main weapon was direct action on the part of the black masses. The MOWM took as its major concern the economic problems of urban slum-dwellers.[69]

Although overlooked by most recent writers on civil rights, mass militancy became common among American Negroes in World War II. This new development was personified by the MOWM and was the reason for its wide appeal. Furthermore,

---

[66] Baltimore *Afro-American*, August 16, 1941.

[67] The Negro press generally recognized that the MOWM represented something new. Commenting on the success of the MOWM, the Pittsburgh *Courier*, July 5, 1941, claimed: "We begin to feel at last that the day when we shall gain full rights . . . of American citizenship is not far distant." The Chicago *Defender*, June 28, July 12, 1941, felt that the white man will be convinced that "the American black man has decided henceforth and forever to abandon the timid role of Uncle-Tomism in his struggle." The tactics of the MOWM had "demonstrated to the doubting Thomases among us that only mass action can pry open the iron doors that have been erected against America's black minority."

[68] Garfinkel, *When Negroes March*, 8.

[69] August Meier and Elliott M. Rudwick, *From Plantation to Ghetto: An Interpretative History of American Negroes*, 222.

older Negro organizations found themselves pushed from below into militant stands. For example, the NAACP underwent a tremendous growth in its membership and became representative of the Negro masses for the first time in the organization's history. From 355 branches and a membership of 50,556 in 1940, the NAACP grew to 1,073 branches with a membership of slightly less than 450,000 in 1946.[70] The editors of the Pittsburgh *Courier* recognized that a new spirit was present in black America. In the past Negroes "made the mistake of relying entirely upon the gratitude and sense of fair play of the American people." Now,

we are disillusioned. We have neither faith in promises, nor a high opinion of the integrity of the American people, where race is involved. Experience has taught us that we must rely primarily upon our own efforts. . . . That is why we protest, agitate, and demand that all forms of color prejudice be blotted out.[71]

---

[70] Frazier, *The Negro in the United States*, 537; Charles Radford Lawrence, "Negro Organizations in Crisis: Depression, New Deal, World War II" (unpublished Ph.D. dissertation, Columbia University, 1953), 103; Myrdal, *An American Dilemma*, 851–52. Such close observers of American race relations as Will Alexander, Edwin Embree, and Charles S. Johnson recognized the changing character of Negro protest. They believed that "the characteristic movements among Negroes are now for the first time becoming proletarian, as contrasted to upper class or intellectual influence that was typical of previous movements. The present proletarian direction grows out of the increasing general feelings of protest against discrimination, especially in the armed forces and in our war activities generally. The present movements are led in part by such established leaders as A. Philip Randolph, Walter White, etc. There is likelihood (and danger) that the movement may be seized upon by some much more picturesque figure who may be less responsible and less interested in actual improvement of conditions. One of the most likely of the potential leaders is A. Clayton Powell, Jr." Memorandum of Conferences of Will Alexander, Charles S. Johnson, and Edwin Embree on the Rosenwald Fund's Program in Race Relations, June 27, 1942, Race Relations folder, Rosenwald Fund Papers, Fisk University.

[71] Pittsburgh *Courier*, September 12, 1942. Among the numerous articles recognizing the growth in militancy and spirit of black protest are: Roscoe E. Lewis, "The Role of Pressure Groups in Maintaining Morale Among Negroes," *Journal of Negro Education*, 12 (Summer, 1943), 464–73; Earl Brown, "American Negroes and the War," *Harper's Magazine*, 184 (April, 1942), 545–52; Roi Ottley, "Negro Morale," *New Re-*

By the time of the Japanese attack on Pearl Harbor, many in America, both inside and outside of the government, were worried over the state of Negro morale. There was fear that the Negro would be disloyal.[72] The depth of white ignorance about the causes for the Negro's cynicism and low morale is obvious from the fact that the black press was blamed as the cause of the widespread discontent. The double victory attitude, constantly displayed in the Negro press throughout the war and supported by most black Americans, was considered as verging on disloyalty by most whites. White America, ignorant of the American Negroes' reaction to World War I, thought that black citizens should subdue their grievances for the duration of World War II.

During World War II there was pressure upon the White House and the Justice Department from within the Federal Government to indict some Negro editors for sedition and interference with the war effort. President Roosevelt refused to sanction this action, however. There was also an attempt to deny newsprint to the more militant Negro newspapers, but the President put an end to this when the matter was brought to his attention.[73] The restriction of Negro newspapers from military installations became so widespread that the War Department had to call a halt to this practice in 1943.[74] The critics failed to realize that, although serving to unify black opinion, the Negro press simply reflected the Negro mind.

One of the most widely publicized attacks on the Negro press was made by a white liberal in the South, Virginius Dabney,

public, 105 (November 10, 1941), 613–15; Thomas Sancton, "Something's Happened to the Negro," *New Republic*, 108 (February 8, 1943), 175–79; Stanley High, "How the Negro Fights for Freedom," *The Reader's Digest*, 41 (July 1, 1942), 113–18; H. C. Brearley, "The Negro's New Belligerency," *Phylon*, 5 (4th Quarter, 1944), 339–45.

[72] Memorandum, G-2, to Assistant Secretary of War McCloy, June 27, 1942, ASW 291.2, NARG 335.

[73] White, *A Man Called White*, 207–8; R. Keith Kane to Ulric Bell, May 14, 1942, Office of Facts and Figures (OFF), 002.11, NARG 208; memorandum, John J. McCloy to Robert A. Lovett, March 6, 1942, ASW 291.2, NARG 335.

[74] Baltimore *Afro-American*, September 30, 1941; Pittsburgh *Courier*, March 8, 1941, November 13, 1943.

editor of the Richmond *Times Dispatch*. He charged that "extremist" Negro newspapers and Negro leaders were "demanding an overnight revolution in race relations," and as a consequence they were "stirring up interracial hate." Dabney concluded his indictment by warning that "it is a foregone conclusion that if an attempt is made forcibly to abolish segregation throughout the South, violence and bloodshed will result."[75] The black press reacted vigorously to such charges. Admitting that there were "all-or-nothing" Negro leaders, the Norfolk *Journal and Guide* claimed they were created by the "nothing-at-all" attitude of whites.[76] The Chicago *Defender* and Baltimore *Afro-American* took the position that they were only pointing out the shortcomings of American democracy, and such criticism was certainly not disloyal.[77] The NAACP and the Urban League claimed that it was patriotic for Negroes to protest against undemocratic practices; those who sought to stifle this protest were unpatriotic.[78]

[75] Virginius Dabney, "Nearer and Nearer the Precipice," *The Atlantic Monthly*, 171 (January, 1943), 94–100; also see Dabney's "Press and Morale," *Saturday Review of Literature*, 25 (July 4, 1942), 5–6, 24–25. White columnist Westbrook Pegler made a similar attack that was answered by the Pittsburgh *Courier*, May 9, 1942.

[76] August 15, 1942. Also see *Journal and Guide* editorials of October 17, April 25, 1942, March 6, 1943, for a defense of Negro militancy.

[77] Chicago *Defender*, December 20, 1941; Baltimore *Afro-American*, January 9, 1943.

[78] Pittsburgh *Courier*, May 8, June 19, 1943. A few conservative Negroes joined whites in criticizing the growing militancy. James E. Shepard, Negro President of North Carolina College for Negroes, asked the Administration to do something to undercut the growing support of the militants among young Negroes: "Those who seek to stir them up about rights and not duties are their enemies." Shepard to Secretary of the Navy Knox, September 28, 1940, OF 93, FDRL. Frederick D. Patterson, President of Tuskegee Institute, made it clear in his newspaper column and in talks with Administration officials that he believed in all-out support for the war effort by Negroes regardless of segregation and discrimination. Stimson Diary, January 29, 1943, and columns by Patterson in the Pittsburgh *Courier*, January 16, July 3, 1943. Such conservatives were bitterly attacked in the Negro press. The black leader who urged his people to relax their determination to win full participation in American life was a "misleader and a false prophet," the *Journal and Guide*, May 2, 1942, proclaimed. Such people "endangered" the interests

The Negro masses simply did not support a strategy of moderating their grievances for the duration of the war. After attending an Office of Facts and Figures conference for Negro leaders in March, 1942, Roy Wilkins of the NAACP wrote:

... it is a plain fact that no Negro leader with a constituency can face his members today and ask full support for the war in the light of the atmosphere the government has created. Some Negro educators who are responsible only to their boards or trustees might do so, but the heads of no organized groups would dare do so.[79]

By 1942 the Federal Government began investigating Negro morale in order to find out what could be done to improve it. This project was undertaken by the Office of Facts and Figures and its successor, the Office of War Information.[80] Surveys by these agencies indicated that the great amount of national publicity given the defense program only served to increase the Negro's awareness that he was not participating fully in that program. Black Americans found it increasingly difficult to reconcile their treatment with the announced war aims. Urban Negroes were the most resentful over defense discrimination,

---

of Negroes by "compromising with the forces that promote and uphold segregation and discrimination," wrote the editor of the Chicago *Defender*, April 5, 1941. *The Crisis* charged that those Negroes who succumbed to segregation as "realism" provided a rationale for those whites who sought to perpetuate segregation. "Government Blesses Separation," *The Crisis*, 50 (April, 1943), 105.

[79] Memorandum, Roy Wilkins to Walter White, March 24, 1942, Stephen J. Spingarn Papers, Harry S Truman Library.

[80] Memorandum, R. Keith Kane to Archibald MacLeish, February 14, 1942; Ulric Bell to Edwin R. Embree, February 23, 1942, both in OFF 002.11, NARG 208. Some government agencies displayed timidity when it came to a subject as controversial as the race question. In April, 1942, Jonathan Daniels, Assistant Director in Charge of Civilian Mobilization, Office of Civilian Defense, urged his superior, James Landis, to do something about minority morale. Daniels wanted a "go" sign to initiate a program that would indicate the Federal Government's concern. One of his suggestions called for the creation of a "Division of American Unity" within the Office of Civilian Defense. This proposal got nowhere as Daniels' superiors decided Negro morale was "too hot a potato." Memoranda to James Landis, April 1, 7, 1942; Daniels to Howard W. Odum, August 24, 1942, Jonathan Daniels Papers, University of North Carolina.

particularly against the treatment accorded black members of the armed forces. Never before had Negroes been so united behind a cause; the war had served to focus their attention on their unequal status in American society. Black Americans were almost unanimous in wanting a show of good intention from the Federal Government that changes would be made in the racial *status quo.*[81]

The government's inclination to take steps to improve Negro morale, and the Negro's desire for change, were frustrated by the general attitude of white Americans. In 1942, after two years of militant agitation by Negroes, six out of ten white Americans felt that black Americans were satisfied with the *status quo* and that Negroes were receiving all of the opportunities they deserved. More than half of all whites interviewed in the Northeast and West believed that there should be separate schools, separate restaurants, and separate neighborhoods for the races. A majority of whites in all parts of the country believed that the Negro would not be treated any better after the war than in 1942 and that the Negro's lesser role in society was due to his own shortcomings rather than anything the whites had done.[82] The white opposition to racial change may have provided the rationale for the government to do very little during the war to raise Negro morale. Furthermore, the white obstinance must have added to the bitterness of black Americans.

Although few people recognized it, the war was working a revolution in American race relations. Sociologist Robert E. Park felt that the racial structure of society was cracking and the equilibrium reached after the Civil War seemed "to be under

---

[81] "Reports from the Special Service Division Submitted April 23, 1942: Negro Organizations and the War Effort"; Cornelius Golightly, "Negro Morale in Boston," Special Services Division Report No. 7, May 19, 1942; Special Services Division Report No. 5: "Negro Conference at Lincoln University," May 15, 1942; Special Services Division Memorandum, "Report on Recent Factors Increasing Negro-White Tension," November 2, 1942. All are in Office of Facts and Figures and Office of War Information files in NARG 44.

[82] "Intelligence Report: White Attitudes Toward Negroes," Office of War Information, Bureau of Intelligence, August 5, 1942; same title, dated July 28, 1942, both in NARG 44. Hazel Erskine, "The Polls: Race Relations," *Public Opinion Quarterly*, 26 (Spring, 1962), 137–48.

attack at a time and under conditions when it is particularly difficult to defend it."[83] Sociologist Howard W. Odum wrote from the South that there was "an unmeasurable and unbridgeable distance between the white south and the reasonable expectation of the Negro."[84] White Southerners opposed to change in the racial mores sensed changes occurring among "their" Negroes. "Outsiders" from the North, Mrs. Roosevelt, and the Roosevelt Administration were all accused of attempting to undermine segregation under the pretense of wartime necessity.[85]

Racial tensions were common in all sections of the country during the war, and a series of major race riots erupted across the United States in 1943.[86] Tensions were high because Negro Americans were challenging the *status quo*. When fourteen prominent Negroes, conservatives and liberals, Southerners and Northerners, were asked in 1944 what they thought the black American wanted, they were almost unanimous! Twelve of the fourteen said they thought that Negroes wanted full political equality, economic equality, equality of opportunity, and full social equality, with the abolition of legal segregation.[87] The war had stimulated the race consciousness and the desire for change among Negroes.

Most American Negroes and their leaders wanted the government to institute a revolutionary change in its race policy. Whereas the policy had been acquiescence in segregation since the end of Reconstruction, the government was now asked to set the example for the rest of the nation by supporting integration. This was the demand voiced by the great majority of the

[83] Robert E. Park, "Racial Ideologies," William F. Ogburn, ed., *American Society During Wartime*, 174.

[84] Howard W. Odum, *Race and Rumors of Race: Challenge to American Crisis*, 7; for a similar view, see Charles S. Johnson, *To Stem This Tide*, ix–x, 67–68, 73, 89–105, 106–7, 113–17.

[85] John Temple Graves, "The Southern Negro and the War Crisis," *Virginia Quarterly Review*, 18 (Autumn, 1942), 500–517; Clark Foreman, "Race Tension in the South," *New Republic*, 107 (September 21, 1942), 340–42.

[86] Alfred McClung Lee and Norman D. Humphrey, *Race Riot*; Carey McWilliams, "Race Tensions: Second Phase," *Common Ground*, 4 (Autumn, 1943), 7–12.

[87] Rayford W. Logan, ed., *What the Negro Wants*.

Negro leaders called together in March, 1942, by the Office of Facts and Figures.[88] *The Crisis* magazine summarized the feelings of many black Americans: Negroes "have waited thus far in vain for some sharp and dramatic notice that this war is not to maintain the status quo here." [89]

The White House — and it was not alone — failed to respond to the revolutionary changes occurring among the nation's largest minority. When the Fraternal Council of Negro Churches called upon President Roosevelt to end discrimination in the defense industries and armed forces, the position taken was that "it would be very bad to give encouragement beyond the point where actual results can be accomplished." [90] Roosevelt did bestir himself over especially outrageous incidents. When Roland Hayes, a noted Negro singer, was beaten and jailed in a town in Georgia, the President dashed off a note to his Attorney General: "Will you have someone go down and check up . . . and see if any law was violated. I suggest you send a northerner." [91]

Roosevelt was not enthusiastic about major steps in the race relations field proposed by interested individuals within and without the government.[92] In February, 1942, Edwin R. Embree of the Julius Rosenwald Fund, acutely aware of the growing crisis in American race relations, urged Roosevelt to create a

---

[88] Memorandum, Roy Wilkins to Walter White, March 23, 1942, Spingarn Papers, Harry S Truman Library; Pittsburgh *Courier*, March 28, 1942; Norfolk *Journal and Guide*, March 28, 1942.

[89] "U.S.A. Needs a Sharp Break With the Past," *The Crisis*, 49 (May, 1942), 151.

[90] "A Statement to the President of the United States Concerning the Present World Crisis by Negro Church Leaders Called by the Executive Committee of the Fraternal Council of Negro Churches of America," February 17, 1942; M. H. McIntyre to Dr. Malcolm MacLean, Chairman of the President's Committee on Fair Employment Practice, February 19, 1942, both in OF 93, FDRL.

[91] Memorandum, the President to the Attorney General, August 26, 1942, OF 93, FDRL.

[92] F.D.R.'s conservative and "leave well enough alone" attitude toward Negro rights is discussed in Arthur M. Schlesinger, Jr., *The Age of Roosevelt: The Politics of Upheaval*, 421; Frank Freidel, *F.D.R. and the South*, 73, 81, 97; Mary McLeod Bethune, "My Secret Talks with F.D.R.," *Ebony*, 4 (April, 1949), 42–51. Perhaps Roosevelt's conservative attitude is responsible for his privately expressed dislike of the NAACP.

commission of race relations experts to advise him on steps the government should take to improve matters. The President's answer to this proposal indicates that he felt race relations to be one of the reform areas that had to be sacrificed for the present in order to prosecute the war. He thought such a commission was premature and said, "We must start winning the war . . . before we do much general planning for the future." The President believed that "there is a danger of such long range planning becoming projects of wide influence in escape from the realities of war. I am not convinced that we can be realists about the war and planners for the future at this critical time."[93]

After the race riots of 1943, numerous proposals for a national committee on race relations were put forward. But Roosevelt refused to change his position toward the suggested committee of experts on race relations. Instead, the President simply appointed Jonathan Daniels to gather information from all government departments on current race tensions and what was being done to combat them.[94] This suggestion for what would

[93] Roosevelt to Edwin R. Embree, March 16, 1942, in answer to Embree to Roosevelt, February 3, 1942; both in OF 93, FDRL.

[94] In June, 1943, Edwin Embree and John Collier, Commissioner of Indian Affairs, developed an idea for a committee established by the President "to assume special responsibility in implementing the Bill of Rights of the Constitution, particularly in defending racial minorities at a time of crisis." Memorandum, Embree to Charles S. Johnson and Will Alexander, June 16, 1943, Race Relations folder, Rosenwald Fund Papers, Fisk University. See also John Collier and Saul K. Padover, "An Institute for Ethnic Democracy," *Common Ground*, 4 (Autumn, 1943), 3–7, for a more elaborate proposal.

Embree probably passed along his idea to Professor Howard W. Odum of the University of North Carolina so that he could discuss it with a fellow North Carolinian in the White House, Jonathan Daniels, Administrative Assistant to the President. Odum and Daniels had a conference in August, 1943, from which emerged a recommendation for a "President's Committee on Race and Minority Groups." Odum to Daniels, August 23, 1943; memorandum, Odum to Daniels, August 30, 1943, Howard W. Odum Papers, University of North Carolina.

Although Daniels apparently gave Odum the impression that he was in favor of a national committee, this was not the case. "It has been suggested that a committee of prominent men be named to study this situation," he wrote the President. "I am sure the naming of such a committee would not now halt the procession of angry outbreaks which are

eventually become the President's Committee on Civil Rights was forced to wait for a President who recognized that a revolution in race relations was occurring and that action by the government could no longer be postponed. In the interim, many would share the shallow reasoning of Secretary of War Stimson that the cause of racial tension was "the deliberate effort . . . on the part of certain radical leaders of the colored race to use the war for obtaining . . . race equality and interracial marriages." [95]

The hypocrisy and paradox involved in fighting a world war for the four freedoms and against aggression by an enemy preaching a master race ideology, while at the same time upholding racial segregation and white supremacy, could not be overlooked. The war crisis provided American Negroes a unique opportunity to point out, for all to see, the difference between the American creed and practice. The democratic ideology and rhetoric with which the war was fought stimulated a sense of hope and certainty in black Americans that the old race structure was destroyed forever. In part, this confidence was also the result of the mass militancy and race consciousness that developed in these years. When the expected white acquiescence in a new racial order did not occur, the ground was prepared for the Civil Rights Revolution of the 1950's and 1960's.

---

occurring. I doubt that any report could be made which would be so effective as a statement now from you would be. I am very much afraid, indeed, that any committee report would only serve as a new ground for controversy." Memorandum, Daniels to the President, August 2, 1943, Daniels Papers. Roosevelt agreed with Daniels' assessment, and Odum was informed that "my boss does not think well of the idea that we discussed." Daniels to Odum, September 1, 1943, Howard W. Odum Papers, University of North Carolina.

Daniels' appointment as White House coordinator of information on race relations was actually suggested by him to the President in June, 1943. Memorandum, Daniels to the President, June 29, 1943, Daniels Papers. By July, 1943, FDR had approved of the new role for his Administrative Assistant, and Daniels was hard at work gathering information. Daniels to Secretary of War Stimson, July 28, 1943, ASW 291.2, NARG 335.

[95] Stimson Diary, June 24, 1943.

CHAPTER VII

The Postwar Situation
and the Postwar President

THERE WERE IMPORTANT CHANGES by the end of World War II that made it more difficult to maintain the racial *status quo* in the United States. The ballots of American Negroes had become a potent political force; the militant spirit that matured during the war made Negroes determined to fight segregation wherever it stood in the way of full citizenship. The United States was now the leader of the non-Communist world, and its race problem was a weakness in its Cold War efforts to influence the emerging nations. A new President took office in the midst of the changing situation, a man who realized that the *status quo* in American race relations had to give way to a new order. Unlike his predecessor, this President would have found it difficult to take a passive stand on Negro rights even if he had desired to do so.

The race tensions in civilian life reached a new peak as the war ended, especially in the South where there was fear that the *status quo* in race relations would be further upset by the many returning Negro veterans. There was evidence that Negro veterans were affected by the war's slogans of democracy and by the more democratic treatment accorded them by foreign civilians. In Atlanta, Georgia, several hundred veterans met and pledged themselves to follow a program of action that would bring the "full share of democracy" for which they had fought.[1] In Birmingham, Alabama, one hundred Negro veterans marched on the courthouse, protesting the fact that they had been denied the right to register to vote.[2] Throughout the South there were reports of violence against Negro veterans by white Southerners. A veteran who attempted to register to vote in a small Mississippi town was beaten. The racist Senator Theodore Bilbo of Mississippi demanded that "red-blooded Anglo Saxon" men stop Negroes from voting by "any means"; and "if you don't know what that means, you are just not up on your persuasive measures."[3] Many Southerners were determined to keep the Negro veterans in "their place." One indignant former national commander of the American Legion wrote to Army Chief of Staff Eisenhower after seeing pictures of black soldiers dancing with German girls:

My dear General, I do not know . . . where these negroes come from, but it is certain that if they expect to be returned to the South, they very likely are on the way to be hanged or to be burned alive at public lynchings by the white men of the South.[4]

Racial violence was also in evidence in the North, where wartime employment had brought many Negro newcomers. In Gary, Indiana; Youngstown, Ohio; and in New York there were riots between white and Negro pupils of the public high schools. There were fears that race riots would erupt in Chicago and other Northern cities.[5] The Justice Department and the Negro press issued reports that the Ku Klux Klan was being revived in various parts of the country. The Klan's revival was not confined to the South;

---

[1] Pittsburgh *Courier*, December 8, 1945.

[2] Pittsburgh *Courier*, February 2, 1946.

[3] *The New York Times*, June 25, 1946. For the white fear of Negro veterans in the South, see article by Harold R. Hinton in *The New York Times*, September 1, 1946.

[4] Alvin M. Owsley, Chairman of the American Legion National Americanism Endowment Fund, to General Eisenhower, September 16, 1946, CS291.2, NARG 319.

[5] Pittsburgh *Courier*, October 6, 1945, for school riots; *The New York Times*, December 11, 1946.

there were reports of its growth in California and New York as well.[6] Many people were sure that a wave of race riots would sweep the country as they had after World War I. Among those who remembered the riots after World War I and who feared they would be repeated was President Harry Truman. Two particularly violent attacks persuaded President Truman that some significant action to protect civil rights was needed. In February, 1946, Isaac Woodard, a newly discharged veteran still in uniform, was blinded when South Carolina policemen pulled him off a bus and jabbed their night sticks into his eyes. In July, 1946, two Negro veterans and their wives were taken from a car near Monroe, Georgia, by a mob of white men; the four Negroes were lined up and killed by approximately sixty shots pumped into their bodies. To put a halt to this kind of violence President Truman appointed the President's Committee on Civil Rights on December 6, 1946, to examine the nebulous authority of the Federal Government in the civil rights area and to recommend appropriate legislation.[7]

What were the beliefs on civil rights of this man from Missouri with a Southern heritage? Truman recalled later, "I was raised amidst some violently prejudiced Southerners myself"; perhaps he reflected his own transformation on this matter when he stated his belief that "the vast majority of good southerners understand that the blind prejudices of past generations cannot continue in a free republic."[8] It is clear that Truman had support from Negro voters as early as 1926. He inherited black

[6] Pittsburgh *Courier*, April 27, May 25, 1946; Norfolk *Journal and Guide*, April 6, 20, August 10, 1946; *The New York Times*, June 23, August 1, 1946.

[7] Truman's fear that a tense post-World War II race situation similar to post-World War I was developing and his indignation over these two particular incidents are expressed in Harry S Truman, *Memoirs*, Vol. II, 180–81; White House assistant on minority affairs, Philleo Nash, interview August 20, 1964, verified Truman's shock over these incidents and recalled that studies made for the President indicated that Negro soldiers returning to the South would not readily accept the *status quo*. The two incidents described here, as well as others, are detailed in Florence Murray, ed., *The Negro Handbook, 1949*, 93–94, 102.

[8] Truman, *Memoirs*, Vol. II, 184.

support from the Pendergast machine of Kansas City, and he managed to maintain this support throughout his career as a senator.[9]

At President Truman's first news conference a Negro reporter asked him what stand he would take on civil rights matters. Truman replied: "I will give you some advice. All you need to do is to read the Senate record of one Harry S Truman."[10] As a candidate for the Vice-Presidency in 1944 Truman had also directed interested persons to his Senate record. Obviously he was proud of his position on civil rights. "Without exception," one student of Truman's Senate record has concluded, "Senator Truman acted to provide greater protection for minorities and to afford equal treatment under the law."[11] Truman consistently supported antilynching bills, signed petitions for cloture, and voted for the amendments to the Selective Service Act of 1940 designed to prevent discrimination.

Truman the Senator had also been familiar with the wartime grievances of American Negroes. In 1939 he had supported legislation that assured training for Negroes as well as whites under the Civilian Pilot Training Program.[12] He had agreed to an NAACP proposal that the Truman Committee, investigating defense contracts, would look into the extent of discrimination against minorities in defense plants.[13] Truman also indicated an interest in the Negro and the armed forces: In 1941 he introduced in the Senate a bill proposed by the Pittsburgh *Courier*,

---

[9] Eugene Francis Schmidtlein, "Truman the Senator" (unpublished Ph.D. dissertation, University of Missouri, 1962), 98, 134, 222–23. Professor Richard S. Kirkendall informs the writer that the Kansas City NAACP opposed Truman when he ran for a local Independence office in 1924. When he ran for a countywide judgeship in 1926, however, Truman definitely had the support of Kansas City Negroes.

[10] *Public Papers of the Presidents of the United States, Harry S Truman, 1945*, 10–11. Cited hereafter as *Public Papers* for specific years.

[11] David S. Horton, *Freedom and Equality: Addresses by Harry S Truman*, xiv–xv.

[12] Lee Nichols, *Breakthrough on the Color Front*, 83.

[13] Walter White, *A Man Called White*, 189. Truman recalled later the anxiety of Southerners over integrating the construction workers building training camps in the South during World War II. See Truman, *Memoirs*, Vol. II, 182.

calling for a combat command for General Benjamin O. Davis; in 1943, as a member of the Senate Military Affairs Committee, he supported passage of a resolution that would have provided for an investigation of the effect of segregation on the opportunities of Negroes in the armed services.[14] Truman's experience with Negroes in the armed services went even further back than his Senate days. After leaving the White House, he recalled that his unit had served next to the unsuccessful all-Negro Ninety-second Division in World War I. Truman was puzzled why this unit had not succeeded, while the reports on the Negro Ninety-third Division, which was attached to the French Army, indicated that it had fought well.[15]

An examination of Senator Truman's speeches on the Negro indicates that he was a firm believer in equality of opportunity and equality before the law. At the same time he expressed himself as opposing social equality, an attitude not uncommon in the North as well as the South at the time. In a 1940 campaign speech, Truman expressed his belief "in the brotherhood of man; not merely the brotherhood of white men, but the brotherhood of all men before the law," and he maintained that "in giving to the Negroes the rights that are theirs, we are only acting in accord with our ideals of a true democracy." Truman went on to make it clear that, while he believed in equality before law, Negroes' "social life, will, naturally, remain their own."[16] Truman, then, as a senator was a traditional conservative on the issue of civil rights; he opposed restrictions on Negro political, legal, and civil rights because they violated traditional American principles, but at the same time he was opposed to social integration. Truman at this time believed in the separate-but-equal doctrine that had long been the law of the land. Unlike the racists, he believed strongly in the *equal* part of the phrase.[17]

---

[14] Pittsburgh *Courier*, June 28, 1941, April 17, 1943.

[15] Nichols, *Breakthrough on the Color Front*, 85.

[16] *Congressional Record*, 76th Cong., 3d Sess. (1940), appendix 4546. Also see Truman's speech to the Convention of the National Colored Democratic Association in 1940 in Horton, ed., *Freedom and Equality*, 1–7, where the same ideas were expressed.

[17] Truman's "traditionalist" view of civil rights before he became President has been generally recognized by those who have studied this

Some people have labeled Truman's early view of civil rights as "traditionalist," but they have gone on to commit an error by saying that he remained consistent in his civil rights views after he became President. For example, Jonathan Daniels has claimed that Truman's presidential civil rights activities "never involved any proposal even approximating the mixing of the races."[18] By focusing on Truman's statements in the Senate of a belief in social segregation, Daniels failed to perceive a significant change in Truman's attitude on civil rights after he became President. Others simply appear to have overlooked his change in attitude.

As President, Truman consistently took positions in favor of social integration. He appointed a Committee on Civil Rights whose report declared that segregation was invariably unequal and that separate but equal was "one of the outstanding myths of American history"; he appointed the Commission on Higher Education whose report declared, "Although segregation may not legally mean discrimination . . . it usually does in fact"; he appointed the Committee on Equality of Treatment and Opportunity in the Armed Services to end military segregation; he allowed the Justice Department to submit *amicus curiae* briefs in behalf of ending the separate-but-equal formula in housing, interstate transportation, and public schools. When a reporter asked Truman in 1950 if he agreed with his Attorney General's statement that all forms of segregation are discriminatory, Truman answered: "I think we have been working for that for some time past. Haven't you read any of my messages on that subject?" In 1951 Truman vetoed a bill for federal aid to schools that contained a Southern-backed amendment requiring the maintenance of segregation in schools on federal property in those states where school segregation was required

---

problem. See William Carl Berman, "The Politics of Civil Rights in the Truman Administration" (unpublished Ph. D. dissertation, Ohio State University, 1963), 49; Charles R. Bush, "The Truman Civil Rights Program" (unpublished Senior Honors thesis, Harvard University, 1964), 60; Jonathan Daniels, *The Man of Independence*, 336–39. Truman himself supports this view in his *Memoirs*, Vol. II, 183.

[18] Daniels, *The Man of Independence*, 339.

by law. "This proposal, if enacted into law," the President stated, "would constitute a backward step in the efforts by the Federal Government to extend equal rights and opportunities to all our people."[19]

The failure to see a change in Truman's beliefs on civil rights after he became President obscures the revolution that occurred in the relationship between the Federal Government and Negro rights. The Truman Administration marked a rapid change away from the Federal Government's policy of supporting or condoning segregation. Truman, together with other forward-looking individuals and the Supreme Court, began to realize that separate but equal was a contradiction, that as long as there was segregation there would be discrimination. This change in attitude by the President and by the government is made more remarkable because the majority of whites opposed any altera-tion in the racial *status quo*. A National Opinion Research Center Poll of 1946 indicated that 66 per cent of the American white population believed that Negroes were treated fairly; only 25 per cent said Negroes were not treated fairly. The gap be-tween the white and Negro analysis of the situation is indicated by the fact that 66 per cent of the Negro population were con-vinced they were not being treated fairly in American society.[20]

In addition to the increasing evidence supplied by the Presi-dent's committees against the separate but equal doctrine, the President was moved toward a new position by the effect of the United States' race problem on international relations. "The top dog in a world which is over half colored ought to clean his own house," Truman said while still President.[21] In prac-tically every speech President Truman made on civil rights, he pointed out the necessity for Americans to practice what they

[19] President's Committee on Civil Rights, *To Secure These Rights*, 79–87; President's Commission on Higher Education, *Higher Education for American Democracy*, 34; President's Committee on Equality of Treatment and Opportunity in the Armed Services, *Freedom to Serve*; the *amicus curiae* briefs are discussed in Berman, "The Politics of Civil Rights," 155–56, 159–60, 189–90; *Public Papers, 1950*, 86; *Public Papers, 1951*, 616.
[20] *The New York Times*, August 4, 1946.
[21] Daniels, *The Man of Independence*, 336.

preached, since the world was watching. "More and more we are learning . . . ," Truman told representatives of the Negro press in 1947,

how closely our democracy is under observation. We are learning what loud echoes both our successes and our failures have in every corner of the world. That is one of the pressing reasons why we cannot afford failures. When we fail to live together in peace, the failure touches not us, as Americans alone, but the cause of democracy itself in the whole world. That we must never forget.[22]

Cold War propaganda against the United States hit hard at the race problem; State Department experts estimated that nearly half of the Russian propaganda against the United States was focused on this issue alone.[23]

The ingredient of political power also played a part in making civil rights a prominent national issue in the Truman years. Black Americans had played an important role in the Roosevelt coalition during the 1930's and 1940's. Negroes had also been a force in Truman's success at the polls in Missouri senatorial politics. Truman and his advisers were aware that the black vote had, by 1948, become a strategic part of Democratic national politics. The necessity of keeping this vote Democratic in 1948 was made doubly important by the Progressive party and the insurrection of the Dixiecrats. This political fact is well known, but to draw from this the implication that the Truman Administration's civil rights program was entirely the result of the political exigencies of 1948 is a distortion.[24] A more accurate view is

---

[22] *Public Papers, 1947,* 162. Also see Nichols, *Breakthrough on the Color Front,* 84, which points out that Special Adviser to the President Clark Clifford later recalled Truman's belief that this country's failure to assure equal rights to Negroes was one of its weakest points in the struggle with communism.

[23] Nichols, *Breakthrough on the Color Front,* 9. For more on this, see Robert E. Cushman, "Our Civil Rights Became a World Issue," *The New York Times Magazine* (January 11, 1948), 12, 22–24; William A. Rutherford, "Jim Crow: A Problem in Diplomacy," *The Nation,* 175 (November 8, 1952), 428–29.

[24] Berman, "The Politics of Civil Rights," indicates Truman's early interest in Negro rights and the forces pushing change on this matter, but constantly infers that the well-spring of his civil rights activity was

that Truman was basically sympathetic to civil rights and that the times and the Negro demanded some kind of action. The Negro vote had become important in national politics, and the Democrats were as determined to hold onto it as the Republicans were to retrieve it.

The political side of the equation was not unimportant. The Negro opinion of Truman as a national political figure had been mixed. Negro delegates to the 1944 Democratic convention had supported Henry Wallace for nomination as Vice-President.[25] Wallace's defeat and Truman's nomination initiated a further hostile reaction from Negroes, because this move was viewed as a compromise with the South. The Norfolk *Journal and Guide* declared that "Senator Truman is a conservative Democrat, who it appears was given the nomination . . . for reasons of party expediency."[26] The managing editor of the Pittsburgh *Courier* admitted that he did not know much about Truman's record on civil rights, but "it can be said from what I do know . . . , that he is a long way from being a Henry Wallace."[27] Another Negro editor felt that Truman was "an unknown quantity on minority questions."[28] Truman attempted to reassure colored Americans: "Of course Negroes will lose

political. For example, Berman claims that the appointment of the President's Committee on Civil Rights was designed to recoup his party's losses after the 1946 election. Yet, Berman's own evidence indicates that Truman had planned the committee before the elections because of his concern over racial violence and the Federal Government's lack of power to do anything (see pp. 35–45, 67). Again, this emphasis leads Berman to distort Truman's actions concerning the report of his Committee on Civil Rights; he says that Truman was hesitant about what to do with the committee's report until Clark Clifford persuaded him to seize the initiative in the 1948 campaign by sending a special message on civil rights to Congress (pp. 64, 70–71). Yet Clark Clifford recalled later that Truman had wanted to send a message to Congress at once. Nichols, *Breakthrough on the Color Front*, 83.

[25] Pittsburgh *Courier*, July 22, 1944; Norfolk *Journal and Guide*, July 29, 1944.

[26] Norfolk *Journal and Guide*, August 5, 1944.

[27] Pittsburgh *Courier*, July 29, 1944.

[28] Norfolk *Journal and Guide*, July 29, 1944.

nothing by my nomination as Vice President," he told a Negro White House correspondent.[29]

To find out more about how Truman stood on the issues that most interested Negroes, the Pittsburgh *Courier* sent a correspondent to interview him. Truman assured the reporter that he had always supported equal opportunity and equal rights for Negroes: "I have a record of fair play toward my Negro fellow-citizens that will stand examination," he exclaimed. The *Courier* proceeded to check Truman's record around his home town. Following up a rumor that Truman had belonged to the Ku Klux Klan in the 1920's, the reporter found that the Klan had actually opposed Truman in an election for county judge. A Negro playmate of Truman's when he was young, a former maid in the Truman household, and the head of a county school for Negro boys when Truman was county judge all testified that he had a good and fair record toward black people. "Harry Truman is not a Henry Wallace," the reporter concluded his story:

But he is not a John Nance Garner, either. If his personal relationships with Negroes and Negro problems have been few, they seem at least to have been fair. He has, of course, yet to demonstrate on a national scale his full position on the Negro question.[30]

As the election neared, the *Courier*, a Republican paper, disputed the evidence of its own reporter and charged repeatedly that Truman had been a member of the Klan. In the few weeks before the election, the *Courier* printed articles and editorials with the following titles: "South Has Little to Fear From Truman," "Truman Supports Ku Klux Congressional Candidate," and "From the Klan to the White House."[31] Republicans were conducting a whispering campaign in Harlem: "Roosevelt is old and may die and you will then have a Ku Klux Klansman in the White House."[32]

---

[29] Norfolk *Journal and Guide*, July 29, 1944.

[30] Pittsburgh *Courier*, August 5, 1944.

[31] Pittsburgh *Courier*, October 21, 28, November 4, 1944.

[32] Norfolk *Journal and Guide*, November 11, 1944. For the opposition of the Klan to Truman in the 1920's, see Daniels, *The Man of Independ-*

Franklin D. Roosevelt's death was mourned deeply by most Negroes, even by those who had opposed his election in 1944. The Pittsburgh *Courier's* editor recalled that "the New Deal philosophy that government is . . . responsible for the social and economic well-being of the individual, gave Negroes a protection never afforded them." But what was to happen now with a "Southerner" in the White House?[33] The Norfolk *Journal and Guide* lamented that Truman "does not seem to be the man to carry Mr. Roosevelt's mantle of humanitarianism" and that Negroes knew he was the choice of the "reactionary and conservative forces of his party."[34] Not only the literate Negro press mourned Roosevelt and at the same time wondered about Truman. "I am speaking for 13 million Negroes," a Negro woman wrote Stephen Early shortly after Roosevelt's death;

you know what Mr. Rosevlet ment to Negroes[.] the thing I am riting you for, is will you try to make clear to Mr. Trueman what the Negroes want. and that is first class citicinship. we know Mr. Rosevelt would have give us that. . . . Most Negroes believe Mr. Trueman is a Negro Hater. the town he came frome is very unfair to Negroes. I feail you can explain to him that God crated all men Equal.[35]

It was clear that President Truman would have to prove himself to black Americans in order to hold this part of Roosevelt's coalition intact. Truman began his efforts at his first news conference as President by making a point of shaking the hand of the Associated Negro Press White House correspondent and telling him to be sure to look up his Senate record.[36] There followed strong support for a permanent Fair Employment Practices Commission in his special message to Congress on reconversion in September, 1945; his radio report to the nation on the status of his reconversion program on January 3, 1946;

ence, 124–27, 256; Alfred Steinberg, *The Man from Missouri: The Life and Times of Harry S Truman*, 64, 79–80, 85, 224.

[33] Pittsburgh *Courier*, April 21, 1945.
[34] Norfolk *Journal and Guide*, April 21, 1945.
[35] Mrs. Lora J. Haynes to Stephen Early, April 13, 1945, OF 93, HSTL.
[36] Norfolk *Journal and Guide*, April 28, 1945.
[37] *Public Papers, 1945*, 282, and *Public Papers, 1946*, 6, 52.

and his State of the Union message on January 21, 1946.[37] Interlaced with these public pronouncements were some significant federal appointments. In October, 1945, Truman appointed Irvin C. Mollison, a Chicago lawyer, to a judgeship on the United States Customs Court, the first Negro appointed to a federal judgeship within the United States. In January, 1946, William Hastie was appointed Governor of the Virgin Islands, believed by Negroes to be the highest appointment of one of their race by a President.[38]

Negroes were pleased with these early indications of Truman's support for their cause. The Republican Pittsburgh *Courier* admitted that Negroes' fears of the new President had been somewhat allayed and that "his support of Negro legislation and appointments far excelled the late Franklin D. Roosevelt." His record of good intentions had not brought any major accomplishment, however. Negroes were alarmed over the Southern congressmen's dominance of the Democratic Congress.[39] Black Americans remained undecided about Truman. At the same time that he spoke good words, there was evidence of discrimination within his Administration. The Veterans Administration discriminated against Southern Negro veterans; the Department of Agriculture announced that no black 4-H Club members would be allowed to attend the national convention.[40] Violence directed at veterans and black civilians continued in the South, and the Federal Government appeared unable to control it. Reports in the Negro press indicated that segregation remained the policy of the Army. Furthermore, the War Department had adopted a discriminatory policy of requiring Negroes to score 99 on the qualifying test to enlist, whereas whites were required to score only 70.[41]

By the 1946 congressional elections, Negroes, like other groups of the Democratic coalition, were ambivalent toward both the

[38] Norfolk *Journal and Guide*, October 13, 1945, and January 12, 1946.
[39] Pittsburgh *Courier*, April 27, 1946. For praise of Truman's support of FEPC, see editorial in Norfolk *Journal and Guide*, September 15, 1945.
[40] Pittsburgh *Courier*, May 18, 1946.
[41] Pittsburgh *Courier*, October 12, 26, November 9, 1946.

new President and his party. Truman had tried to conciliate all significant groups in the country and had ended by antagonizing most of them.[42] Negroes were concerned about what they perceived as Southern dominance in the Democratic party, or "Bilboism." They pointed to James E. Byrnes, Will Clayton, George E. Allen, and John W. Snyder as Southerners in prominent positions within the Administration. The recent racist campaigns of Governor Eugene Talmadge of Georgia and Senator Theodore Bilbo of Mississippi angered Negroes. There was a feeling among black Americans that they had fared better politically under Roosevelt, that their votes had been appreciated more. Mrs. Truman was certainly not so concerned about Negroes as Mrs. Roosevelt had been. When the elections of 1946 came, many Negro voters either switched to Republican candidates or failed to vote.[43]

Truman had been moving toward a new policy on civil rights before the election of the Eightieth Congress, however. "The ballot is both a right and a privilege," the President said in his message to the 1946 annual convention of the NAACP. "The right to use it must be protected and its use by everyone must be encouraged. Lastly, every veteran and every citizen . . . must be protected from all forms of organized terrorism."[44] In August, 1946, after the atrocity at Monroe, Georgia, the President announced that he had instructed the Justice Department to "proceed with all its resources to investigate this and any other crimes of oppression so as to ascertain if any Federal statute can be applied."[45] The incident in Georgia shocked Truman, and the inability of the Federal Government to act in cases of mob violence led him to accept the idea of a committee

---

[42] Barton J. Bernstein, "The Truman Administration and the Steel Strike of 1946," *Journal of American History*, 52 (March, 1966), 791–803, illustrates how Truman managed to antagonize many groups in society while trying to conciliate them all.

[43] *The New York Times*, October 18, 1946, contains an article detailing Negro grievances against the Democratic party and the Administration. Walter Johnson, *1600 Pennsylvania Avenue: Presidents and the People Since 1929*, 228, points out that many Democrats failed to vote in 1946.

[44] *The New York Times*, June 27, 1946.

[45] *Public Papers, 1946*, 368.

on civil rights to chart a course of action for all levels of government in this field.[46]

Although the appointment of the President's Committee on Civil Rights was not announced until December, 1946, the decision had been made months earlier. When a delegation of the National Emergency Committee Against Mob Violence had called upon the President on September 19, Truman hinted that he was considering such a committee.[47] The President's thinking about a new role for the Federal Government in civil rights was revealed in a message to the National Urban League a few days later. The government has "an obligation to see that the civil rights of every citizen are fully and equally protected"; and "if the civil rights of even one citizen are abused, government has failed to discharge one of its primary responsibilities," Truman said.[48] In his letter of instructions to the President's Committee, Truman made it clear that protection of civil liberties was the duty of every level of government, that the Federal Government had the obligation to act in this area when state or local authorities failed to do so, and that the Federal Government's authority was now hampered by inadequate statutes. The Committee was to recommend legislation and other means by which government could protect civil rights.[49] No longer would the Federal Government play a passive role in the area of Negro rights.

Truman was convinced, therefore, that some federal action on civil rights was needed. Soon after the Republican victory of 1946, a group of liberal Administration figures took it upon themselves to prepare a coherent program for the President's campaign in 1948, and, since this included civil rights, Truman's convictions were fused with the necessities of winning a presidential election. Oscar Ewing, then Acting Chairman of the Democratic National Committee, was convinced that Truman had failed to identify with major groups of voters; he felt that the political strategy for 1948 called for the President to enunci-

---

[46] Interview with Philleo Nash, August 20, 1964.
[47] Pittsburgh *Courier*, September 28, October 5, 1946.
[48] *The New York Times*, September 25, 1946.
[49] *To Secure These Rights*, vii.

ate his program in such a way as to appeal to the various voting blocs.[50]

In December of 1946 Ewing, now Director of the Federal Security Agency, brought together Clark Clifford, Leon Keyserling, C. Girard Davidson, David A. Morse, and Charles S. Murphy, all Administration figures. Their aim was to use their influence to see that the President followed a liberal approach in domestic affairs and to counter the predominantly conservative influence of the Cabinet and the Democratic leaders in Congress. In addition, their goal was the election of Truman in 1948. This group met each week to discuss and decide the programs they would attempt to get the President to support and the strategy they would use to further their plans. Clark Clifford, former Special Counsel to Truman, has described the aims of the group:

Our interest was to be exclusively on domestic affairs. . . . We wanted to try to develop not only policies that would be good for the country, but especially those that would have a high political appeal. We wanted to create a set of goals that truly met the deepest and greatest needs of the people, and we wanted to build a liberal, forward-moving program around those goals that could be recognized as a *Truman* program.[51]

Late in November, 1947, Clark Clifford gave the President a forty-page memorandum representing the liberal group's analysis of how the 1948 campaign should be conducted. Civil rights had a prominent place in this strategy. The Negro vote was crucial for success, along with the farm and labor vote. The Wallace supporters represented a distinct threat to Truman's success, as far as the black vote was concerned, and civil rights would have to be emphasized to hold this element of the Democratic coalition. A significant miscalculation was that "the South, as always, can be considered safely Democratic."[52] This false assumption helps to explain much of the apparent inconsistency

[50] Nichols, *Breakthrough on the Color Front*, 84.

[51] Cabell Phillips, *The Truman Presidency*, 163. The most detailed discussion of this group in print can be found in Phillips, 162–65.

[52] Phillips, *The Truman Presidency*, 197–99.

of the Administration's actions during 1948 — the strong emphasis on civil rights, which had the effect of alienating the South, and the subsequent unsuccessful attempt to write a moderate civil rights plank at the Democratic convention to forestall a Southern bolt.

Truman's civil rights record as a senator was not well known. Many Negroes had developed a sympathetic attitude toward Henry Wallace because they believed he had been sacrificed for the South in 1944; Truman had been acceptable to Southerners as a vice-presidential candidate, and this was one strike against him as far as Negroes were concerned. When Truman became President there was considerable suspicion among Negroes concerning his stand on civil rights. Although he attempted to reassure Negroes by his support of a permanent FEPC and by Negro appointments, Truman was not able to overcome the Southern image of him and of his Administration among Negroes by the end of 1946. The political strategy for a Truman victory in 1948, however, made the Negro vote crucial. Added to these political factors was the growing conviction of Truman and others during these same years that the Federal Government must assume a leading role in civil rights. A fusion of practical politics and democratic idealism set the stage for civil rights to become a national political issue.

CHAPTER VIII

Policy and Politics Again

T HE CIRCUMSTANCES surrounding the 1948 election made the
Negro vote vitally important to the Democratic party. The prospect of a revolt in the South by the Dixiecrats made the Northern Negro vote crucial in the states with a large electoral vote.
The Wallace Progressives threatened to slice off this portion of support. Furthermore, the Republicans were sure to
present stiff competition after their resurgence in the 1946 congressional elections. Added to this political pot was the old
grievance of segregation in the armed forces, which was inten-
sified by the Army's stand-pat attitude and the attempt to pass
a new peacetime draft bill.

As the War Department had waited for the responses to its
questionnaire of May, 1945, officials within the office of the
Assistant Secretary of War continued to think about the Army's
postwar Negro troop policy. Civilian Aide Gibson was concerned that the General Staff's questionnaire did not take
prejudices into account and called principally for subjective
opinions.[1] Gibson's concern was justified as the results began
to come in from various Army commands. Most of the reports
contained the old racial stereotypes of black troops: The Negro
soldier is a coward in combat; he is inherently inferior in mental
aptitude; his performance as a soldier is adversely affected by

---

[1] Memorandum, Gibson to McCloy, May 30, 1945, WDSSP 291.2,
NARG 319.

---

cold weather; he is afraid of the dark; and he is peculiarly suited for labor duty.[2] Rare indeed was a recommendation like that from General Joseph T. McNarney, Commander of the Mediterranean Theater of Operations, that an immediate experiment be conducted by integrating Negroes into white squads:

I am convinced that had it been possible to put this proposal to a test . . . , there would have been no measurable loss in combat efficiency, and we would have been able to demonstrate that the colored soldier individually can be made into a good combat man, whereas we have in general failed to accomplish this using colored troops collectively in segregated units.[3]

Gibson also warned that a new Negro policy should not be based on the old racist ideas. Any study of this problem should come to grips with two important questions: What effect did the policy of segregation itself have on the performance of Negro troops? and, What was the effect of concentrating large numbers of low AGCT personnel in one unit? Gibson felt that any new study of black soldiers should also consider the experiences during the war with unsegregated hospitals and officer candidate schools, the integrated platoons in Europe, and the Navy's experience with integration.[4] McCloy was impressed with Gibson's analysis and forwarded it to the new Secretary of War, Robert P. Patterson, with the recommendation that a special board of officers be appointed to consider this matter. "This whole subject has to be dealt with rather soon and it is a matter in which I feel the Secretary of War must become involved," McCloy wrote.[5]

Secretary Patterson appointed a board of three general officers to investigate the Army's present Negro policy and to prepare a new one that would efficiently utilize this segment of the

---

[2] These reports are in WDSSP 291.2 (1945), NARG 319.

[3] General Joseph T. McNarney to the Chief of Staff, August 13, 1945, WDSSP 291.2, NARG 319.

[4] Memorandum, Gibson to McCloy, August 8, 1945, ASW 291.2, NARG 335.

[5] Memorandum, Colonel Sommers to McCloy, August 28, 1945; memorandum, McCloy to Patterson, September 17, 1945, both in ASW 291.2, NARG 335.

nation's manpower. This group, known as the Gillem Board after its chairman, General Alvan C. Gillem, Jr., held its first meeting on October 1, 1945. For four months the board heard the testimony of sixty-nine military and civilian witnesses and examined the various studies of Negro manpower made between the two world wars. The Gillem Board report was the most extensive inquiry ever made by the Army into its Negro policy. The report and recommendations were issued in April, 1946, as the Army's "Utilization of Negro Manpower in the Postwar Army Policy," superseding the policy announced in October, 1940.[6]

The Gillem Board recognized the right and obligation of Negroes as citizens to participate in the armed forces and assumed that the Army must make the most effective use of its manpower. The board candidly admitted that the Army had failed to utilize efficiently this potential 10 per cent of its manpower during World War II. Negroes were not used adequately in combat units; often units without any definite mission were formed just to absorb Negro troops. Hitting at the many criticisms of Negro units, the Gillem Board stated that "official reports on Negro units do not reflect many factors which may have been contributing causes of the substandard performance in combat." The board recognized the rapidly increasing educational achievements of American Negroes and concluded that wider opportunities within the Army were in order. The goal of the Army's future policy should be to "eliminate, at the earliest practicable moment, any special consideration based on race."

The Gillem Board also recommended the steps it felt were necessary to improve the Army's utilization of black manpower. Among the most important were: Negroes should be integrated in duty assignments in special and overhead units (post housekeeping and administrative jobs); Negroes should form 10 per cent of the Army; a special staff group should be formed within the War Department to see that Negro policy was implemented;

---

[6] This was published as War Department Circular No. 124, April 27, 1946. All reference to the Gillem Report in the following paragraphs, unless otherwise noted, is from this document.

Negro officers should be accorded equal opportunities for advancement and assignment; groupings should be made of smaller Negro units with larger white units in "composite organizations"; War Department policy that the use of the post recreational facilities must be without regard to race should continue; and commanders of Negro troops should be fully cognizant of the Army's Negro policy.

The Gillem Board did not question the traditional premise of the Army's Negro policy — segregation. True, it did recommend that Negroes be integrated into overhead units, but this was for duty hours only, with off-duty housing remaining segregated. The report appeared to leave integration for some far-off time — at some "unknown date" and against "an undetermined aggressor," manpower was to be used "without regard to antecedents of race." This failure to spell out clearly the policy toward integration resulted in confusion. In 1946 Secretary of War Patterson told the Negro press that the new policy meant that segregation was no longer required. Patterson's successor Kenneth Royall said, in 1948, that the policy meant "equality of opportunity on the basis of segregation."[7] The Personnel and Administration Division of the War Department (G-1), which was given the responsibility of seeing that the new policy was implemented, had another idea of the policy's ultimate goal. G-1 officials believed that integrating small Negro units into larger white units was the goal envisioned by the Gillem Board.[8]

The lack of a clear statement about segregation in the Gillem report was not the only cause for confusion. The report called for maximum utilization of Negro manpower and at the same time imposed a quota of 10 per cent Negro strength. This was contradictory. Maximum utilization was also contradicted by continuing segregation. Negroes failed to see anything strikingly new in the Army's policy. "This new Army directive indi-

[7] Baltimore *Afro-American*, March 9, 1946; Margaret L. Geis, *Negro Personnel in the European Command: 1 January 1946 to 30 June 1950* (Historical Division, European Command, 1952), 3.

[8] Memorandum, G-1 to the Secretary of War, December 24, 1946, OSW 291.2, NARG 335.

cates that the Army command has undergone no real change of heart . . . ," the Pittsburgh *Courier* exclaimed.[9] The Norfolk *Journal and Guide* felt that it was a step in the right direction, but reserved its judgment until it saw how the policy was implemented.[10] Roy Wilkins of the NAACP and Lester Granger of the National Urban League both condemned the policy as "inadequate" because it did not end segregation.[11]

The test of any policy is how it is put into practice, and the Army's new Negro policy suffered from lack of implementation from the beginning. The Gillem Board's recommendation that a special staff group be appointed to be a watchdog over the new policy was refused by the War Department. Instead, this function was given to the Welfare Branch of G-1, a relatively insignificant office. The War Department, in a letter sent to the major commands calling their attention to the new policy, stated that "it is desired that it be initiated without delay."[12]

There were immediate indications, however, that the policy was not being followed. Three months after the announcement of the new policy, a group of Negro newspaper publishers toured Europe at the invitation of the Secretary of War. This body reported that they saw neither composite mixed units nor Negro combat units; except for two generals they found no officers with official knowledge of the Army's new policy.[13] Marcus H. Ray, Truman Gibson's successor as Civilian Aide to the Secretary of War, toured European Theater Army installations six months after the new policy became official. Ray found no Negroes being integrated in overhead duty assignments; the only nonservice Negro units were four bands. Furthermore, no black units had been assigned to police duty in the European Theater because of the racial ideologies of the

---

[9] Pittsburgh *Courier*, May 11, 1946.

[10] Norfolk *Journal and Guide*, March 9, 1946.

[11] *The New York Times*, March 5, 1946.

[12] The Adjutant General to Army Ground Forces, Army Air Forces, and Army Service Forces, May 6, 1946, WDAG 291.2, NARG 319.

[13] "Report of the Negro Newspaper Publishers' Association to the Honorable Secretary of War . . . on Troops and Conditions in Europe," July 18, 1946, WDGPA 291.2, NARG 319.

Germans. "To accept the racial prejudices of the German people," Ray wrote, "as a reason for non-utilization of the American soldier who happens to be non-white is to negate the very ideals we have made part of our re-education program in Germany."[14]

The Personnel and Administration Division (G-1) of the Army General Staff, whose job it was to monitor the implementation of the new program, was called upon by the Secretary of War to explain Ray's findings. G-1 officials replied that they had not asked the overseas theaters to implement the new policy because of other problems they faced. Furthermore, the officials had decided that the Gillem report's ultimate objectives "should be set far in the future, and that very little could be accomplished toward these objectives . . . unless and until the Army rids itself of many thousands of substandard Negroes . . . and raises the general intellectual level of the Army Negro population." Prejudice "held by some Army personnel of all grades" had also proved to be a factor in not implementing the policy. The War Department should make further efforts to obtain "intelligent and willing cooperation" on this matter, because "attempts to force compliance by specific and detailed directives could well lead to misunderstanding, resentment and obstructionist tactics."[15]

The fact is that, from April, 1946, to 1948, little progress was made in implementing the Army's new Negro policy. This failure was particularly true of the two most important points: assignment of Negroes to overhead units and assignment of small Negro units to larger white units. Both of these objectives were designed to secure broader job opportunities for black soldiers, so that the range of opportunity would approach that for white soldiers. One comprehensive study of the implementation of the Gillem Board policy, based on the official records, found that there existed within the Army "no consistent

---

[14] "Report of Tour of European Installations," November 16 to December 17, 1946, by Marcus H. Ray, WDGPA 291.2, NARG 319.

[15] Memorandum, G-1 to the Chiefs of Staff, January 21, 1947, WDGPA 291.2, NARG 319.

enthusiasm for, and very often active opposition to, any positive measures for implementing the policies of the Gillem Board."[16]

The unwillingness of the Army to implement the Gillem policy, however, was not the only reason for its failure. There was a basic contradiction between the goal, full utilization of Negro manpower, and the policy of segregation. The Gillem Board had failed to face this fact, and the Army was continuing to dodge it. The limited number and type of segregated black units could not begin to provide the range of jobs offered to white soldiers. If there were no Negro units calling for certain specialties, Negro soldiers could not be sent to schools for training in these jobs. As a result, over half of all courses in Army schools had no quotas for Negro soldiers, regardless of their qualifications and training. If Negro soldiers possessing the necessary skills were not available, it could be argued that there was no use opening these jobs to Negro soldiers. The plight of black soldiers was similar to that of the vicious circle encountered by an inexperienced man seeking employment when every employer wants only workers with experience.[17]

When politics was added to the other forces favoring a change in the racial *status quo*, the armed forces policy of continued segregation appeared more and more to be an anachronism. It was in the fluid political situation of a presidential election that segregation in the armed forces again became an important political issue. This issue was emphasized for Negroes because of the consideration of a Universal Military Training bill by Congress in 1947–1948. In June, 1947, the President's Advisory Commission on Military Training reported that segregation should have no place in any program enacted by Congress:

[16] "Report on Gillem Board Policy and Implementation," n.d. [1949], 112, typewritten manuscript prepared by and in the files of the President's Committee on Equality of Treatment and Opportunity in the Armed Services, HSTL. This committee is hereafter referred to by its popular title, the Fahy Committee. This conclusion is exhaustively documented in 70–122. The failure of the Army to implement the Gillem policy is detailed in memorandum, G-1 to the Deputy Chief of Staff, December 16, 1947, CSGPA 291.2, NARG 319, and Geis, *Negro Personnel in the European Command*, 20–60.

[17] "Report on Gillem Board Policy and Implementation," 91–94.

Nothing could be more tragic for the future attitude of our people, and for the unity of our Nation, than a program in which our Federal Government forced our young manhood to live for a period of time in an atmosphere which emphasized or bred class or racial difference.[18]

When the legislation to institute Universal Military Training was introduced in Congress, however, there was no provision in it to bar segregation. As originally written, the bill had contained a nonsegregation clause, but this had been deleted before it was introduced in Congress.[19] The reason for the deletion was opposition from the Army. It felt that "progressive experimentation" according to the Gillem Board policy "will in time accomplish the purpose of the proposed legislation."[20] *The Crisis* summarized the feeling of the majority of Negroes about a draft law that allowed segregation:

. . . the vast body of Negro Americans is opposed to this training as long as it is to be on a segregated basis. They had enough of segregation in World War II. The scars of Jim Crow service are still fresh upon their young men and families.[21]

Negro opinion was ripe for some action on this point, and Congress was due to hold hearings on Universal Military Training in 1948. Sensing that the time was right, A. Philip Randolph and Grant Reynolds, a state official of New York, organized the Committee Against Jim Crow in Military Service and Training in November, 1947. Their purpose was to form a pressure group to ensure that segregation would not be a part of any new draft law.[22]

On October 29, 1947, the President's Committee on Civil Rights issued its report. In addition to condemning segregation

---

[18] Quoted in Pittsburgh *Courier*, June 7, 1947.

[19] Pittsburgh *Courier*, July 26, 1947.

[20] Secretary Patterson to Walter G. Andrews, Chairman of the House Committee on Armed Services, April 3, 1947, CS 291.2, NARG 319.

[21] *The Crisis*, 55 (February, 1948), 41. See editorials opposing any segregated draft law in Pittsburgh *Courier*, February 15, April 12, 1947, January 3, 10, 1948.

[22] L. D. Reddick, "The Negro Policy of the American Army Since World War II," *Journal of Negro History*, 38 (April, 1953), 199.

wherever it existed and labeling "separate but equal" a myth, the committee spoke out strongly against segregation in the armed forces. "Prejudice in any area is an ugly, undemocratic phenomenon," the committee said, but "in the armed services where all men run the risk of death, it is particularly repugnant."[23] The report recognized that all of the services had recently adopted policies with objectives of equality of opportunity, but much discrimination still remained. Segregation had no place in the military forces. The committee made a point of contradicting an old armed forces' defense of segregation — that the services were not social laboratories:

During the last war we . . . found that the military services can be used to educate citizens on a broad range of social and political problems. The war experience brought to our attention a laboratory in which we may prove that the majority and minorities of our population can train and work and fight side by side in cooperation and harmony.[24]

Finally, the committee recommended legislation and administrative action "to end immediately all discrimination and segregation based on race, color, creed or national origin, in . . . all branches of the Armed Services."[25]

The political strategy of the Administration called for using the committee's report for a special message on civil rights to Congress. The President could thereby seize the initiative in the 1948 campaign.[26] Work began almost immediately to boil the Civil Rights Committee's recommendations down into those requiring legislative action and those requiring administrative action. The Administration began writing an "omnibus" civil rights bill that would include all of the committee's suggestions for legislation. Ending segregation in the armed forces was mentioned in all of these proposals, but there was indecision over

[23] President's Committee on Civil Rights, *To Secure These Rights*, 41.
[24] *To Secure These Rights*, 47.
[25] *To Secure These Rights*, 162.
[26] William Carl Berman, "The Politics of Civil Rights in the Truman Administration," 71.

whether it should be done by administrative action or by legislation.[27]

Before the President's special message to Congress on civil rights, it was decided that discrimination and segregation in the armed forces would be dealt with by administrative action. The situation was complicated further by an agreement that action by the President must apply to the government's civil employees as well as to the military. Should the President issue one executive order covering both, or should he issue two separate orders? The decision was not made before delivery of the President's civil rights message, but the important point is that the Administration had decided to move against segregation in the armed forces, although the method and the timing to be used had not been decided.[28]

In his historic special civil rights message on February 2, 1948, President Truman announced that he would soon issue an executive order banning discrimination in federal employment and federal services and facilities. Truman also stated that he had

instructed the Secretary of Defense to take steps to have the remaining instances of discrimination in the armed services eliminated as rapidly as possible. The personnel policies and practices of all the Services in this regard will be made consistent.[29]

Secretary of Defense Forrestal was thinking about the President's instructions and wanted "to see if we can't apply the same

---

[27] Memorandum, G. Girard Davidson, Assistant Secretary of the Interior, to Senator J. Howard McGrath, December 6, 1947, Democratic National Chairman folder, McGrath Papers, HSTL, recommended ending segregation in the armed forces by executive order. Stephen J. Spingarn, "Suggested Outline of Omnibus Civil Rights Bill of 1948," January 22, 1948, Stephen J. Spingarn Papers, HSTL, had originally included ending military segregation by legislative action; a penciled note says that, as of January 25, 1948, this part was taken out of bill and would be considered for executive action.

[28] Oscar R. Ewing to the author, July 22, 1964. Confirming Mr. Ewing's recollection that the decision had been made to act against segregation in the armed forces at this early date, is Ewing to Charles R. Murphy, January 2, 1948, Charles R. Murphy Papers, HSTL.

[29] *Public Papers, 1948,* 125–26.

method in the larger area of the three Services as we did in the Navy — in other words, get the results and talk about them afterward." [30] To aid in accomplishing this change, Forrestal planned to call a meeting of Negro leaders to talk about integration.[31]

The impact of the President's message was described in glowing terms by David K. Niles, adviser on minority matters:

Strong favorable language was the rule in the editorials. The President was described as the new champion of human freedom. The program as a whole was hailed as the strongest civil rights program ever put forth by any President. The message was referred to as the greatest freedom document since the Emancipation Proclamation. The language of the message was described as Lincolnesque.[32]

This enthusiasm was only part of the story, however, because incensed Southerners immediately began to talk of revolt.

The Army appeared to recognize that change was in the air, but it gave no indication of accepting it willingly. When Secretary of the Army Kenneth C. Royall was asked to comment on the Committee on Civil Rights' report, he would say only that the Gillem policy was the one the Army followed, and it would be continued.[33] In late 1947 the Army stirred itself to action in an effort to implement the Gillem policy. Increased quotas for Negroes in Army schools were ordered. In November, 1947, the first major attempt to form composite units of whites and Negroes was made public when it was announced that some black units would be included in the Eighty-second Airborne Division.[34] Inquiries to the Army about how the Committee on Civil Rights' report affected Army policy prompted a message to be sent to all Continental army commanders: "Recent newspaper

---

[30] Forrestal to Lloyd K. Garrison, February 16, 1948, Correspondence, Box 79, James V. Forrestal Papers, Princeton University Library.

[31] Walter White to Forrestal, February 17, 1948; memorandum, Marx Leva to Forrestal, February 24, 1948, both in D54-1-3, NARG 330.

[32] Memorandum, Niles to the President, February 16, 1948, Philleo Nash Papers, HSTL.

[33] Pittsburgh *Courier*, November 8, 1947.

[34] Memorandum, G-1 to The Adjutant General, December 8, 1947, G-1 291.2, NARG 319; Pittsburgh *Courier*, November 29, 1947.

and magazine accounts have highlighted portions of the Report of the President's Committee on Civil Rights. . . . Such accounts taken out of context might be misunderstood."[35]

The Army's recalcitrance served to embarrass the Administration a few days after the President's civil rights message to Congress. Governor Alfred E. Driscoll of New Jersey announced on February 4, 1948, that the Department of the Army had forbidden his state to integrate its National Guard, despite a clause in the state's new constitution forbidding segregation in the militia.[36] The reaction from Negroes was immediate. Walter White sent a telegram to the Secretary of Defense, quoting that portion of the President's civil rights message about instructions to the Secretary to end remaining discrimination in the military. How could the Army's action be consistent with this? "We urge conformance to President's instruction," White concluded.[37]

The problem related to the National Guard actually had its beginning in 1947. Negroes, congressmen from Northern states, and Civilian Aide Marcus Ray suggested that integration of National Guard units be allowed if the individual states so desired. The answer was always that the National Guard, as a reserve component of the Army, had to follow the Gillem policy, which did not allow integration. The Army General Staff, including Chief of Staff General Dwight Eisenhower, agreed that federal recognition should be withdrawn from those National Guard units which integrated Negroes into white units.[38] Eisenhower decided, however, that Negro companies could be included in white battalions. The Army's Operation and Training Division (G-3) and the Air Force opposed even this concession. If Negroes gained an opening in the National Guard, "the next step by Negro leaders conceivably will be to

[35] Attachment to memorandum, G-1 to Under Secretary of the Army, April 29, 1948, G-1 291.2, NARG 319.

[36] *The New York Times*, February 5, 1948.

[37] Telegram to Forrestal from White, February 5, 1948, OSA 291.2, NARG 335.

[38] Secretary of War Patterson to Walter White, February 14, 1947; Patterson to Senator Brien McMahon of Connecticut, March 7, 1947; memorandum, Assistant Deputy Chief of Staff to G-3, May 17, 1947, all in WDSCA 291.2, NARG 319.

demand the integration of Negroes into Regular Army units as individuals."[39]

The political implications of the Army's action in the New Jersey case were recognized immediately by the Administration. Secretary of Defense Forrestal's assistant, Marx Leva, advised his chief that he should have a talk with Secretary Royall: "This is a serious matter both from the standpoint of practical considerations and the standpoint of the political implications."[40] After his talk with Forrestal, Royall wrote Governor Driscoll that "for the present" the Army would continue to recognize the New Jersey National Guard. It must be clear, however, that this recognition of integration in the New Jersey militia did not change the segregation policy of the Regular Army, because segregation "was considered to be in the interest of national defense, and both the staff and I feel that this is still the case," Royall concluded.[41]

The storm continued. Walter White wrote Secretary Forrestal to express his disappointment that the Army believed only segregated units were in the national interest. In the past the Army had stated that its policy was to conform to local laws and customs when refusing to violate the Southern etiquette of segregation. "How, then," White said, "can the imposition of segregation upon northern states having clear-cut laws and policies in opposition to such practices be justified by the Army?"[42] Henry A. Wallace, campaigning hard for the Negro vote in Harlem, charged that the President was insincere on the question of civil rights; if he really wanted to end segregation in the armed forces he would ask Secretary of the Army Royall to resign.[43]

The New Jersey incident set off a chain reaction in other northern states. The Governor of Connecticut wrote President

[39] Memorandum, Assistant Secretary of War to Secretary of War, May 24, 1947, ASW 291.2, NARG 335; memorandum, G-3 to Deputy Chief of Staff, May 28, 1947, WDGOT 325, NARG 319.

[40] Memorandum, Leva to Forrestal, February 5, 1948, D54-1-2, NARG 330.

[41] *The New York Times*, February 9, 1948; memorandum, Forrestal to Royall, February 5, 1948, OSA 291.2, NARG 335.

[42] White to Forrestal, February 17, 1948, D54-1-1, NARG 330.

[43] *The New York Times*, February 16, 1948.

Truman that for over a year he had tried to integrate his state's National Guard, only to be told that, if he did so, such action would jeopardize federal recognition and support. The Governor requested that the President direct the Army to change its policy to conform with the report of the Committee on Civil Rights.[44] In New York a special legislative committee began investigating how segregation could be ended in that state's National Guard, and another political opponent of Truman's, Governor Thomas E. Dewey, supported this action.[45] The Governor of Minnesota soon wrote that he wanted to integrate the National Guard units of his state by executive order.[46]

The National Guard issue caused enough concern at the White House that Secretary Royall was told not to answer any of these inquiries until his replies were approved by Clark Clifford.[47] Under pressure from the White House and against the wishes of the Army General Staff and the National Guard Bureau, Royall agreed to adopt a position that any state forbidding segregation in the militia by constitutional amendment or legislative act would continue to receive Army recognition and support, but to end segregation by a governor's executive order would not be accepted.[48] Royall insisted, against the arguments of Forrestal and Clifford, on including a defense of segregation in his letters to the governors of Minnesota and Connecticut: "It is the opinion of the Staff — with which I concur — that in the interest of national defense the policy of April 27, 1946 [segregation],

[44] Telegram, Governor James L. McConaughy to the President, February 9, 1948, OF 155, HSTL.

[45] *The New York Times*, February 10, 11, March 14, 1948.

[46] Governor Luther W. Youngdahl to Forrestal, March 6, 1948, OSA 291.2, NARG 335.

[47] Memorandum, Royall to Forrestal, February 23, 1948; memorandum, Marx Leva to Royall, March 19, 1948, both in OSA 291.2, NARG 335; memorandum, Philleo Nash to Clark Clifford, April 9, 1948, Nash Papers, HSTL.

[48] Memorandum, Marx Leva to Forrestal, March 8, 1948, OSA 291.2; memorandum, G-3 to Deputy Chief of Staff, April 8, 1948, WDSCA 291.2, NARG 319; memorandum, Royall to Forrestal, May 6, 1948, and memorandum, Leva to Forrestal, May 7, 1948, both in OSA 291.2, NARG 335.

should be uniformly applied throughout the Federal forces of the Army."[49]

Agitation for action to permit integration of the National Guard by a governor's executive order continued.[50] Secretary Royall wanted to answer these letters with a firm reaffirmation of the Army Staff's opposition to any deviation from the policy of segregation, but including a statement that constitutional or legislative action would be reluctantly accepted.[51] Chief of Staff Omar Bradley felt that "from the military point of view, I still think that any integration of Negroes . . . in the National Guard will create problems which may have serious consequences in case of national mobilization of those units."[52]

The issue was hot politically, however, and the White House refused to let Royall mail his letters.[53] Clark Clifford informed Royall that "the President has suggested that this entire matter be studied carefully in the light of recent happenings"; and he wanted to "discuss the subject thoroughly."[54] Secretary Royall knew of nothing in recent events that would change the policy he had announced earlier. "The staff and myself strongly feel that this policy cannot be changed without adversely affecting national defense . . . ," Royall answered.[55] The "recent happenings" referred to by the President and Clifford was the

---

[49] Memoranda, Leva to Forrestal, May 5, 20, 1948, both in D54-1-1, NARG 330; Royall to Governors of Connecticut and Minnesota, May 20, 1948, OSA 291.2, NARG 335.

[50] Representative John A. Blatnik to Secretary Royall, May 29, 1948, Representative Harold C. Hagen to Royall, May 28, 1948, both in OSA 291.2, NARG 335; Governor of Connecticut to Royall, June 29, 1948; telegram, Governor of Minnesota to the President, both in OSA 291.2, NARG 335.

[51] Draft of proposed letter to Governor of Connecticut from Secretary of the Army, n.d., OSA 291.2, NARG 335.

[52] Memorandum, Bradley to Royall, July 7, 1948, OSA 291.2, NARG 335.

[53] Memoranda, Royall to Clark Clifford, July 8, 19, 1948, OSA 291.2, NARG 335.

[54] Memorandum, Clifford to Royall, July 8, 1948, OSA 291.2, NARG 335.

[55] Memorandum, Royall to Clifford, July 20, 1948, OSA 291.2, NARG 335.

Democratic convention. A liberal plank against segregation in the armed forces had been adopted and the Administration was required to act.

About the time that the National Guard issue was developing, A. Philip Randolph and his Committee Against Jim Crow in Military Service and Training were proceeding with their campaign against provision for segregation in any new draft law. The Democratic National Committee had promised this group in December, 1947, that it would issue a statement against segregation in the draft.[56] This had not been done to Randolph's satisfaction, and he met again with Democratic party officials on February 5, 1948. Randolph and his committee wanted a strong statement against segregation in the Universal Military Training act under consideration by Congress; amendments barring segregation in the draft and in interstate travel by draftees; amendments making attacks against a soldier in uniform a federal offense; and a ban of the poll tax for draftees in federal elections. The Democratic party official who met with Randolph and his group was noncommittal; he quoted the pertinent portion of the President's civil rights message and assured them that "careful consideration" would be given to the proposed amendments.[57]

On March 22 a group of Negro leaders called at the White House and urged Truman to insist on antisegregation amendments in the draft law. Randolph was among those present. "In my recent travels around the country," Randolph told the President, "I found Negroes not wanting to shoulder a gun to fight for democracy abroad unless they get democracy at home."[58] Truman was disturbed but told Randolph and the others that he was doing the best that he could. On March 27 twenty Negro organizations met in New York at the invitation of the NAACP

---

[56] Randolph to Senator J. Howard McGrath, Chairman of the Democratic National Committee, February 2, 1948, McGrath Papers, HSTL.

[57] Committee Against Jim Crow in Military Service and Training List of Ideas They Would Like Incorporated in H. R. 4278, n.d., and memorandum, R. M. Moore to Senator McGrath, February 5, 1948, both in McGrath Papers, HSTL.

[58] *The New York Times*, March 23, 1948.

and issued the "Declaration of Negro Voters." Their statement endorsed Truman's civil rights program. As a first step to get Negro voter support, they demanded "that every vestige of segregation and discrimination in the armed forces be forthwith abolished." In a statement obviously aimed at Secretary Royall, this group insisted that "any public official . . . who fails to act against these evils be removed from office."[59]

The Committee Against Jim Crow in Military Service and Training decided to take some action of its own after failing to obtain any important concessions. On March 30 the committee's national chairman, Grant Reynolds, told the Senate Armed Services Committee: "Our grievances are being tossed around Washington . . . , and we have no alternative but to fight with the . . . weapons of truth and non-cooperation against any form or variety of compulsory Jim Crow."[60] A. Philip Randolph was explicit about what this meant: Negroes would refuse to serve if the new draft law did not forbid segregation. "I personally pledge myself," Randolph vowed, "to openly counsel, aid, and abet youth, both white and Negro, to quarantine any Jim Crow conscription system."[61] Senator Wayne Morse, Republican of Oregon, was upset over Randolph's threat. Would the Negro leader counsel disobedience to the draft if the United States was at war? Randolph's answer was "Yes." Senator Morse pointed out that this would be treason, to which Randolph answered, "I would be willing to face that . . . on the theory . . . that we are serving a higher law than the law which applies to the act of treason."[62]

The reaction of the Negro community to Randolph's threat of civil disobedience was mixed. Negro editors generally opposed it, while admitting that Randolph and Reynolds did not exaggerate the bitterness of Negroes toward military segregation.[63]

[59] Norfolk *Journal and Guide*, April 3, 1948.
[60] U.S. Senate, Committee on Armed Services, *Hearings . . . on Universal Military Training*, 678.
[61] *Hearings . . . on Universal Military Training*, 688.
[62] *Hearings . . . on Universal Military Training*, 689.
[63] See Pittsburgh *Courier*, April 10, 1948; Norfolk *Journal and Guide*, April 10, 17, 1948.

Earl Brown, a columnist for the New York *Amsterdam News*, stated that many Negroes "feel even more bitter about the raw undemocratic deal they got and are still getting in the armed services than Reynolds and Randolph."[64] A poll among Negroes in New York City indicated that a majority felt Randolph was right in urging civil disobedience as long as the country was not at war.[65] Walter White and the NAACP did not disavow Randolph's proposal completely; the NAACP would not advise youth to boycott the draft, "but those who expected them to be enthusiastic soldiers should remember that their memories of mistreatment in the last war are bitter green."[66] Representative Adam Clayton Powell, Jr., Democrat of New York, announced that he would support the civil disobedience movement if the draft law did not abolish segregation.[67]

For several weeks prior to Randolph's threat, Secretary Forrestal and Lester Granger had been planning a "National Defense Conference on Negro Affairs." The purpose was to bring together a group of Negro leaders who would advise the armed services how to overcome their race problem.[68] Sixteen Negro leaders met Forrestal and representatives of the three services on April 26. Lester Granger, acting as chairman for the Negroes, summarized their feelings. Unless the armed forces ended segregation soon, "there will be a reaction among our Negro public resulting in irreparable damage to the national welfare."[69]

The Negro conferees were pleased to hear from the Secretaries of the Air Force and Navy that their services were working on plans to eliminate all segregation and discrimination. But Secretary of the Army Royall pointedly told the Negro delegation that the Army was of the opinion that segregation could exist without

---

[64] This and other Negro reactions are printed in *Congressional Record*, 80th Cong., 2d Sess. (1948), 4314–18.

[65] *Congressional Record*, 80th Cong., 2d Sess. (1948), 4314–18.

[66] *Congressional Record*, 80th Cong., 2d Sess. (1948), 4314–18; and "Fighting the Jim Crow Army," *The Crisis*, 55 (May, 1948), 136.

[67] Pittsburgh *Courier*, April 10, 1948.

[68] Granger to Forrestal, March 2, 1948, D54-1-4, NARG 330; Pittsburgh *Courier*, April 10, 1948.

[69] "Transcript of National Defense Conference on Negro Affairs," April 26, 1948, copy in Fahy Committee Papers, HSTL.

discrimination. Furthermore, the General Staff, under the leadership of Chief of Staff Omar Bradley, had recommended the maintenance of segregation. "But," Royall told the group, "even if my general staff had not recommended segregation, I would have continued it as a policy." [70] The attitude of the Army and of Royall so infuriated the Negro conferees that they refused to serve as advisers to the Defense Department. "Our group is concerned with elimination of segregation, not its perpetuation," Negroes told the press. Although not condoning the extreme action recommended by A. Philip Randolph, most of these black leaders expressed sympathy with the motivation behind his proposal.[71]

Congress provided the next forum for the issue of segregation in the armed forces. Southern congressmen were apparently ready to threaten the passage of the Administration-backed draft bill in order to force the President to back down on a part of his civil rights message. They also wanted to counteract Randolph's threat of civil disobedience. Senator Richard B. Russell of Georgia attempted to attach an amendment in committee that would have made it mandatory for the armed forces to permit the transfer of all men who requested assignment to military units composed of members of their own race. After the Republican-controlled Senate Committee on Armed Services defeated this amendment, Southerners threatened to filibuster when the draft law reached the floor of Congress.[72] Truman refused to back down, saying that his instructions to the Secretary of Defense to end military discrimination still stood. Furthermore, Truman told a press conference, he made no distinction between "discrimination" and "segregation." [73]

The threat raised by the Southerners provided a good opportunity for those who were opposed to any kind of draft law. Among these were Senator William Langer, Republican of

---

[70] "Transcript . . . on Negro Affairs," April 26, 1948.

[71] "Transcript . . . on Negro Affairs," April 26, 1948; *The New York Times*, April 27, 1948; Norfolk *Journal and Guide*, May 1, 1948; "Stonewall Against America," *The Crisis*, 55 (May, 1948), 136.

[72] *The New York Times*, May 12, 13, 24, 1948.

[73] *The New York Times*, May 28, 1948.

North Dakota, who announced on May 26 that he was going to offer amendments to the draft bill that would incorporate the complete civil rights program of the President. One of these amendments proposed to eliminate all racial segregation in the drafting and assignment of men in the military.[74] Senator Glen H. Taylor of Idaho, the vice-presidential running mate of Henry Wallace, joined Langer in conducting a short filibuster for civil rights amendments to the draft bill.[75]

The Langer amendments were defeated easily, but the Southern congressmen took the opportunity to point out what they saw as the failure of the Negro soldier. Senator Burnet R. Maybank of South Carolina claimed that "the wars of this country have been won by white soldiers and I defy any member . . . to challenge this statement."[76] Senator Allen Ellender of Louisiana proclaimed that the Negro was inherently inferior, and this was the reason he had proven to be a poor soldier in combat.[77] Senator Russell of Georgia repeated these ideas, and said there was no doubt in his mind that the President was determined to end segregation in the armed forces.[78] Most of the Southerners quoted the former Army Chief of Staff, General Eisenhower, against military integration. He had once told the Senate Committee on the Armed Services: "I do believe that if we attempt merely by passing a lot of laws to force someone to like someone else, we are just going to get into trouble."[79]

The Southerners' filibuster failed to materialize, but the new Selective Service law did not ban segregation. Secretary Royall and Army Chief of Staff Bradley made it clear that the controversy over the new draft law had not changed their minds. Segregation would continue to be Army policy.[80]

Segregation in the military was still an important political issue. The Republicans thought so too, and they adopted a plat-

---

[74] *The New York Times*, May 27, 1948.

[75] *The New York Times*, June 18, 19, 1948.

[76] *Congressional Record*, 80th Cong., 2d Sess. (1948), 7366.

[77] *Congressional Record*, 80th Cong., 2d Sess. (1948), 7489–93.

[78] *Congressional Record*, 80th Cong., 2d Sess. (1948), 7355–57.

[79] *Hearings . . . on Universal Military Training*, 996. This statement would plague Eisenhower in 1952 and 1956.

[80] *The New York Times*, June 22, 29, 1948.

form plank stating, "We are opposed to the idea of racial segregation in the armed services of the United States."[81] The annual meeting of NAACP was riddled with dissension between the supporters of Wallace and the supporters of Truman. There was no dissension, however, over resolutions calling for the resignation of the Secretary of the Army and a national meeting of Negroes to formulate plans for fighting segregation in the military.[82] Lester Granger told the Secretary of Defense that military segregation was a definite political issue and that it was "impossible for any group of Negroes mindful of their public standing to relax in the slightest from a position of unfaltering opposition to the principle of enforced segregation in the armed services."[83]

By May the Administration was contemplating further steps it could take on this issue. On May 12 Clark Clifford proposed to Forrestal that a committee be created to put into effect the President's aim as announced in his civil rights message. Forrestal was evidently concerned about moving too rapidly on this matter. "I think we are all fully aware of the difficulties and the fact that the world is not going to be changed overnight," Clifford assured Forrestal, "but I also think the time has come when we must make a start and that the movement must be in the direction laid down in the President's message." Specifically, Clifford proposed a board composed of both service and civilian personnel, including Negroes. This board should be concerned with implementation as well as policy, and "it should be more than advisory . . . ," Clifford believed.[84]

Meanwhile, after receiving no satisfaction from the White

---

[81] *The New York Times*, June 23, 1948.

[82] *The New York Times*, June 27, 1948; "Annual Conference," *The Crisis*, 55 (August, 1948), 246–47. See *The New York Times*, March 20, 1948, for the division within NAACP chapters between Wallace and Truman supporters.

[83] Granger to Marx Leva, May 14, 1948, D54-1-4, NARG 330.

[84] Memorandum, David K. Niles to Clark Clifford, May 12, 1948, Nash Papers, HSTL. This is a draft memorandum from Clifford to Forrestal elaborating on a meeting just held between the two. There is no evidence that it was sent to Forrestal, but it does represent Clifford's thinking at the time.

House or Congress, A. Philip Randolph decided to take some action. On June 26 he announced a new organization, the League for Non-violent Civil Disobedience Against Military Segregation. The immediate purpose of this new group was to get the President to issue an executive order ending segregation in the armed forces. If this was not done before August 16, the date the new draft law went into effect, the league would call upon whites and Negroes to refuse to register. Randolph wrote the President informing him of the group's intentions. Unless the executive order was issued immediately, he warned the President, "Negro youth will have no alternative but to resist a law, the inevitable consequences of which would be to expose them to un-American brutality so familiar during the last war." [85]

Support for Randolph's proposal appeared to be growing among young Negroes. The NAACP conducted a poll among male Negro college students and found 71 per cent were sympathetic to civil disobedience against the draft. *Newsweek* magazine made a survey and reported that among Negro college youth "there were indications of strong sympathy and support for Randolph." [86] The arrest, three months before the election, of young Negroes who refused to register for segregated military duty would have been a political calamity. Long before Randolph's threat, however, the Administration had decided to take action to end military segregation. Soon after the report of the President's Committee on Civil Rights, as we have seen, plans were under way to issue an executive order. Then, in May, 1948, there was discussion of creating a committee to see that a program of military integration was implemented. The urge to act was present and only waiting for an opportune time.

The course of the civil rights plank at the Democratic convention called for a reassessment of the Administration's political strategy on this issue. Still following the campaign strategy of holding the South, as formulated by the liberal White House junta, the President wanted a general civil rights plank to be

[85] Pittsburgh *Courier*, July 3, 1948; Grant Reynolds and A. Philip Randolph to the President, June 29, 1948, D54-1-14, NARG 330.

[86] *The New York Times*, June 5, 1948; "Crisis in the Making," *Newsweek*, 31 (June 7, 1948), 28–29.

adopted by the convention. One similar to the 1944 plank, it was felt, would not unduly antagonize the South. But the Democratic liberals, whose spokesman on the platform committee was Mayor Hubert H. Humphrey of Minneapolis, were determined that the civil rights plank would be a strong one containing the actual recommendations of the President's Committee on Civil Rights. Specifically, the liberals wanted the plank to call for federal legislation to provide for an antilynching law, equal opportunity for employment, the right to vote, and equal treatment in the armed forces.[87]

President Truman's wishes prevailed over those of the liberals, and the four specific recommendations were voted down by the platform committee by a substantial voice vote. Mayor Humphrey tried immediately to save the one calling for abolition of segregation in the armed forces, but it was voted down, 28 to 36.[88] The liberals did not accept defeat, however, and they carried the fight to the convention floor. In a most unusual action, the convention voted 651½ to 582½ to overrule the platform committee and the Administration in favor of the liberal civil rights plank.[89] Several Southern delegations walked out of the convention immediately as a result of this liberal victory.

Oscar Ewing now advised the President to do everything within his power immediately to carry out the liberal civil rights plank of the platform or he would lose the Negro vote. Other liberals were writing the President, urging the same course upon him. President Truman decided to issue the two executive orders that had long been planned, one banning discrimination in federal employment and one ending military segregation. Although these ideas had been around the White House for several months, the Democratic convention made it necessary to take quick action. Philleo Nash, Clark Clifford, and Oscar Ewing set

---

[87] *The New York Times*, July 11, 12, 13, 1948; Clifton Brock, *Americans for Democratic Action: Its Role in National Politics*, 91, 97. Oscar R. Ewing to the author, July 22, 1964, states that the mild civil rights plank supported by the Administration was designed to prevent a Southern bolt.

[88] *The New York Times*, July 14, 1948.

[89] *The New York Times*, July 15, 1948.

to work drafting the orders. While this was being done, it was decided that a presidential committee to implement the order on desegregating the armed forces should be included. This was also an idea that had been floating around the White House for several months and that was now acted upon.[90]

On July 26, 1948, the eve of the special session of the Republican Eightieth Congress called by the President, Truman issued his executive order. Executive Order 9981 stated in part:

1. It is hereby declared to be the policy of the President that there shall be equality of treatment and opportunity for all persons in the armed services without regard to race, color, religion, or national origin. This policy shall be put into effect as rapidly as possible, having due regard to the time required to effectuate any necessary changes without impairing efficiency or morale.

2. There shall be created in the National Military Establishment an advisory committee to be known as the President's Committee on Equality of Treatment and Opportunity in the Armed Services, which shall be composed of seven members to be designated by the President.[91]

The order also authorized the committee to confer with and advise the Secretary of Defense and the three service secretaries on how this policy was to be put into effect.

The reaction to the executive order was complicated by the fact that nowhere in it was there any mention of ending segregation; instead it spoke of "equality of treatment and oppor-

[90] Lee Nichols, *Breakthrough on the Color Front*, 85–86, accurately pieces the story together from interviews; Berman, in "The Politics of Civil Rights," 110, points out these orders were considered by the White House a long time before they were issued; Oscar Ewing to the author, July 22, 1964, confirms these two accounts and makes the point that "the adoption of the strong civil rights plank by the Convention . . . created an urgency for prompt action by the President." Liberal pressure upon the President to take immediate action on civil rights after the convention is evident in Leon Henderson, National Chairman of the Americans for Democratic Action, to the President, July 22, 1948, OF 93B, HSTL, and Richard Givens, President of The Students for Democratic Action, to John R. Steelman, July 22, 1948, OF 93B, HSTL.

[91] A copy of the order is in President's Committee on Equality . . . in the Armed Services, *Freedom to Serve*, xi–xii.

tunity." An unnamed federal official pointed this out to *The New York Times* and said it was his opinion that integration was not the goal of the order.[92] This was a crucial point as far as Negroes were concerned, because they had long contended that equality was impossible with segregation. On the other hand, those opposed to integration maintained that separate but equal was indeed possible.

The situation was confused further by a statement made by General Omar Bradley, Army Chief of Staff. The day after the President's order was issued Bradley declared that the Army was no place to conduct social experiments and that desegregation would come to the Army only when it was a fact in the rest of the United States. The press immediately took Bradley's statement to mean that the Army would not obey the President's order if it was intended to end segregation.[93] Actually, General Bradley had not read the order at the time and had not been aware that reporters were in his audience. He assured the President that the press was in error when it implied that his statement meant the Army would stubbornly resist integration: "I assure you that nothing is further from our intent," Bradley wrote Truman in apology.[94] Unfortunately, Bradley underestimated the will to resist integration within the Army.

The Army's opposition to integration was obvious immediately. Secretary of the Army Royall had instructed his staff that they were to make no comment on the President's order.[95] On the same day that the order was made public, however, Army staff officers stated anonymously that no desegregation action was necessary to comply with the order because it did not specifically forbid segregation. Furthermore, they announced their firm support for the Army's policy of separate units for the races.[96] *The New York Times*'s expert on military affairs, Han-

---

[92] *The New York Times*, July 27, 1948.

[93] *The New York Times*, July 30, 1948.

[94] Bradley to the President, July 30, 1948, and Truman to Bradley, August 4, 1948, accepting his apology, both in CS 291.2, NARG 319.

[95] Royall to the President, July 29, 1948, D54-1-16, NARG 330.

[96] *Washington Daily News*, July 26, 1948, Army clippings, Fahy Committee Papers, HSTL.

son W. Baldwin, reflected the Army's attitude. Baldwin said that Bradley's statement had summarized Army feeling and that it was a widely held view within the Army that integration would impair the Army's morale and efficiency.[97]

The Southern Democrats in Congress were severely critical of the President's order, and they praised General Bradley's comments as a defiance of the President. Representative Joseph R. Bryson of South Carolina commended General Bradley "for his courage in continuing the policy of General Eisenhower on segregation."[98] Senator Burnet R. Maybank of South Carolina, a member of the Senate Armed Services Committee, hailed General Bradley's statement and made a frank admission: "It was my understanding with the Army officials at all committee meetings that they would retain segregation."[99] Editorials in the Southern press generally echoed the praise of General Bradley and condemned Truman for mixing politics with the military forces.[100]

The black press's immediate reaction to the order was critical. Most Negro newspapers felt that the language of the executive order was not strong enough; its failure to call explicitly for an end to segregation left a loophole, because the separate-but-equal doctrine could still stand.[101] To allay some of these misgivings, President Truman stated in a press conference three days after his order was issued that it was intended to end segregation in the armed forces.[102]

This statement was not enough for some Negroes, including A. Philip Randolph. The order was "deliberately calculated to obscure" the whole question and Negroes should ignore it, admonished Randolph. To assure Randolph and the League for Non-violent Civil Disobedience Against Military Segregation, Senator J. Howard McGrath met with this group on August 2.

[97] *The New York Times*, August 8, 1948.
[98] *Congressional Record*, 80th Cong., 2d Sess. (1948), 9527.
[99] *Congressional Record*, 80th Cong., 2d Sess. (1948), 9456.
[100] See clippings in the Fahy Committee Papers, HSTL.
[101] These generalizations are based on the extensive clippings from the Negro press in the Fahy Committee Papers, HSTL.
[102] *Public Papers, 1948*, 422.

McGrath told them that the committee to be appointed by the President would "initiate its activities and functions on the basis of non-segregation."[103] Randolph was satisfied at last that the President meant to end segregation in the armed forces, and he announced that the civil disobedience campaign had ended.[104]

The skepticism of Negroes about the motives behind Truman's civil rights program melted away with the Dixiecrat revolt from the Democratic party. Most Negroes came to feel that their grievances against Truman were minor and that he merited their support. "The formation of the Dixiecrat party," *The Crisis* editorialized, "and its bitter attacks upon the President indicate that Truman's pronouncements on civil rights are regarded as something more than barn-storming slogans."[105] President Truman's executive order on equality of treatment and opportunity in the military, together with the rest of his civil rights program, was instrumental in keeping the Negro vote a part of the Democratic coalition in 1948.[106] More important for the future was the fact that Executive Order 9981 marked a move by the Federal Government to support integration rather than segregation. Concern for civil rights, campaign strategy, and the demands of a politically important minority group were fused in 1948 to produce a democratic achievement.

---

[103] Grant Reynolds, "A Triumph for Civil Disobedience," *The Nation*, 167 (August 28, 1948), 228–29.

[104] Pittsburgh *Courier*, August 28, 1948.

[105] "Wallace's Southern Tour," *The Crisis*, 55 (October, 1948), 297.

[106] Memorandum, Donald S. Dawson to the President, September 9, 1948, Nash Papers, HSTL, describes the good reception by Negroes of the President's order.

CHAPTER IX

The Fahy Committee

B ECAUSE OF THE EXCITEMENT generated in the closing days of the 1948 campaign, little attention was given to the appointment, in September, 1948, of the members to the President's Committee on Equality of Treatment and Opportunity in the Armed Services. Negroes, however, were skeptical of what could be achieved by such a committee, and not without reason. The Army had let it be known that it did not interpret Executive Order 9981 as requiring the end of segregation. But even before the President's committee held its first meeting, it was clear that the Army was to be in the minority in fighting to retain its policy of segregation. The Navy hastened to announce that it was extending its policy of integration begun in the closing months of World War II. The Air Force leaked to the press that it had completed plans for full integration that only waited approval.[1] The Army would be on the defensive, but its determination to maintain segregation would not be easy to break. Despite the opposition, the end of the Fahy Committee, as it came to be known, would come only after the Army had officially adopted a policy of integration.

The White House had considerable trouble determining who should be appointed to the President's committee. Dr. Frank Graham, white moderate of North Carolina, was wanted as the

---

[1] Announcements of Navy and Air Force reported in Pittsburgh *Courier*, October 9, 1948, and January 22, 1949.

chairman, but he declined to serve. Charles E. Wilson of General Motors, former chairman of the President's Committee on Civil Rights, was also approached unsuccessfully for the chairmanship.[2] In addition to the problem of finding a chairman, Secretary of the Army Royall felt that many of the people under consideration had expressed themselves as being opposed to segregation in the armed services. Lester Granger, being pushed by Forrestal, was in this category. "I feel strongly that no person should serve on this Committee who has formed a fixed opinion on this subject on either side," Royall complained to the President.[3]

Despite the problems of personnel, the White House announced the names of the members of the President's committee on September 18, 1948. Appointed as chairman was Charles Fahy, a Georgia-born Catholic who had held many posts in Democratic administrations since the 1930's and who was known to be liberal on the race issue. Other members were Dwight R. G. Palmer, president of the General Cable Corporation, active in the National Urban League, and proponent of equal employment opportunities; William E. Stevenson, president of Oberlin College; Lester Granger, Negro head of the Urban League and close friend of Secretary of Defense Forrestal; and John H. Sengstacke, Negro publisher of the Chicago *Defender*, the only major Negro newspaper to support Truman in 1948.[4] Two other appointed members never took an active part in the committee's work: Alphonsus Donahue, a prominent Catholic layman, was ill, and Charles Luckman of Lever Brothers never indicated any interest. E. W. Kenworthy, a former newspaperman and secretary of the American Embassy in London, was later chosen as executive secretary. Basically, the President's committee was a liberal one.

The President's executive order created ripples on the surface

---

[2] Forrestal to the President, August 3, 1948, D54-1-16, NARG 330, contains a list of suggested names; memorandum, Marx Leva to Forrestal, August 31, 1948, OSA 334, NARG 335.

[3] Royall to the President, September 17, 1948, OSA 334, NARG 335.

[4] *The New York Times*, September 19, 1948; Lee Nichols, *Breakthrough on the Color Front*, 89–90.

of the segregation policy and had some effect before the Fahy Committee held its first meeting in 1949. In August, 1948, Secretary Royall called in Negro sociologist Charles S. Johnson and asked his advice on how the Army could solve its Negro problem. Royall reportedly admitted that "segregation in the Army must go," although this could not be accomplished immediately. Royall had in mind the creation of an experimental integrated unit that would indicate how integration would affect the Army.[5]

Over the Army General Staff's objections that an experimental unit "did not prove anything on the subject," Secretary Royall made his formal proposal for an experiment in integration to the Secretary of Defense in December, 1948. For the Army to carry out its proposal, however, the Navy and the Air Force must agree to conduct similar experiments.[6] The Navy refused to go along with Royall's proposal; it took the position that such an experimental unit was of interest only to the Army, because the Navy had already made considerable progress with integration on a permanent basis.[7]

The Air Force also refused to cooperate with Royall's experiment because it was already planning a policy of integration of its own. The development of a new racial policy for the Air Force began soon after it became an independent service within the new National Defense Establishment in 1947. Lieutenant General Idwal E. Edwards, the new Air Force's Deputy Chief of Staff for Personnel, had served on the McCloy Committee in World War II and was aware of the waste of manpower that resulted from the Army's segregation policy. General Edwards reviewed the policy of segregation for the new Air Force and concluded that maximum efficiency required that all Air Force personnel should be assigned on the basis of merit and ability,

---

[5] Pittsburgh *Courier*, August 14, 1948.

[6] The Staff's opposition is indicated in Chief of Staff to General Bull, October 11, 1948, G-1 291.2, NARG 319; Royall's proposals are set forth in memoranda, Royall to Forrestal, November 18, 1948, G-1 291.2, NARG 319, and December 2, 1948, OSA 291.2, NARG 335.

[7] John Nicolas Brown, Acting Secretary of the Navy, to Secretary Forrestal, December 28, 1948, OSA 291.2, NARG 335.

regardless of race. He faced bitter opposition to a policy of integration among Air Force officers, but Edwards' willingness to support a change was reinforced by the first Secretary of the Air Force, Stuart Symington.[8]

Secretary Symington committed himself to basing Air Force personnel policy on merit alone and instructed that planning for a policy of integration begin. President Truman's executive order gave these Air Force efforts a boost when it was issued in July, 1948. Symington later recalled that he went to the President, told him what he proposed to do, and asked if he had the President's backing. "With no reservations," Truman replied. With this firm support, Symington informed his staff that, regardless of the opposition, the Air Force was to draw up a policy of integration. By December, 1948, this policy was on Secretary of Defense Forrestal's desk, awaiting his approval. Although some units would remain all-Negro, Negro personnel would generally be assigned strictly on the basis of qualifications. To implement this policy, the Air Force proposed opening all of its schools to Negroes and breaking up certain all-Negro units and distributing their personnel to white units. There was delay in approving this new policy, however, because the Army was aware that its acceptance would leave the Army alone among the services in maintaining and defending segregation.[9]

The armed forces were attempting to arrive at some definite decisions before the President's committee met. Fahy was also thinking about how he would conduct the committee and what its goals should be. Before the committee held its first meeting in January, 1949, Fahy discussed his ideas with the President. It was important, Fahy felt, that the final policy be agreed upon by both the committee and the armed forces. The armed forces should be persuaded to adopt a nondiscriminatory policy. The persuasion would take time, but issuing a committee report

[8] Nichols, *Breakthrough on the Color Front*, 75, 77–78; "A Report on the First Year of Implementation of Current [Air Force] Policies Regarding Negro Personnel," n.d., PPB 291.2, NARG 330.

[9] Nichols, *Breakthrough on the Color Front*, 75–81; memorandum, Secretary Symington to Secretary Forrestal, January 6, 1949, OSA 291.2, NARG 335; Pittsburgh *Courier*, February 5, 1949.

without the military's approval would accomplish little. President Truman agreed with Fahy's proposed tactics and told him to take whatever time was needed. Furthermore, the President told Fahy, he could count on Truman's full support to get the military services to adopt the committee's suggestions.[10]

On January 12, 1949, the committee held its first meeting with the President and the Secretaries of the Army, Navy, Air Force, and Defense. President Truman told those present he did not see the committee's role as a publicity stunt. He wanted "concrete results . . . not publicity on it. I want the job done and I want it done in a way so that everybody will be happy to cooperate to get it done." The President hoped that he would not have to "knock somebody's ears down," but if that should be necessary, he would do it.[11] After meeting with the President and the service secretaries, the Fahy Committee met privately and expressed concern over its public image. Lester Granger pointed out that Negroes were skeptical about what the committee could accomplish; they "expect us to look for an easy way out and to curve around the main issue [segregation]." Mr. Fahy was fearful that, since the committee's offices were in the Pentagon, people might think it was under the Pentagon's control. It was obvious from the beginning that the committee's members were resolved to be an independent body.[12]

The Fahy Committee held its first hearings on January 13 when representatives from the military staffs of each of the three services appeared before it. The representatives from the Army General Staff said that the prime concern of the Army was "the desire to achieve maximum effective utilization of all its available manpower." There was no discrimination against the Negro, despite the fact of segregation — there were equal opportunities and equal facilities. Segregation of the Negro into separate units "has been the thing that has given the Negro far greater opportunity than any business or profession in the United

---

[10] Interview with Judge Charles Fahy, August 10, 1964.

[11] "Testimony before the Fahy Committee," Vol. I, 2–3, Fahy Committee Papers, HSTL. Cited hereafter as "Testimony."

[12] "Testimony," Vol. II, 12–18, January 12, 1949.

States can point to."[13] This argument was an often-repeated defense of segregation. The reasoning behind it was that there were more Negro commissioned and noncommissioned officers in a segregated system, because the "inferior" Negroes did not have to compete with whites for these positions. The Army spokesmen apparently failed to understand that this was a poor argument for their stated goal of maximum efficiency.

The Marine Corps, which was supposed to be under the control of the Navy Department, had a difficult time explaining why it had failed to follow the Navy's integration policy. The Marine representative told the committee that its policy of segregation had been adopted as the best, following an investigation of all of the records of the Army on the subject. Questioning by the committee's members revealed that the Marine Corps had only one Negro officer among eighty-two hundred, and that no thought had been given to changing the policy of segregation. When asked what he thought of integration, the Marine representative replied, "I think you'd be making a problem instead of solving one."[14]

The Navy reiterated its policy of integration, and the Air Force extolled its new policy of integration pending before the Secretary of Defense. The committee was favorably impressed by both services, but they spotted weaknesses in their programs. The Air Force's proposed policy, for example, called for a maximum 10 per cent quota of Negroes in any one unit. The committee felt that this arbitrary quota would lead to discrimination. In addition to the rigid segregation policy of the Marines, there were other indications that the Navy's policy had not been fully implemented: Two thirds of the Negro sailors were segregated in the Steward's Branch, and there were only five Negro officers out of forty-five thousand on active duty with the Navy.[15]

After this first hearing, Fahy and his colleagues realized that there were many questions to which answers would have to be found before it could go much further. One of the most important questions was how to interpret the President's order. Was

[13] "Testimony," Vol. III, 32, 204, January 13, 1949.
[14] "Testimony," Vol. IV, 9, 12–13, 15.
[15] "Testimony," Vol. II, 39ff, and Vol. III, 69–84.

its intent to have the committee seek the end of segregation as well as of discrimination? Most of the committee members interpreted the order in this way, which appeared to answer for the moment the second question the committee had posed for itself: Could there be equality of treatment and opportunity in the armed forces without the elimination of segregation? Was there such a condition as separate but equal? Chairman Fahy suggested that the members would be wise to wait for more information about the services' policies before taking a definite stand on these issues.[16]

On March 28 the three service secretaries appeared before the committee. Secretary Symington of the Air Force and Secretary John L. Sullivan of the Navy pointedly stated that they were opposed to segregation and had policies of integration. The Air Force's policy was only awaiting the approval of the Secretary of Defense. Symington and Sullivan made it clear that they both believed integration led to more efficient use of manpower, in contrast to the Army's belief that integration would mean a loss of efficiency.[17]

Secretary Royall's statement to the committee was a frank review of the Army's position. The Army was "not an instrument for social evolution." Admitting that an end to segregation would solve a lot of administrative headaches for the Army, Royall felt that the history of Negro troops in two world wars indicated that they were not suited for combat units. On the other hand, they were "peculiarly qualified" for manual labor. "It follows that in the interest of efficient national defense, certain types of units should be entirely or largely confined to white troops." Since voluntary segregation was the normal condition in civilian life, and since a large portion of the Army's volunteers came from the South, Royall felt that integration would seriously disrupt the Army and impede its mission of national defense.[18]

---

[16] "Testimony," Vol. V, 4ff, February 21, 1949; memorandum by Joseph H. B. Evans, Associate Secretary of the Fahy Committee, March 1, 1949, Fahy Committee Papers, HSTL.

[17] "Testimony," Vol. X, 2–35, March 28, 1949.

[18] "Testimony," Vol. IX, 3–8.

To those who argued that segregation meant that the Negro did not have equal opportunity, Royall repeated the old Army arguments in support of segregation. The Negro soldier actually had more opportunity for advancement in a segregated Army than he would have in an integrated one, because he did not have to compete with whites. The committee's criticisms did not seem to shake Royall's position. When asked in conclusion if he thought that the Army was carrying out the policy announced in Executive Order 9981, Royall answered in the affirmative and claimed that this had been the case before the order was issued. "The Army has done so much more and gotten so much less credit for what is done [for the Negro] than any [other] Department of Government . . . ," Royall concluded.[19]

By the end of March it was clear to the Fahy Committee that the Army was firmly wedded to its segregation policy. The members of the committee agreed that their achievements would be limited if they made only the usual criticisms of segregation, because appeals to religious, moral, and political principles against segregation had little impact. The Army did not defend its policy on moral grounds, but maintained that segregation was necessary for social and military reasons. The Fahy Committee decided that it would have to meet the Army on its own terms — military efficiency — and would have to dig deeply into the Army's personnel practices to prove that segregation resulted in both discrimination and inefficient use of manpower. The committee hoped that through this approach the Army could be persuaded to adopt a more liberal policy.[20]

The committee faced the prospect of a long, tedious examination of the Army's records to liberalize a policy of segregation rather than to end it. At this point the committee received unexpected aid from the office of the Secretary of Defense. About the same time that the Fahy Committee was beginning its hear-

[19] "Testimony," Vol. IX, 16–50. Also see "Testimony," Vol. X, 66–73, for Army Chief of Staff General Omar Bradley's testimony that is very similar in reasoning to that of Secretary Royall.

[20] "An Analysis of the Work of the President's Committee . . . Through March 28, 1949"; "Report on Gillem Board Policy and Implementation," 130–31; memoranda, Kenworthy to Fahy, March 9, 10, 1949, all in Fahy Committee Papers, HSTL.

ings, Secretary Forrestal called in Thomas R. Reid, Chairman of the Personnel Policy Board. Forrestal wanted Reid to formulate a general policy for the three armed forces that would end segregation and guarantee equal opportunity. Forrestal and Reid wanted to establish a new policy before the committee dictated one. The new Air Force policy then pending before the Secretary of Defense was considered a good model; it provided for an immediate beginning of integration, but complete transition would be gradual. The Army was reluctant to go along; the Army General Staff opposed Reid's proposed policy, on the grounds that it was "a directive to assign Negro personnel to organizations without regard to race, and, as such, is complete integration. It is the opinion of the Army that integration of individual Negroes in white organizations should not and cannot be undertaken at this time." [21]

Reid, by continuously pointing out the willingness of the Air Force to integrate and the desirability for the armed forces to take the initiative rather than to wait for dictation from the Fahy Committee, secured reluctant approval from the Army civilian leadership for a policy statement. On April 1, 1949, Reid went to the new Secretary of Defense, Louis Johnson. He told Johnson about Forrestal's earlier instructions and the proposed policy he had drawn up. Emphasizing that "this is a matter which has the President's direct interest," Reid persuaded Johnson to issue the proposed policy in the form of a directive to the service secretaries on April 6. [22]

Johnson declared that it was the Department of Defense's policy that there should be equality of treatment and opportunity for all. To guarantee this, all personnel would be considered "on the basis of individual merit and ability" for

[21] Memorandum, G-1 to the Deputy Chief of Staff for Administration, March 30, 1949, CS 291.2, NARG 319. The roles of Mr. Reid and Secretary Forrestal are revealed in Thomas R. Reid to the author, February 12, April 1, 1965; memorandum, Reid to Worthington Thompson, February 15, 1949, and memorandum, Reid to John H. Ohly, March 15, 1949, both in PPB 291.2, NARG 330.

[22] Memorandum, Reid to Secretary Johnson, April 1, 1949; memorandum, Allen to Secretary Johnson, April 5, 1949, both in D54-1-16, NARG 330.

enlistment, attendance at schools, promotion, and assignment. Although some all-Negro units might continue in existence for a while, "all Negroes will not necessarily be assigned to Negro units." Instead, "qualified Negro personnel shall be assigned to fill any type of position . . . without regard to race." [23] In short, the Secretary of Defense took the position, contrary to the Army, that equality of treatment and opportunity required abandonment of rigid segregation. Each of the services was directed to submit individual policies for approval that would meet the broad aims of this directive.

The Fahy Committee was surprised by this initiative from the Secretary of Defense and was not informed of the directive until April 18, the day before it was released to the press. The effect on the committee was profound, for if the directive meant what it said, complete integration would result. No longer did just lowering the degree of segregation in the Army appear to be the only realistic goal. Furthermore, at about the time Johnson issued his memorandum, the committee's examination of the Army's historical record revealed that efficiency had not been one of the results of the Army's Negro policy. It was clear that the Gillem policy had not been implemented and that, contrary to Army claims, segregation by its nature precluded equality of treatment and opportunity. The new policy of the Secretary of Defense and the accumulated evidence pointed to one conclusion: "In my opinion, man-to-man integration has got to come much sooner than I thought a month ago," the committee's executive secretary declared. Now, the proper goal of the committee appeared to be the determination of procedures by which the Army would integrate. [24]

---

[23] Memorandum, Secretary Johnson to the Secretaries of the Army, Navy, Air Force, and Chairman of the Personnel Policy Board, April 6, 1949, copy in Fahy Committee Papers, HSTL. The earlier draft of the proposed policy drawn up by Reid had called for the new policy to begin in July, 1949, and to be completed by July, 1950: "It is the intent of this directive that the maximum integration of members of minority groups throughout the military establishment shall be accomplished by 1 July 1950." Apparently this was deleted because of Army objections. See "Draft of Proposed Directive for the Armed Forces," n.d., PPB 291.2, NARG 330.

[24] Memorandum, Kenworthy to Fahy, April 27, 1949, Fahy Committee

The public reaction to Johnson's order was mixed. One rabid racist wrote the Defense Secretary that "it is my earnest hope that if you enforce this rule in our armed services, that your wife, daughters, or any women dear to you are attacked by these brutes."[25] *The Crisis* saw the directive as ending the policy of segregation while the practice continued, but it was now possible "for armed service officers and civilian groups to work for the elimination of the practices and build a military establishment without a color line."[26] Secretary Johnson took a strong stand in favor of integration in his replies to those questioning his action:

These policies have the support of millions of citizens who feel strongly that segregation in the armed forces is sharply at variance with our democratic principles and ideals and who understand that its practice reduces the efficiency of our military strength. The practice of segregation is damaging to our country's reputation with millions of people around the world.[27]

In replying to the Secretary of Defense's April directive, the Army made clear its disagreement with Johnson's analysis of military segregation. "The Department of the Army," wrote Royall,

has reviewed its practices and procedures . . . and is of the opinion that they are sound in the light of actual experience, and are in accord with the policies of the National Military Establishment and with Executive Order 9981.[28]

In addition, Royall claimed, falsely, that Johnson's requirements for schooling, promotion, and assignment without regard to race were already being followed by the Army. In effect, the Army was continuing to assert — in opposition to the President,

Papers, HSTL, illustrates the change in thinking of the committee and the results of the study of the Army's records.

[25] D.W. McC. to Johnson, April 21, 1949, D54-1-16, NARG 330.

[26] "Armed Service Jim Crow Policy Ends," *The Crisis*, 56 (May, 1949), 137.

[27] Secretary Johnson to Senator Lyndon B. Johnson of Texas, July 8, 1949, D54-1-16, NARG 330. Senator Johnson wanted information to answer the complaint of a constituent.

[28] Quoted in "Report on Gillem Board Policy," 154–55.

the Secretary of Defense, and the Fahy Committee — that equality of opportunity could be achieved with segregation. The Navy's answer was similar to that of the Army in that it claimed that the Secretary of Defense's directive was already being followed by the Navy. The Air Force replied with its detailed policy for integration that had been before the Secretary of Defense since February, 1948.

Apparently aware that the Army's reply would not be readily acceptable, Royall wrote Johnson on April 22, warning him not to act precipitantly against the Army's segregation policy. According to Royall, the preceding spring certain senators on the Senate Armed Services Committee had warned that they would violently oppose the draft law pending before it if they felt that the President would issue a pre-emptory order completely abolishing segregation in the Army. Both he and Secretary Forrestal assured these senators that this would not be the case. "I think you should be advised of these circumstances," Royall told the Secretary of Defense in conclusion, "because if any action were later taken by you or other authority to abolish segregation in the Army, I am confident that these Southern Senators would remember this incident." [29]

Aware of the President's intentions, Secretary Johnson accepted the plan of the Air Force but rejected those of the Army and Navy on May 11. He said that the Army and Navy had not responded to his request for "a detailed plan for such additional forward steps as can and should be made." He was pleased to see that the Army had made progress in the last few years but felt "that much remains to be done and that the rate of progress toward the objectives of the Executive Order must be accelerated." The Army was directed to submit "specific additional actions" which it planned to take in the future by May 25. [30]

At this point, Thomas Reid suggested to the Fahy Committee that it should indicate informally to the Army and Navy the steps that it thought were necessary to get their policies approved

[29] Memorandum, Secretary Royall to Secretary Johnson, April 22, 1949, OSA 291.2, NARG 335.
[30] Quoted in "Report of the Gillem Board Policy," 156; *The New York Times*, May 12, 1949.

by the Secretary of Defense.[31] Fahy and his colleagues readily agreed to this proposal, because it meant that the committee was once again in the middle of things. The committee's recommendations to the Navy called essentially for a campaign to increase the number of Negro officers and for an increase in the number of enlisted men outside of the Steward's Branch. The Army was asked to open all Army jobs (Military Occupational Specialties) on the basis of qualifications without regard to race, to abolish all Negro quotas for Army schools, to assign students to these schools without regard to race, to assign all graduates of Army schools to units without regard to race, and to abolish the 10 per cent racial quota for enlistment.[32]

The Fahy group was aware that the acceptance of its propositions by the Army would mean the end of segregation. "We will have undermined segregation and it will come tumbling down of its own weight," said Executive Secretary Kenworthy.[33] Under the prevailing procedures, for example, a Negro soldier could enroll in an Army school course only if there was an opening waiting for his specialty in a black unit. Since only a comparatively small number of all-Negro units existed and they were of a limited type, many qualified Negro soldiers were not allowed to pursue their interests or aptitudes. Of 106 Army courses open to recruits in April, 1949, only 21 were open to Negroes.[34] To assign black soldiers to schools and subsequently to units without regard to race, as the committee suggested, would require the end of segregation. The Army was also well aware of this fact.

The second reply of the Navy was accepted by the Secretary of Defense, but the Army was again turned down. The latter had made its second reply a lengthy defense of the Gillem policy of segregation and the alleged progress under that policy. In effect, the Army refused to modify its policies of assignment,

---

[31] "Report on Gillem Board Policy," 156.

[32] "Initial Recommendations by the President's Committee . . . ," n.d., Fahy Committee Papers, HSTL.

[33] Memorandum, Kenworthy to Fahy, May 12, 1949, Fahy Committee Papers, HSTL.

[34] Figures are in Fahy Committee Papers, HSTL.

segregation, or the quota system as the Fahy Committee suggested.[35]

The committee's analysis of the Army's second reply indicated that it was full of inaccurate and misleading statements. For example, the Army claimed that Negroes were found in all type jobs; the committee pointed out that the Army's own figures indicated this was not true. The Army asserted that there were no schools from which black soldiers were excluded solely on the basis of color; the committee pointed out that this statement was true as far as it went, but it was basically inaccurate. Although Negroes were not excluded from Army schools, they were excluded from approximately 81 per cent of these schools' courses. The Army claimed that the 10 per cent quota for Negroes was necessary, because if it should be dropped Negroes, the majority of whom were poorly educated, would become 30 to 40 per cent of the Army. After examining the statistical evidence, the committee denied that Negroes could ever make up so large a percentage of the Army.[36] False information such as this from the Army plagued the committee throughout its existence.

The Army concluded its second reply with an attempt to frighten those opposing its policy:

. . . there is a growing concern among many senior officers of the Army that we are weakening to a dangerous degree the combat efficiency of our Army. These officers are familiar with the combat performance of Negro troops during war and feel that we have already gone too far in inserting colored organizations in white combat units.[37]

The basis for this cryptic warning was the old idea, which had become rooted within the Army during World War I, that the Negro was unreliable as a combat soldier because he was cowardly. Although this was not stated so boldly in public, behind

---

[35] The Army's reply is quoted in "Report on Gillem Board Policy," 157–59.

[36] "Report of the Gillem Board Policy," 159–60.

[37] "Report on Gillem Board Policy," 159.

the scenes the Army General Staff constantly expressed this belief and quoted field commanders' statements to this effect. Integration would lead to military inefficiency, the Army reasoned, because it would require the dispersion of inherent cowards throughout the Army's combat units, thus weakening their effectiveness. Segregation allowed inferior Negroes to be used mainly in those roles for which they were "peculiarly" suited — labor and service. The racist belief that the Negro was a natural coward was the real objection to integration by many within the Army. Another argument, more frequently used openly, was that most of the Army's white soldiers would not accept the integration of Negroes into their units. Integration would therefore lead to constant racial conflict, the Army asserted, thus lowering combat efficiency.[38]

In refusing the Army's second reply on June 7, the Secretary of Defense called for another report by June 20, and for the first time he formally asked the Army to take into consideration the proposals of the Fahy Committee. There now began a long series of negotiations between the Fahy Committee and Army officials, with the Army's deadline for its third report being extended several times. The committee fluctuated between optimism and pessimism over the impact of its arguments upon the Army. At a meeting with Chief of Staff Bradley on June 13, Dwight Palmer and Fahy saw hope that the Army was beginning to see

[38] Interview with Judge Charles Fahy, August 10, 1964; Thomas R. Reid to the author, April 1, 1965; E. W. Kenworthy, "The Case Against Army Segregation," *The Annals*, 275 (May, 1951), 27–33. This belief in the inherent cowardice of the Negro soldier is stated openly only infrequently in the documents of the period, but it is always just below the surface of Army arguments against integration. For example, the Army's second reply to the Secretary of Defense also contained this argument for retaining segregation: "The soldier on the battlefield deserves to have, and must have, utmost confidence in his fellow soldiers. They must eat together, sleep together, and all too frequently die together. There can be no friction in their every-day living that might bring on failure in battle. A chain is as strong as its weakest link, and this is true of the Army unit on the battlefield." In this statement both the arguments of "confidence" and "friction," or racial conflict, are merged. Quoted in "Report on Gillem Board Policy," 158.

things their way.[39] By June 23, reports reaching the committee were that "the Army cannot yield on the segregation principle."[40]

On July 5, Fahy and Palmer met with General Bradley and Royall's successor as Secretary of the Army, Gordon Gray. The committee was presented with an "Outline Plan for Utilization of Negro Manpower to Provide Further Equality of Opportunity." The new proposal provided for the opening of all Army job classifications to Negroes and for increasing the number of Negro units. Fahy and his colleagues were disappointed, because their recommendations to ease complete segregation in units and to abolish the 10 per cent quota were again ignored. Furthermore, the Army had refused to adopt their position on assignment; although the Army's new proposal would allow Negroes to attend all of its schools, the fact that the black soldier could be assigned only to an all-Negro unit meant that he might not be assigned to a job for which he was trained.[41]

The members of the committee resolved that the Army proposals were not acceptable and would not be until the quota system was abolished and Negro soldiers were assigned to units on the basis of their training, regardless of race. In short, equality of treatment and opportunity could be accomplished only by ending segregation. There was now a stalemate between the committee and the Army, and the former was determined that the Army policy as it stood should not be accepted by the Secretary of Defense as fulfilling Executive Order 9981 or the Defense Department's directive of April 6. The Secretary of Defense, the Secretary of the Army, and the President were informed of this position.[42]

There followed two months of talks between the Army and

---

[39] Kenworthy to W. E. Stevenson, June 13, 1949; Fahy to Secretary Johnson, June 14, 1949, both in Fahy Committee Papers, HSTL.

[40] Kenworthy to Fahy, June 23, 1949, Fahy Committee Papers, HSTL.

[41] "Minutes of the Meeting of the President's Committee," July 11, 1949, Fahy Committee Papers, HSTL.

[42] Fahy to Secretary Johnson, July 25, 1949; Fahy to Secretary Gray, July 25, 1949; Fahy to the President, July 27, 1949; all in Fahy Committee Papers, HSTL.

the committee, with neither side willing to compromise. During this period Fahy thought he had assurances from the White House that no Army proposal would be accepted unless it met the committee's demands on assignment and on the quota.[43] On September 27 the Army informed Fahy that they were sending their proposed policy to the Secretary of Defense. Without furnishing the committee a copy, Army officials assured Fahy that they were adopting the committee's suggestions on assignment.[44]

The next thing the committee heard was the announcement on September 30 that the Secretary of Defense had approved the Army's proposals. The committee was angry, however, when it learned that, as announced to the press, the Army had not accepted its policy on assignment or the quota. Furthermore, the Army had given the impression that its proposal had received the approval of the Fahy Committee.[45] Negro and liberal organizations blasted the Army's policy for not ending segregation. If the Air Force and the Navy could integrate, why could not the Army? Was this all the Fahy Committee could accomplish?[46]

The reason for the acceptance of the Army's proposal by the Secretary of Defense over the objections of the committee is not clear. Perhaps the Army implied to the Secretary of Defense that the Fahy Committee had agreed to its statement; this was the implication to the press by Army officials. It is clear that officials within the Department of Defense who would normally see such a release before it was issued to the press did not see

---

[43] Fahy to members of the committee, August 3, 1949; Fahy to Secretary Gray, September 9, 1949; memorandum, E. W. Kenworthy to members of the committee, September 19, 1949; all in Fahy Committee Papers, HSTL.

[44] Memorandum, Kenworthy to the committee, September 27, 1949.

[45] *Washington Post*, October 1, 1949.

[46] Pittsburgh *Courier*, October 8, 15, 1949; Press Release of the Committee Against Jim Crow in Military Service and Training, October 6, 1949, and Elmer W. Henderson, Director of American Council on Human Rights, to Fahy, both in Fahy Committee Papers, HSTL. Charles M. LaFollette, National Director of Americans for Democratic Action, to the President, October 1, 1949, OF 190T, HSTL.

this one.[47] Perhaps the Army's stubborn insistence that integration would be detrimental to its combat effectiveness frightened the Defense Department into acceptance. Thomas R. Reid recalled that "this was the most difficult argument to handle because it implied we were in effect asking them to run the risk of military ineffectiveness or something less than the full defense of the United States against an enemy." Reid admitted that "the Army position was so well documented and so strongly presented that my own conviction that we were doing the right thing was shaken from time to time."[48]

Whatever doubt existed within the Defense Department about forcing the Army to integrate was not shared by Fahy and his cohorts. The committee sent a memorandum to the President, explaining that the Army's plan as accepted did not provide for assignment without regard to race, a point that was crucial to guarantee equality. Unrestricted assignment would provide for "the beginning of integration by a slow and practical process and provide for a better Army." If the committee was to resume discussions with the Army, the Secretary of Defense should be told that the committee's recommendations conformed to the requirements of Executive Order 9981.[49] Meanwhile, Truman was aware of the Fahy Committee's anger over the approval of the Army statement and the fact that it was "arousing a good deal of controversy."[50] At his October 6 press conference the President moved to allay any anxiety. He labeled the Army's statement a "progress report" and made it clear that there would be further recommendations from the Fahy Committee. In addition, Truman once again stated that his goal was integration of the Army.[51]

---

[47] Memorandum, Kenworthy to Fahy, October 2, 1949, Fahy Committee Papers, HSTL.

[48] Reid to the author, April 1, 1965. The trepidation within the Defense Department over forcing the Army to do something that it considered detrimental to its effectiveness is also indicated in memorandum to Reid from Colonel J. F. Cassidy, August 23, 1949, PPB 291.2, NARG 330.

[49] Memorandum, Charles Fahy to the President, October 11, 1949, Fahy Committee Papers, HSTL.

[50] Memorandum, David K. Niles to the President, October 5, 1949, Philleo Nash Papers, HSTL.

[51] *Public Papers of the Presidents: 1949*, 501.

The opposition to integration within the Army, however, was by no means ready to give in. The third Army reply had contained concessions to the effect that all Army jobs and schools would be opened to Negroes, but integrated assignment was to be allowed only in overhead positions or in positions where there were critical shortages of specialists. On October 1 the Army sent this new policy to all major commands. Several weeks later an anonymous person left with the Fahy Committee a copy of a second order that had been issued by the Army on October 27. This one stated that the limited integration authorized in Secretary Gray's order of October 1 should be disregarded; Negroes would be assigned only to Negro jobs.[52] Gray was outraged that such an order was issued without his knowledge, and on November 3 he issued a statement that the second order violated the Army's announced policy. Some qualified Negro specialists would indeed be assigned to white units, Gray emphasized.[53] The whole episode was indicative of the opposition to integration that the Fahy Committee had to overcome.[54]

The Army now began preparing a major new policy on Negro troops that would incorporate its approved third reply and replace the Gillem policy. The angry reaction of the Fahy Committee and of the public to the approval of the Army's statement of October 1 put the White House on guard. Word was passed to the Army and to the Fahy Committee that any new Army policy must have the committee's approval before it would be acceptable.[55] These assurances were needed to quiet the Negro members of the committee, Granger and Sengstacke, who were

[52] The two orders are quoted in "Report on Gillem Board Policy," 171–72.

[53] *The New York Times*, November 4, 1949.

[54] This incident can be traced in Nichols, *Breakthrough on the Color Front*, 93; memorandum, Kenworthy to Fahy, October 29, 1949; memorandum, Kenworthy to committee members, October 29, 1949; memorandum, Kenworthy to Philleo Nash; memorandum, Kenworthy to the committee, November 3, 1949, all in Fahy Committee Papers, HSTL. Secretary Gray's reaction is discussed in memorandum, Worthington Thompson to Marx Leva, November 3, 1949, D54-1-61, NARG 330.

[55] Memorandum, Kenworthy to Fahy, October 18, 1949; memorandum, Kenworthy to Fahy, October 26, 1949; memorandum, Kenworthy to committee, October 29, 1949, all in Fahy Committee Papers, HSTL.

calling for a press release detailing the impasse between the Army and the committee.[56]

By the end of November the Army finished its revision of the Gillem policy and carried it to the White House for approval. David K. Niles told the Army officials that if it was satisfactory to the President's committee it would be satisfactory to the White House.[57] It was not acceptable to the committee, however, because it maintained segregation and the quota and allowed only a few Negro specialists to be integrated into white units.[58] Fahy warned the Army that if it officially issued this revised policy he would notify the White House of the committee's disapproval and would issue a statement to the press condemning it.[59] Fahy and his colleagues were impatient, as it appeared that another stalemate would develop, and they thought seriously about releasing a public statement to indicate why no progress had been made.[60]

The committee informed Philleo Nash, the White House's adviser on minority matters, that it would issue a statement soon unless the Army retreated. Nash advised against a statement and suggested that the committee send its proposal on assignment to the Army and to the White House. In Nash's opinion, "the White House would indicate to the Army that it should move to meet the recommendations of the President's Committee."[61] The committee sent its recommendations for modification of the Army's proposed policy to the President on Decem-

[56] Sengstacke to Fahy, November 8, 1949, Fahy Committee Papers, HSTL.
[57] Memorandum, Kenworthy to Fahy, November 22, 1949, Fahy Committee Papers, HSTL.
[58] "Utilization of Negro Manpower in the Army," November 16, 1949, copy in Fahy Committee Papers. The committee's unfavorable analysis of this proposed policy is summarized in memorandum, Kenworthy to Fahy, November 28, 1949, Fahy Committee Papers, HSTL.
[59] Memorandum for the record by Kenworthy, November 27, 1949, Fahy Committee Papers, HSTL.
[60] See John H. Sengstacke to Fahy, November 29, 1949; Dwight R. G. Palmer to Kenworthy, November 28, 1949, in Fahy Committee Papers, HSTL.
[61] Memorandum for the record by Kenworthy, December 9, 1949, Fahy Committee Papers, HSTL.

ber 15. They proposed an end to the racial quota and a statement specifying that Negroes would be assigned to units without regard to race.[62] The Defense Department next told the Army that the Fahy Committee's recommendations on the quota and assignment should be accepted.[63] The White House and the Defense Department were now definitely opposed to further obstinance on the part of the Army.

The reports of the success of the Navy and Air Force integration programs left the Army further isolated in defending segregation. In December, 1949, the Air Force reported that its integrated units increased from 273 in June, 1949, to 797 in August. Furthermore, there had been no racial conflict within the newly integrated units.[64] *Ebony* magazine described Air Force integration as "the swiftest and most amazing upset of racial policy in the history of the U.S. military."[65] The Navy reported that it had issued an order stating that "all personnel will be enlisted or appointed, trained, advanced or promoted, assigned duty and administered in all respects without regard to race, color, religion, or national origin." In addition, it had appointed more Negro officers, had made special efforts to obtain more Negro enlistees, and had instituted a program to upgrade the status of the Steward's Branch and to allow qualified Negroes to transfer from this branch to general service. Finally, all separate training for Negroes in the Marines had been abolished. "The results attained during a comparatively brief period," Navy officials concluded, "indicate forcibly that racial tolerance is spreading and it is only a question of time until it will no longer present a problem within the Navy."[66]

---

[62] Memorandum, the President's Committee, to the President, December 15, 1949, Fahy Committee Papers, HSTL.

[63] Memorandum, Kenworthy to Fahy, December 19, 1949, Fahy Committee Papers, HSTL.

[64] Memorandum, the Assistant Secretary of the Air Force to the Chairman of the Personnel Policy Board, December 5, 1949, PPB 291.2, NARG 330. For accounts of the integration at various Air Force bases, see *The New York Times*, September 18, November 28, 1949.

[65] "The Air Force Goes Interracial," *Ebony*, 4 (September, 1949), 15–18.

[66] Memorandum, the Under Secretary of the Navy to the Chairman of the Personnel Policy Board, December 22, 1949, PPB 291.2, NARG 330.

Events moved rapidly now. Secretary of the Army Gray asked for a meeting with Fahy on December 27. At this meeting Gray admitted that the White House had given him the committee's recommendations for revision of the Gillem policy, and the Army had rewritten its proposed policy with these suggestions in mind. There was still concern with the committee's proposed language on assignment, which stated simply that Negroes be assigned to any unit on the basis of need and ability and without regard to race. Gray said he was in agreement in principle with this, but wanted language that would allow integration to take place gradually, starting with skilled Negroes and working down. After this meeting Fahy informed the committee members: "I feel we are much closer to agreement than at any time in the past, and I am very hopeful that by some modification in the language we can reach agreement."[67]

Fahy felt that the Army was sincere, and he agreed to compromise the language on assignment so that integration would be gradual.[68] On January 14, 1950, the full committee met and approved of the Army's revision of its Gillem policy. The compromise involved acceptance of the committee's language on assignment: Negroes "will be utilized in accordance with . . . skills and qualifications, and will be assigned to any . . . unit without regard to race or color." To this was added the Army's suggestions for "additional steps" toward the attainment of the goal stated by the committee, which involved beginning with the integrated assignment of Negroes to specialty jobs for which there was a shortage of qualified personnel. The committee informed the President of its approval of the Army policy on January 16, and on the same day the Army issued its successor to the Gillem policy. Only the committee's recommendation for an end to the racial quota was left unresolved, and discussion began immediately on this point.[69]

---

[67] Memorandum, Fahy to the committee members, December 27, 1949, Fahy Committee Papers, HSTL; Nichols, *Breakthrough on the Color Front*, 96.

[68] These negotiations can be followed in memoranda to the committee members, December 29, 30, 1949, January 5, 6, 1950, Fahy Committee Papers, HSTL.

[69] Memorandum, Fahy to the President, January 16, 1950, Fahy Com-

The reaction of Negroes to the announcement of the new policy was mixed. The Pittsburgh *Courier* saw it as a "victory"; on the other hand, the Norfolk *Journal and Guide* claimed that a "basic flaw" of the new policy was the fact that it made individual commanders responsible for its implementation.[70] A. Philip Randolph was critical of the new policy because he felt that it did not end segregation. Others apparently felt this was the case too, because several congressmen introduced bills calling for an end to segregation in the armed forces.[71]

The President's committee was convinced that it had done the best it could under trying circumstances, and it continued to negotiate over the last obstacle — the racial quota. There was considerable support within the Office of the Secretary of Defense, however, for ending the Fahy Committee immediately and allowing the Army a free hand in implementing its new policy. The Fahy Committee was opposed to this step until it had achieved the end of the quota. They had powerful support within the White House in Clark Clifford and David Niles, who advised the President that the committee should remain in existence until the quota was abolished.[72]

The President agreed that the committee would continue until the quota was ended.[73] President Truman apparently told Secretary Gray of his desire that the quota be abolished, and the Army agreed to do so if the President would agree that a racial quota could be reinstituted if the percentage of Negroes in the Army became too great. "If as a result of this new system," Secretary Gray wrote the President, "there ensues a disproportionate

---

mittee Papers, HSTL. The Army's new policy was released as Special Regulations No. 600-629-1, a copy of which is in Fahy Committee Papers. An accurate account of these final negotiations with the Army is contained in *The New York Times*, January 16, 1950.

[70] Pittsburgh *Courier*, January 28, 1950; Norfolk *Journal and Guide*, February 4, 1950.

[71] *The New York Times*, February 15, May 22, 25, 1950.

[72] Memorandum, J. F. Cassidy to Admiral McCrea, January 18, 1950, PPB 291.2, NARG 330; memorandum, Clark Clifford to the President, n.d. [January, 1950], Nash Papers, HSTL.

[73] Memorandum, Fahy to committee members, February 1, 1950, Fahy Committee Papers, HSTL.

balance of racial strength . . . , it is my understanding that I
have your authority to return to a system which will . . . control
enlistment by race." President Truman approved.[74] The Fahy
Committee was never informed of this agreement, but by
March 13 the Army had agreed to abolish the 10 per cent quota
on Negro strength, beginning in April, 1950. Reassuring the
Army that it had nothing to fear, President Truman wrote Secretary Gray that he appreciated the Army's action: "I am sure
everything will work out as it should," he concluded.[75]

The Fahy Committee began preparation of its final report
with a feeling of a job well done.[76] The committee's Executive
Secretary accurately summed up the sentiments of the individual
members when he claimed in a magazine article that the new
racial programs of the services were not "millennial": "Much
remains to be done. But I think it is fair to say that they represent
an unprecedented stride toward the solution of a problem that
has embarrassed the nation since its beginning." [77] The committee's final report, *Freedom to Serve*, was submitted to the President May 22, 1950. In receiving it, President Truman said that
he had followed the committee's work closely since its beginning
and had confidence that its recommendations would be carried
out and that "within the reasonably near future, equality of
treatment and opportunity for all persons within the armed
services would be accomplished." [78]

To ensure that the new racial policies would actually be carried
out — something that had not always been done in the past —
most of the committee members wanted a successor body appointed.[79] This was opposed by Secretary of Defense Johnson,

[74] Secretary Gray to the President, March 1, 1950, OF 1285, HSTL.

[75] Memorandum, the President to Secretary Gray, March 27, 1950,
OSA 291.2, NARG 335.

[76] For the feeling of individual committee members, see Fahy to William Stevenson, March 30, 1950; Kenworthy to John H. Sengstacke,
April 25, 1950; Sengstacke to Fahy, May 25, 1950; all in Fahy Committee Papers, HSTL.

[77] E. W. Kenworthy, "Taps for Jim Crow in the Services," *New York
Times Magazine* (June 11, 1950), 12, 24–27.

[78] *The New York Times*, May 23, 1950.

[79] Memorandum, Kenworthy to Philleo Nash, April 26, 1950; memo-

however, who felt rather strongly about having a watchdog committee over him. Instead, Johnson wanted the services to make semiannual progress reports to his Personnel Policy Board.[80] The President went along with his Secretary of Defense and informed the committee on July 6, 1950, that it was being discontinued: "The necessary programs having been adopted, I feel that the Armed Services should now have an opportunity to work out in detail the procedures which will complete the steps so carefully initiated by the Committee." He was leaving Executive Order 9981 in effect, however, because "at some later date, it may prove desirable to examine the effectuation of your Committee's recommendations."[81]

Had the Fahy Committee really overcome the widespread opposition to integration among the high-ranking officers within the Army? Secretary Gray had committed himself to integration by releasing the new policy in January, 1950. About three weeks after this policy was inaugurated, however, a board of generals that had been appointed somewhat earlier made its report to him. "Amalgamation would place the Negro in a competitive field he is not prepared to face . . . ," and "there would be widespread resentment on the part of most white soldiers with a consequent destruction of combat effectiveness," the generals reported. They had interviewed many officers who had commanded black troops, and "almost without exception they vigorously opposed amalgamation and strongly urged the retention of the Negro unit. This Board concurs."[82] Clearly the civilian leadership had committed the Army to a policy that many officers did not support.

What had the Fahy Committee accomplished? The executive

---

randum, Kenworthy to Fahy, April 28, 1950, Fahy Committee Papers, HSTL.

[80] Memorandum, David Niles to the President, May 22, 1950, Nash Papers, HSTL; memorandum, Kenworthy to Fahy, July 10, 1950, Fahy Committee Papers, HSTL.

[81] President Truman to Fahy, July 6, 1950, Fahy Committee Papers, HSTL.

[82] "Report of the Board of Officers on Utilization of Negro Manpower in the Army to the Secretary of the Army," February 9, 1950, OSA 291.2, NARG 335.

order creating it had provided the impetus for the Air Force to move rapidly to a policy of integration. The committee's examination of the Navy's failure to completely implement a progressive policy led that service to take steps to bring practice in line with policy. The committee's conviction and proof that segregation led to discrimination encouraged it to resist doggedly Army pressure for something less than integration. Important in all of this was the initiative of the President. Truman's issuance of the executive order and his insistence that its purpose was to end segregation weakened resistance in the armed services. Furthermore, the President's backing for all of the Fahy group's recommendations to the Army enabled the committee to overcome the almost total opposition to integration in this service. Throughout this period it was the support of civilian leaders within the military establishment for integration that proved decisive. The significance of the committee's achievements is that at its beginning the Army had an official policy of segregation and at its conclusion the Army was officially committed to integration. Would practice, however, lag far behind policy, as it had in the past?

CHAPTER X

Korea

THE FAHY COMMITTEE was discontinued only after the Army had given up its policy of rigid segregation. Throughout the Army, however, the practice of segregation continued. Many high-ranking officers took the position that integration should be gradual, *very* gradual. Some talked of complete integration coming only after fifty or more years. Clearly, such a delay was not what the President's committee envisioned. The continuing resistance within the Army to integration has led many to conclude that the Fahy Committee had actually accomplished little and that integration came to the Army only as the result of the Korean War.[1] There is no doubt that the Korean War pushed the Army to complete integration much sooner than would have been the case without a war, but this occurred only because of the foundation laid down by the Fahy Committee. Without a policy of rigid segregation to stop them, many commanders in Korea during the first days of the war adopted a policy of assigning desperately needed replacements without regard to race.

E. W. Kenworthy, Executive Secretary of the Fahy Committee, was very pessimistic about the Army's intentions, in the last week of the committee's existence. Six months had passed since the Army had adopted its policy ending complete segregation in January, 1950, and the Army had done little to implement

---

[1] Lee Nichols, *Breakthrough on the Color Front*, 96.

201

this policy. In contrast, the Air Force had integrated over half of its Negro personnel within the first six months of its new policy. "I can only conclude from the little progress that has been made . . . ," Kenworthy wrote Fahy in his last memorandum, "that the Army intends to do as little as possible toward implementing the policy which it adopted and published."[2]

Kenworthy was too pessimistic; the fact that the Army no longer had an official policy barring integration was enough for some Army commanders. Fort Ord, California, had been reactivated in 1949 to train the increasing number of recruits supplied by the new draft law of 1948. In the West, black recruits were comparatively few in number, and maintaining training staffs of forty to sixty men and officers to handle only a few Negroes in separate training companies seemed impracticable. To prevent this inefficiency, officers at Fort Ord took it upon themselves to integrate the training companies. The Department of the Army learned about this action through the newspapers. Although nothing was done to halt the integration at Fort Ord, the Army did not consider this experience a guide for the future, as it was on a small scale and not in the South.[3]

A new element was introduced, however, when the Fahy Committee persuaded the Army to abolish the racial quota in April, 1950. The committee had always insisted that the racial quota maintaining the Army's Negro strength at no more than 10 per cent be abolished because it was discriminatory. Negro enlistments had been 8.2 per cent of the total in March, 1950; without the quota they shot up to 22 per cent of the total in April. By July, 1950, Negro enlistments accounted for 25 per cent of the total. The crux of the matter was that the number of Negro units in the Army was geared to contain a maximum of 10 per cent Negro strength. The only way to maintain segregation with the increasing number of black soldiers was to maintain Negro units at overstrength — place more Negroes in black units than was called for in the tables of organization for those units. But

---

[2] Memorandum, Kenworthy to Fahy, July 25, 1950; see also Kenworthy to Philleo Nash, July 25, 1950, both in Fahy Committee Papers, HSTL.

[3] Nichols, *Breakthrough on the Color Front*, 108–9; Pittsburgh *Courier*, August 26, 1950.

this solution was hard to justify when many white units were actually short of personnel. To solve this problem and maintain segregation, the Personnel and Administration Division (G-1) of the Army General Staff requested in September, 1950, that the racial quota be reinstated and that more black units be established to take care of the Negro overstrength. The request was denied by the Secretary of the Army for the moment.[4]

The racial quota had been the key that allowed segregation to function in an orderly manner in the past. With it, the Army could predict the number of Negroes that would have to be trained and the number of segregated units that would have to be provided. The problem of operating without a quota was made even more difficult, beginning in June, 1950, with the outbreak of the Korean War. Recruits flooded Army training installations, and officials found it impossible to predict the number of each race that would arrive. This situation developed at Fort Jackson, South Carolina, in August, 1950. The post commander found that it was "totally impractical to sort them out" and proposed integration of the training units to solve the problem. When a member of his staff questioned this move as not being in line with Army policy, the post commander pointed to the appropriate wording in the Army statement of January, 1950, as all the authority he needed. The very ambiguity of the Army-Committee compromise worked to the advantage of integration in this case. Here was an example of integration within the South, and it worked. When word of this success story reached the Department of the Army, commanders and the staffs of other training posts were asked to visit Fort Jackson. Soon, all of the Army's basic training was integrated.[5]

The same forces for change were at work in Korea. The garrison troops from Japan originally sent to Korea and the forces later sent from the United States included Negro units. Because of the old practice of assigning Negroes mainly to service or noncombat units, black units at first were stationed mostly behind the lines. As a result, they did not suffer proportionate

---

[4] Memorandum to the Chief of Staff from G-1, September, 1950, CS 291.2, NARG 319.

[5] Nichols, *Breakthrough on the Color Front*, 109–11.

casualties. Furthermore, because of the absence of a racial quota and the large percentage of Negro volunteers, replacement troops sent to Korea contained more Negroes than there were spaces in segregated black units. Assigning black soldiers only to Negro units meant that the percentage overstrength of Negro units in Korea was increasing at the same time that white units were begging for replacements.[6]

The pragmatic solution to this problem was obvious to combat commanders in Korea: Take the excess black soldiers in Negro units and integrate them as replacements in white combat units. The Ninth Infantry Regiment was composed of two white battalions desperately short of men, due to casualties, and one Negro battalion that was 10 per cent overstrength. The regiment's commander reasoned, "We would have been doing ourselves a disservice to permit [Negro] soldiers to lie around in rear areas at the expense of still further weakening our [white] rifle companies." The excess black strength was therefore integrated into the white units. There were no racial incidents, and the Negroes seemed to become better soldiers.[7] Integration also frequently came about in Korea because of the accidental assignment of Negroes as replacements in white units. Because the men were needed, they were not refused on the basis of their color.

The old charges of the unreliability of large all-Negro combat units were revived in Korea, and this also led many officers to recommend integration as the only feasible solution. The all-Negro Twenty-fourth Infantry Regiment, particularly, was cited to prove this point. This unit was charged by one of the battalion commanders with fleeing "like rabbits" before the enemy.[8] Here again, as in World Wars I and II, the truth of the charges against Negro combat units is hard to determine. Many white units fled

---

[6] H. S. Milton, ed., *The Utilization of Negro Manpower in the Army*, 181. This report is the result of "Project Clear," which will be discussed in detail later in this chapter.

[7] Nichols, *Breakthrough on the Color Front*, 111–12.

[8] Harold H. Martin, "How Do Our Negro Troops Measure Up?" *Saturday Evening Post*, 223 (June 16, 1951), 30–31, 139, 141, repeated these charges in arguing that Negroes made better soldiers in integrated units.

"like rabbits" during the first months of the Korean War, but race did not figure in the explanation as it did for black units.[9] On the other hand, Negro units suffered from the same handicaps as in the past — a concentration of poorly educated personnel, low morale, and a tendency for commanders to blame their units' failures on race. The available evidence suggests that the Twenty-fourth Infantry Regiment's performance was a mixture of success and failure.[10] Regardless of the circumstances, General William B. Kean, Commander of the Twenty-fifth Division, of which the Twenty-fourth Infantry was a part, recommended in September, 1950, that this unit be abolished and its black soldiers be integrated throughout other units in Korea. At the same time, he made it clear that he was criticizing Negro units and not Negro soldiers who did well in integrated units.[11]

Although General Kean's request to break up the Twenty-fourth was not acted on immediately, piecemeal integration continued in Korea as individual black soldiers were used for replacements in white units. By January, 1951, Eighth Army Headquarters in Korea had adopted an unofficial policy of integrating the excess strength of Negro units.[12] This action was the result of the reports of the noted military historian General S. L. A. Marshall, who was then serving as Infantry Operations Analyst for the Eighth Army. Marshall had witnessed integrated units in action during the retreat from the Yalu River in November, 1950, and was convinced that integration was

[9] T. R. Fehrenbach, in *This Kind of War*, points out the general unpreparedness of the American soldier at the beginning of the Korean War.

[10] Colonel John T. Corley, former commanding officer of the Twenty-fourth Infantry, gave an interview to the Pittsburgh *Courier* in which he claimed that *The Saturday Evening Post* article cited in note 8 distorted the unit's record by magnifying the failures and overlooking the successes. Pittsburgh *Courier*, June 23, 30, July 7, 1951.

[11] Roy E. Appleman, *United States Army in the Korean War: South to the Naktong, North to the Yalu*, 485–86. The official Army view of the Twenty-fourth Infantry is set forth in Appleman. For a strong dissent from Appleman, see John P. Davis, "The Negro in the Armed Forces of America," in John P. Davis, ed., *The American Negro Reference Book*, 648–52.

[12] Milton, ed., *The Utilization of Negro Manpower*, 182.

successful enough to be extended throughout the Army. "In my opinion," Marshall told the press, "those [integrated] companies handled themselves as efficiently and courageously as any companies in the war."[13]

All officers in Korea, however, were not convinced that integration was the answer to the Army's "Negro problem." S. L. A. Marshall's suggestion that integration be extended was received with a "completely negative view" at General Douglas MacArthur's headquarters in Tokyo. Marshall did not talk to MacArthur personally, but a member of the United Nations Commander's staff told him that Negroes would never make good combat soldiers. In Korea General Edward M. Almond, Commander of the Tenth Corps and a former Commander of the Negro Ninety-second Division during World War II, issued directives to resegregate Negroes that had been successfully integrated in units under his command.[14] By early 1951, then, there was no definite assignment policy for Negroes in Korea. Some units were integrating at the same time that others were attempting to maintain segregation.[15]

The reports of integration and segregation at the same time resulted in a confused reaction in the Negro press. The Pittsburgh *Courier* claimed that the Twenty-fourth Infantry was being "framed" and used as a "scapegoat," and it called for an immediate end to segregation. In the very same issue the *Courier* praised the integration in Army combat units in Korea.[16] The

[13] Nichols, *Breakthrough on the Color Front*, 112–13; *The New York Times*, December 17, 1950.

[14] Nichols, *Breakthrough on the Color Front*, 113–14. In an interview by the Pittsburgh *Courier*, June 2, 1951, after he was relieved by President Truman, General MacArthur claimed that the segregation that existed in his command had been "dictated from Washington." Perhaps MacArthur was unaware of the actions of his staff on this matter. Nichols, p. 14, says that Pentagon officials told him that MacArthur "showed no interest in integration of Negro and white troops." The member of MacArthur's staff who told S.L.A. Marshall that he was opposed to any integration was probably General Almond, at that time MacArthur's Chief of Staff. Norfolk *Journal and Guide*, August 11, 1951.

[15] Milton, ed., *The Utilization of Negro Manpower*, 182.

[16] Pittsburgh *Courier*, September 16, 1950. The earliest mention of

NAACP charged that there was discrimination in courts-martial of black soldiers in Korea. Thurgood Marshall, the chief lawyer for the NAACP, went to Korea to investigate.[17] Negro leaders called upon the President to end segregation in the Army at once.[18] Negroes were obviously not aware of the extent of the revolution occurring within the Army in Korea.

There was also confusion within the Pentagon as integration continued at a faster pace both in training units in the United States and in combat units in Korea. In February, 1951, a special board of three general officers was created to consider the best use of the Army's Negro manpower in the light of the integration experience in Korea. This board granted that statements from the integrated combat units indicated that integration was a success and that Negro-white friction actually decreased. The generals had serious reservations, however, about the continued absence of a racial quota and the resulting increase of Negroes in the Army. They feared that the increased number of black soldiers within the Army could not be assimilated and that the increased number of poorly educated Negroes would dangerously reduce the fighting efficiency of combat units. The board concluded on a negative note: The racial quota should be reinstituted and segregated units should be maintained. The Army General Staff was divided over whether the board's recommendations should be approved.[19]

Seeking further guidance about the course to follow, the Personnel and Administration Division (G-1) of the Army Staff asked for the opinions of twenty-two officers and two civilian officials who had had recent experience with integration. Most of these were cautious in agreeing that Korea furnished only a limited test of integration, but the general conclusion of the majority was that integration furnished the most effective way to utilize Negro soldiers. Seventeen of the officers favored com-

integration in Korea in the Negro press is Pittsburgh *Courier*, July 29, 1950.

[17] Pittsburgh *Courier*, January 6, February 24, 1951.

[18] Pittsburgh *Courier*, January 6, 20, 1951; Norfolk *Journal and Guide*, March 10, 1951; *The New York Times*, March 1, 1951.

[19] Milton, ed., *The Utilization of Negro Manpower*, 568.

plete integration and only two were in favor of maintaining complete segregation.[20] Clearly the spontaneous integration occurring within the Army was changing the views of many officers.

Liberal congressmen added their voices to those of Negroes and of officers who were calling for a definite end to segregation. Senators Hubert H. Humphrey of Minnesota and Herbert H. Lehman of New York led a group of congressmen who called upon the Army and the Defense departments to end segregation once and for all. Defense officials informed these congressmen that integration of the Army was being gradually accomplished in Korea and in basic training. But Senator Humphrey thought the experience of the Air Force and Navy indicated that integration of the Army could move faster. "You've got to decide who you want trouble with, the southerners or us," he told officials.[21] After satisfactory assurances were given, the liberal congressmen agreed to keep integration out of the public arena in return for periodic progress reports.[22]

Another problem pushing the civilian officials of the Department of the Army toward a definite stand in favor of integration was the increasing waste of manpower in the overstrength all-Negro units. In early 1951 Assistant Secretary of the Army Earl D. Johnson expressed alarm over the fact that the overstrength in some Negro units had reached as high as 62 per cent. This was indefensible, since there was a shortage of personnel throughout Korea. The obvious solution was to take the

[20] Milton, ed., *The Utilization of Negro Manpower*, 582.
[21] Quoted in Nichols, *Breakthrough on the Color Front*, 137.
[22] Memorandum, Chief of Staff General J. Lawton Collins for the Assistant Chief of Staff, G-1, March 1, 1951, SD 291.2, NARG 330; memorandum for the record by Major M. O. Becker, March 13, 1951, G-1 291.2, NARG 319; Assistant Secretary of Defense to Senator Herbert Lehman, June 26, 1951, and July 23, 1951, and Senator Humphrey to Assistant Secretary of Defense, July 11, 30, 1951, all in OASD 291.2, NARG 330. Democratic senators associated with Humphrey and Lehman in pressuring Defense officials were: Paul H. Douglas of Illinois, William H. Benton of Connecticut, Harley M. Kilgore and Matthew M. Neely of West Virginia, Warren G. Magnuson of Washington, and John Pastore of Rhode Island.

excess Negro strength and distribute it throughout the other units of the Army. "If non-segregation works as well as it has in certain units, I can see no good reason why it should not work for other units," Johnson told Secretary of the Army Frank Pace.[23]

Whereas the Army General Staff had earlier used the over-strength of Negro units as an argument for reimposing the Negro quota and thereby strengthening segregation, Johnson used the overstrength problem to argue for complete integration. The Army General Staff and General Mark Clark, Commander of the Army Field Forces, took the position that the integration in Korea had not been proven a definite success and continued to argue that the best way to reduce the overstrength in Negro units was to reimpose the racial quota. Secretary Pace followed Johnson's recommendation, however, and refused to reimpose the quota for the time being.[24]

Integration continued to spread both in Korea and in training divisions at home in the spring of 1951. Although still indecisive about an over-all policy, the Pentagon did acquiesce in the integration of all basic training within the United States and announced that this had been accomplished on March 18, 1951.[25] The mixture of integration and segregation was as confusing as ever, however. Many Negroes received integrated basic training but were later assigned to segregated units. If integration worked in combat units in Korea and in basic training, why did not the Army adopt integration as a general policy and abolish all remaining segregated units, Negroes reasoned. It was "integration in slow motion," the Pittsburgh *Courier* claimed in frustration.[26]

Acting as deliberately as ever in adopting a new racial policy,

[23] Memorandum, Secretary Johnson to Pace, April 3, 1951, G-1 291.2, NARG 319.

[24] Memorandum, Secretary Johnson to Secretary Pace, n.d. [May or June], 1951, CS 291.2, NARG 319.

[25] *The New York Times,* March 19, 1951.

[26] Pittsburgh *Courier,* March 31, 1951. The Pittsburgh *Courier* sent a reporter to various military installations in 1951, and he reported on the mixture of segregation and integration. For example, see the issues of April 7, 14, 21, 28, May 12, June 9, 1951.

the Army called in a team of social scientists in March, 1951, to study the effects of integration and segregation upon the Army. This undertaking was known by the code name of "Project Clear." Research teams, under the direction of the Operations Research Office of The Johns Hopkins University, began by conducting surveys in Korea, Japan, and ten Army posts in the United States. A preliminary report was promised in July, 1951, and a final one in November, 1951. Until this information was in, the Army adopted the position that it was moving toward complete integration, but "the advance would have to be taken cautiously." [27]

Meanwhile, the officers in Korea who had experienced integration knew that it worked. General Matthew B. Ridgway was one of these officers, and soon after he replaced General MacArthur as Far Eastern Commander in April, 1951, he requested that the Pentagon allow him to integrate all Negroes within his command. Approximately two months passed while the various sections of the General Staff studied the proposal and finally approved. Army Chief of Staff General J. Lawton Collins and Assistant Secretary of the Army Earl D. Johnson convinced the powerful Southerners on the House and Senate Armed Services Committee, particularly Senator Richard Russell and Representative Carl Vinson of Georgia, that integration was in the interest of efficiency. Secretary Frank Pace, Jr., got the approval of the President. [28] A big factor in the willingness of the Pentagon to give General Ridgway the approval he needed was the preliminary report of Project Clear, proclaiming inte-

[27] These are the words of Secretary Pace in memorandum for the record, June 9, 1951, OASD 291.2, NARG 330. H. S. Milton, ed., *The Utilization of Negro Manpower*, is the final report of Project Clear. This study remained classified until recently and is still not readily available. For convenient summaries of this report, see Alfred H. Hausrath, "Utilization of Negro Manpower in the Army," *Journal of the Operations Research Society of America*, 2 (February, 1954), 17–30; Leo Bogart, "The Army and Its Negro Soldiers," *The Reporter*, 11 (December 30, 1954), 8–11; Paul B. Foreman, "The Implications of Project Clear," *Phylon*, 16 (September, 1955), 263–74.

[28] Memorandum, the Acting Chief of Staff to Secretary Pace, May 28, 1951, OSA 291.2, NARG 335.

gration to be an unqualified success and recommending that it be extended Army-wide. On July 26, 1951, the Army announced publicly that integration would be completed in about six months in Japan, Korea, and Okinawa and that the all-Negro Twenty-fourth Infantry was being disbanded.[29]

The Army was anxious about the reception of the Korean announcement in the South. Actually, only a few major Southern papers commented on it editorially, and not always unfavorably. Southern congressmen had made only half-hearted attempts to turn back the tide of integration. A few weeks before the beginning of the Korean War, Senator Russell of Georgia had attached an amendment to the draft extension bill calling for soldiers to be allowed a choice of whether or not they would serve in integrated units. Administration forces, however, led the fight that defeated this amendment rather handily.[30] Arthur Krock of *The New York Times* claimed that the defeat of the Russell amendment reflected the belief of most of the country that "establishing racial inferiority among Americans who have assumed the risk of dying for their country . . . is a system as repugnant to decency as to democracy."[31]

In the spring of 1951 Representative Arthur Winstead of Mississippi had introduced an amendment similar to Russell's in the House. This one was also easily defeated.[32] The successful integration that had already taken place within the armed services left the Southerners divided. Representative Carl Vinson of Georgia, the powerful Chairman of the House Armed Services Committee, for example, requested that the Defense Department furnish him with a statement in opposition to the Winstead amendment based on military grounds rather than "social reasons."[33] By the time of the announcement in July, high military and civilian officials of the Army had done a good job

[29] Milton, ed., *The Utilization of Negro Manpower*, viii; *The New York Times*, July 27, 1951.

[30] *The New York Times*, June 9, 22, 1950.

[31] *The New York Times*, June 23, 1950.

[32] *The New York Times*, April 13, 1951.

[33] Memorandum, Office of Legislative Liaison to Assistant Secretary of Defense Rosenberg, March 17, 1951, G-1 291.2, NARG 319.

of convincing the Southerners. Buoyed by the preliminary report of Project Clear, the officials argued that the demands of efficiency required integration. To impress the Southerners further, the point was made that segregation meant that whites experienced more than their share of casualties in Korea. Most of the important Southern congressmen adopted the attitude that integration had come to the armed forces, and they remained silent.[34]

The announcement that all Negro soldiers in the Far East would be integrated into the service was generally well received by Negroes. The end of the Twenty-fourth Infantry was looked upon with a "twinge of regret" by the Pittsburgh *Courier*, but this was "definitely a new deal in the armed forces with complete integration becoming more and more an actuality."[35] The Norfolk *Journal and Guide* praised the Army's action, but pointed out that there was still segregation in the Army to be eliminated.[36] The men of the Twenty-fourth Infantry had no regrets about the break-up of their unit and were elated over integration. Those Negro soldiers who had not been home since the beginning of the war wondered if there had been improvements in race relations there commensurate with those they had experienced in the Army.[37]

Unauthorized integration continued to spread to other areas outside of the Far East as commanders, on their own initiative, solved the problem of overstrength Negro units by integrating the excess black soldiers into white units that were generally understrength.[38] When the hitherto dreaded racial conflict did not develop, these commanders urged the Department of the Army to allow them to adopt an official policy of complete inte-

[34] Nichols, *Breakthrough on the Color Front*, 115, 135–36, 140–41.
[35] Pittsburgh *Courier*, August 4, 1951.
[36] Norfolk *Journal and Guide*, August 11, 1951.
[37] Norfolk *Journal and Guide*, August 11, 1951.
[38] Some idea of the extent of this unauthorized integration is indicated by the fact that by August, 1951, 270 Regular Army units had experienced a degree of integration. See Assistant Chief of Staff, G-1, to the Chief of Staff and Secretary of the Army, December 29, 1951, and memorandum, Manpower Control Division, G-1, to General Taylor, September 6, 1951, both in G-1 291.2, NARG 319.

gration. The Commander of the Sixth Army Area, the West Coast, wrote the Pentagon that it was his conviction and experience that "the reaction to integrating colored personnel into white units will be negligible . . . ," and he concluded that "the eventual solution of this continuing problem of the Army is gradual integration."[39] If allowed to establish a policy of integration, the Commanding Officer of the United States Army, Alaska, felt this would "evolve into a harmonious system of full and complete utilization of available manpower based on individual effectiveness on the job and no other consideration."[40] As cautious as ever, the Pentagon informed these commanders that general integration would have to wait until after study of the Project Clear final report, due in November.[41]

Project Clear's social scientists found that black soldiers performed better in integrated than in segregated units. This was the conclusion of the majority of officers with experience in integrated units in Korea. Of these officers, 76 per cent rated Negroes as just about as good fighters as white soldiers; 80 per cent believed that the same Negro would perform better in an integrated unit; six of seven believed that the Negro and white soldier stood up in battle about the same. Officers who expressed opinions contrary to these were usually those who had not had experience in integrated units. White noncommissioned officers and enlisted men exhibited the same range of attitudes, depending on whether or not they had had experience in an integrated unit. The Negro soldier was generally accepted when he was seen as part of the team, but he aroused criticism when viewed as part of a separate group. The expected violent conflict and opposition to integration by white soldiers did not materialize; instead, integration was accepted as the Army's way of doing things.[42]

[39] General J. M. Swing to General A. C. McAuliffe, Assistant Chief of Staff, G-1, September 10, 1951, G-1 291.2, NARG 319.
[40] General J. W. Cunningham to the Department of the Army, September 15, 1951, G-1 291.2, NARG 319.
[41] G-1 to General J. W. Cunningham, October 22, 1951, G-1 291.2, NARG 319.
[42] Milton, ed., *The Utilization of Negro Manpower*, 4, 104, 139.

Integration also solved old problems that had plagued segregated Negro units. Of the Army's black soldiers 62 per cent made low scores on educational tests, as compared with 33 per cent of the white soldiers. With integration, the low-scoring Negro soldiers could be spread out rather than concentrated into a few units. Integration also improved standards of leadership because all officers and noncommissioned officers were judged by the same standards. In the past, white officers of Negro units tended to attribute all of their units' problems to race; integration created a situation in which officers regarded their problems as military ones. Furthermore, experience indicated that under integration officers of both races were accepted across racial lines on the basis of merit. Low morale had been a constant problem with black soldiers who had objected to segregation; since Negro soldiers were overwhelmingly in favor of integration, their morale was raised. At the same time the morale of white soldiers was not affected by bringing Negroes into their units. Although the average Negro soldier was culturally handicapped when compared to the average white soldier, his "efforts are stimulated when he feels he and the white are equal members of the same team."[43]

These findings reflected the acceptance of a new experience under the pressure of combat conditions. What were the results in the less demanding atmosphere of the United States? Integration had been just as successful where it was applied in the United States. Integration of recreational facilities and activities did not present major problems, even in the South. Integration on military installations was generally considered by local civilians as having little impact on their private lives. In the South, where close social relationships between the races were frowned upon, both white and Negro soldiers appeared to conform to local customs informally off the post.[44]

Project Clear also emphasized an old problem — there was great confusion and ignorance throughout the Army about the official policy toward Negroes. An investigation indicated that

[43] Milton, ed., *The Utilization of Negro Manpower*, 4, 209, 265–69.
[44] Milton, ed., *The Utilization of Negro Manpower*, 5, 313–14, 410–11.

few post commanders actually knew the Army's policy on the Negro, and interpretations ranged all the way from complete segregation to complete integration. Although this was partly because of the Army's past lack of vigor in implementing its policy, confusion was also created by the fact that in 1951 the Army contained both segregated and integrated units. The great majority of the white soldiers serving in integrated units thought Army policy was integration; on the other hand, those whites serving in segregated units thought the Army's policy was one of segregation. In short, men generally believed the Army policy was whatever they experienced. This explained, in part, why integration was accepted where it had taken place and opposed where segregation remained the rule.[45]

The conclusions of Project Clear were that "the continued existence of racial segregation limits the effectiveness of the Army" and that "integration enhances the effectiveness of the Army." The success of integration where it was tried indicated that Army units could be composed of a maximum of 15 to 20 per cent black personnel. The social scientists recommended, therefore, that "the Army should commit itself to a policy of full and complete integration to be carried out as rapidly as operational efficiency permits."[46]

Project Clear ended most of the remaining opposition to integration among the Army General Staff.[47] In a conference called by the Department of the Army in December, 1951, the United States and Alaskan Army commanders were ordered to proceed with the orderly integration of all units under their command. No timetable was set, but they were informed that it was the Secretary of the Army's desire that integration should be completed within the next few years.[48] Secretary of the Army Pace

---

[45] Milton, ed., *The Utilization of Negro Manpower*, 401–9.

[46] Milton, ed., *The Utilization of Negro Manpower*, 5–6.

[47] Memorandum, the Assistant Chief of Staff, G-1, to the Chief of Staff and Secretary of the Army, December 29, 1951, G-1 291.2, NARG 319; memorandum, G-1 to the Chief of Staff, January 5, 1952, CS 291.2, NARG 319.

[48] Nichols, *Breakthrough on the Color Front*, 132–33; "Proposed letter to all major commanders from the Chief of Staff," December, 1951, G-1 291.2, NARG 319.

had earlier granted the request of the Commander of the United
States Forces, Austria, to integrate his forces.[49] By the end of
1951 the only major Army command not pursuing an active
policy of integration was United States Army, Europe (France
and Germany).

After World War II, advances in Army racial policy had been
slow to be realized in Europe. As late as April, 1949, a Negro
reporter touring European Army posts found that "integration
policies and programs talked about in Washington are scarcely
heard of in Europe."[50] As Europe was on the front line of the
Cold War, segregated American military forces proved to be
embarrassing confirmation of Communist propaganda. The
experience of Claude Barnett, Director of the Associated Negro
Press, was not uncommon for American Negroes touring Europe. He wrote the Secretary of the Army that

Europeans and members of our own diplomatic staffs in Germany
and Scandinavia told me that the policy of the . . . Army was one
of the greatest handicaps they had to meet in seeking to present the
value and sincerity of democracy as practiced in the United States.[51]

By early 1952, Negroes were disturbed over the fact that integration was taking place rapidly everywhere but in Europe.
Even after information was leaked from the Pentagon that segregation was on its way out in Europe, Collins George, correspondent for the Pittsburgh *Courier*, found that officers in
Europe knew nothing about the change in policy. Furthermore,
George found segregation at all of the Army installations that
he visited in Europe.[52]

The United States Army, Europe, was slow to integrate because of the opposition of its Commander, General Thomas T.
Handy. In the summer of 1951 Dr. Eli Ginzberg of Columbia
University, a consultant for the Army on manpower problems,
was directed to go to Europe and inform General Handy and

---

[49] Nichols, *Breakthrough on the Color Front*, 127–28.
[50] P. L. Prattis in the Pittsburgh *Courier*, April 9, 1949.
[51] Barnett to Secretary Pace, February 23, 1952, CS 291.2, NARG 319.
On this point also, see Raymond Pace Alexander, "The Negro Soldier in
the United States Army," 1950, OF 93, HSTL.
[52] Pittsburgh *Courier*, March 8, 15, 22, 29, 1952.

his staff that the Army had decided to end segregation and that General Handy should prepare a plan to accomplish this decision. Upon his arrival, Dr. Ginzberg told each senior officer with whom he came in contact that it was necessary to begin integration in Europe. "With almost no exception," Ginzberg found, however, these officers refused to believe that the Pentagon actually wanted to end segregation. When informed of the integration taking place in Korea and the United States, many of these officers refused to believe that Ginzberg had correct information. The few officers willing to believe that integration had succeeded under combat conditions in Korea felt that this experience was not typical and did not prove anything with regard to the Army in Europe. The general conclusion of these officers was that integration would come eventually, "but surely not in less than a hundred years."[53]

When Ginzberg reported to the Pentagon, he concluded that it would be necessary to "push" General Handy. This is exactly what the Department of the Army did. In the fall of 1951, General J. Lawton Collins, Chief of Staff, visited Germany and told the commanders what was expected. Shortly after returning to Washington, General Collins, knowing no such plan existed, requested General Handy's integration plan. The European command submitted a proposal in December, 1951, but with several provisions that the Pentagon thought were unsatisfactory. For example, General Handy wanted to integrate only Negro combat units; since the majority of Negroes were in service units, most black soldiers in Europe would remain segregated. The Department of the Army directed that service units must also be integrated, and it made several other suggestions that had the effect of liberalizing General Handy's plan. Integration began in Europe on the first of April, 1952.[54]

Meanwhile, military segregation became a political issue for

---

[53] Eli Ginzberg to Lieutenant Colonel Edward J. Barta, Historical Division, U.S. Army, Europe, n.d., copy in the possession of Dr. Ginzberg, Columbia University.

[54] Nichols, *Breakthrough on the Color Front*, 128–30; Ronald Sher, *Integration of Negro and White Troops in the U.S. Army, Europe 1952–1954*, 11–12.

the last time in the campaign of 1952. Negroes remembered General Eisenhower's statement supporting segregation before the Senate Armed Services Committee in 1948. Some Negro Republicans opposed his nomination because of this statement, and during the campaign Negroes continually asked Eisenhower about his stand on segregation while he was in the Army.[55] President Truman took advantage of this suspicion in his campaigning for Adlai Stevenson. "While the Republican candidate was in uniform," Truman told a Harlem audience, "he told the Armed Services Committee of the Senate that a certain amount of segregation is necessary in the Army. You and I know that this is morally wrong. And what's more, it's even militarily wrong."[56] Eisenhower and his campaign strategists sought to counter this handicap by claiming that he had actually started integration within the Army. As a general, Eisenhower had favored a lessening of the degree of segregation by placing Negro platoons in white companies, for example. Although he had nothing to do with beginning integration, candidate Eisenhower continually conveyed this impression in his statements on the subject.[57]

Actually, the degree of segregation in the armed forces was rapidly diminishing as the 1952 campaign ended. Integration was proceeding in Europe faster than expected, and by September, 1953, the Army announced that 90 per cent of its Negro strength was serving in integrated units. From a high of 385 all-Negro units in June, 1950, there were only 88 in August, 1953.[58] Integration of the Army was practically complete by October, 1953, when it was announced that 95 per cent of the

[55] *The New York Times*, April 5, July 4, August 5, 1952; Norfolk *Journal and Guide*, June 14, 1952; Pittsburgh *Courier*, October 11, 1952.

[56] *The New York Times*, October 18, 1952. This line was repeated by Truman during the campaign. See *The New York Times*, June 14, October 30, 1952.

[57] *The New York Times*, June 13, October 26, 1952; Norfolk *Journal and Guide*, June 14, 1952; Pittsburgh *Courier*, November 1, 1952.

[58] *The New York Times*, September 13, 1953. For an interesting description of how the integration of one particular unit was accomplished in Europe, see Ernest Leiser, "For Negroes, It's a New Army Now," *The Saturday Evening Post*, 225 (December 13, 1952), 26–27, 108, 110–12.

black soldiers were integrated.[59] A quiet racial revolution had occurred with practically no violence, bloodshed, or conflict.

The foresight of the Fahy Committee's recommendations, particularly the removal of the racial quota, had much to do with the spontaneous integration that took place before and after the beginning of the Korean War. The war, with its casualties and consequent needs for replacements, led the combat commanders in the field to adopt the only sensible course — integrate available Negro manpower. The success of this spontaneous integration generated support for a policy of integration. With Project Clear's enthusiastic support for such a policy, the top Army leadership was finally convinced that it was time to join the social revolutionaries.

[59] *The New York Times*, October 13, 1953.

Epilogue

B Y THE END OF 1954, segregation and discrimination were virtually eliminated from the internal organization of the active military forces. Integration and equal treatment was the official policy in such on-base facilities as swimming pools, chapels, barbershops, post exchanges, movie theaters, and dependents' housing as well as in the more direct military areas of assignment and promotion. Military life had developed a unique interracial character unlike that found in the other major institutions of American society. Despite this achievement, however, there remained areas where military life touched the surrounding off-post civilian communities and where discrimination and segregation remained the rule. This was especially true in civilian housing and in schools surrounding military bases. In addition, there remained a problem with the National Guard of several states.[1]

During the Administration of President Eisenhower, the Department of Defense took the position that military integration was an accomplished fact and largely ignored the peripheral areas where discrimination continued.[2] Not until President John F. Kennedy's appointment in June, 1962, of the President's

---

[1] For a recent assessment of military integration, see Charles C. Moskos, Jr., "Racial Integration in the Armed Forces," *American Journal of Sociology*, 72 (September, 1966), 132–48.

[2] United States Commission on Civil Rights, *Employment: 1961 Report*, Book 3, 48–53.

Committee on Equal Opportunity in the Armed Forces, popu-
larly known as the Gesell Committee after its chairman Ger-
hard A. Gesell, did these remaining problem areas receive
adequate attention from the Federal Government.[3] The President was specific in directing the Gesell group to spend a major
portion of its time determining steps that the government could
take "to improve equality of opportunity for members of the
Armed Forces and their dependents in the civilian community,
particularly with respect to housing, education, transportation,
recreational facilities, community events, programs and activities."[4]

The Gesell Committee found that on-base government family
housing was sufficient to house only about half the married
servicemen. Half of all military families — considerably more,
in some installations — thus lived in off-base civilian housing in
communities near the servicemen's place of duty. The armed
forces were even more remiss in failing to provide on-post schools
for military dependents, and the overwhelming majority of
servicemen's children attended the local public school system
whether they lived on or off base. The results were obvious.
Since discrimination because of race in housing was a fact of
life regardless of the section of the country, the black service-
man was forced to live in that part of town reserved for Negroes — the most expensive, dirty, and dilapidated housing
available. Furthermore, Negro dependents were forced to attend
segregated, and usually inferior, schools, especially in the South.
The impact of such conditions on the black soldiers' morale was
profound: "To all Negroes these community conditions are a
constant reminder that the society they are prepared to defend
is a society that deprecates their right to full participation as
citizens," the Gesell Committee stated.[5]

[3] The other members of the committee were Nathaniel Colley, Abe
Fortas, Louis J. Hector, Benjamin Muse, John H. Sengstacke, and
Whitney M. Young, Jr.
[4] The President's Committee on Equal Opportunity in the Armed
Forces, *Initial Report* (mimeographed, June 13, 1963), 1.
[5] President's Committee, *Initial Report*, 45–52, 75–84. For more on
the problem of off-post discrimination, see Ruth and Edward Brecher,

The President's committee concluded its *Initial Report* with the suggestion that the Federal Government use its full power to eliminate these off-base morale-crippling practices. With President Kennedy's backing, Secretary of Defense Robert McNamara announced his support for ending such discrimina- tion in a policy statement issued to each of the armed services. Furthermore, McNamara implied the possibility of imposing sanctions, such as declaring off-limits all public places and housing that persisted in discriminating against Negro person- nel. Southern congressmen and senators immediately charged that any such action by the government would be "economic blackmail" and a "direct invasion of local affairs." Perhaps as a result of this pressure from Southerners, the Department of Defense delayed using its ultimate power in civilian commu- nities. Beginning in June, 1967, however, the Defense Depart- ment began declaring off-limits civilian housing that discrimi- nated on the basis of race.[6] The armed forces thus continue to play a significant part in the Federal Government's role as guarantor of equality for Negro Americans.

In 1964 the Gesell Committee found one segment of the armed forces that had not been fully integrated — the National Guard. In the past, Southern states in particular denied Negroes the opportunity to serve in the National Guard, or provided segregated units. By the time the President's committee dug into the matter, most of these states, anticipating criticism, had eliminated the formal restrictions and provided for token inte- gration. But tokenism was no longer enough. The Gesell Com- mittee pointed out that over 90 per cent of the National Guard's financial support comes from the Federal Government, and since the Defense Department's policy was one of equal opportu-

"The Military's Limited War Against Segregation," *Harper's Magazine*, 217 (September, 1963), 79–92.

[6] For Secretary McNamara's actions and the Southerners' reactions, see John P. Davis, "The Negro in the Armed Forces of America," in Davis, ed., *The American Negro Reference Book*, 658–60; "The Penta- gon Jumps into the Race Fight," *U.S. News and World Report*, 55 (August 19, 1963), 49–50; "Georgia's Vinson: Battling the Pentagon," *U.S. News and World Report*, 55 (September 30, 1963), 16; *The New York Times*, January 28, July 14, 1964, August 27, 1967.

nity and integration, federal support should be withdrawn from the Guard of any state that refused to comply.[7]

By January, 1965, President Lyndon Johnson informed his Secretary of Defense that all discrimination against Negroes in the Guard must be ended. Accordingly, Secretary McNamara issued a twenty-six-page directive detailing the action to be taken — cutting off of federal funds — against the National Guard of any state that persisted in denying equal opportunity. By mid-1965, the full weight of federal authority was on the side of equality in the last stronghold of internal military discrimination. Actual integration of the National Guard continued at a slow pace, however. After the Guard's role in the summer riots of 1967, the spotlight was turned on once again. The President's Commission on Civil Disorders publicly lamented the fact that Negroes made up only 1.15 per cent of the Army National Guard and 0.6 per cent of the Air National Guard.[8]

The conclusion that the United States armed forces are the most integrated institution in American society today is inescapable. This fact, together with the Vietnam War and the black nationalism current among today's Negro radicals, however, poses a number of ironies. The Vietnam conflict is constantly labeled "the most integrated war in American history," a fact that must result in a feeling of a job well done by the Negro radicals of yesterday whose slogan was "the fight for the right to fight." But the black radicals of today charge that the war and the military are too integrated, that Negro soldiers are doing more than their share of dying. Negro soldiers, Stokely Carmichael of the Student Nonviolent Coordinating Commit-

---

[7] The President's Committee on Equal Opportunity in the Armed Forces, *Final Report* (mimeographed, November, 1964), 12–22. Also see Isham G. Newton, "The Negro in the National Guard," *Phylon*, 23 (First Quarter, 1962), 18–28; *The New York Times*, May 10, December 30, 1964.

[8] *The New York Times*, January 9, March 31, April 1, 1965; for criticism of the Guard by the Commission on Civil Disorders, see *The New York Times*, August 11, 1967; William A. McWhirter, "The National Guard — Awake or Asleep?" *Life*, 63 (October 27, 1967), 85–98, reveals a vicious anti-Negro prejudice in some of the National Guard units he infiltrated.

tee and Floyd McKissick of the Congress of Racial Equality proclaim, are "black mercenaries" of a white government fighting against their colored brothers in Vietnam. They call upon the young Negro to resist the draft.[9]

Certainly part of this indictment is a reflection of the general radical and liberal opposition to United States involvement in Vietnam. But the black radical's claim that the military is too integrated has some basis in fact. Comprising 11 per cent of the population, Negroes are only 9.5 per cent of all the armed forces. In Vietnam, however, black soldiers are 14.5 per cent of the combat units and 22.4 per cent of all troops killed in action.[10] The Negro radical of today also finds cause for complaint when he examines the draft statistics: Negroes make up approximately 13.4 per cent of all the draftees inducted. This is especially galling to the radicals because, as of May, 1967, only 1.3 per cent of all local draft board members were Negroes, and there was not a single black member on the draft boards in Alabama, Arkansas, Louisiana, and Mississippi.[11]

There are logical reasons why Negroes make up a larger percentage of the draft, the combat forces, and the battle deaths. The primary cause for the high number of draftees among Negroes is the fact that they do not occupy the position in American life that makes them eligible for deferment. Negroes do not get their share of the college deferments, for example, because relatively few have the opportunity to attend college. The high percentage of Negroes in the combat forces and the resulting high number of battle deaths is explained by the fact that Negroes like the military as a career. This is illustrated by the high re-enlistment rate — approximately 45 per cent black as compared with 17 per cent white. Black Americans are definitely aware that the military is the most integrated institution in

---

[9] For representative statements of Carmichael and McKissick, see *The New York Times*, July 2, 26, 1966.

[10] *The New York Times*, March 5, 1967. For other statistics, see "Only One Color," *Newsweek*, 66 (December 6, 1965), 42–43; "Integrated Society," *Time*, 88 (December 23, 1966), 22; Gene Grove, "The Army and the Negro," *New York Times Magazine* (July 24, 1966), 4–5, 49–51.

[11] *The New York Times*, May 4, 1967.

American life. Recent opinion polls indicate that by a margin of 2 to 1, Negro civilians believe they get a better chance in the services than in civilian life. Furthermore, the black soldier volunteers for hazardous duty in Vietnam because it means extra money, faster promotions, higher status, and a chance to prove himself. Contrary to what the black radicals might hope, the great majority of Negro soldiers and civilians are not angry about carrying a heavy load in Vietnam.[12] The sad truth of this situation is the fact that the best opportunity American society provides for many Negroes to get ahead in life can only be taken by risking one's life.

The thinking of today's black militants is not entirely different from that of the past. In March, 1967, General Lewis B. Hershey, Director of the Selective Service System, was forced from the stage of Howard University by students shouting "America is the black man's battleground." This has been a constant theme of Negroes opposing the Vietnam War, and it recalls the black opposition to American involvement in World War II and the double victory attitude prevalent during that war.[13] There is a double irony here, too. Many of the Negro soldiers now serving in Vietnam, like those who served before them in World Wars I and II, are not likely to be happy with anything less than first-class citizenship when they return home. One black sergeant stated the matter bluntly: "When I get back, I'm as good as any son of a bitch in the States." Those who have talked with the Negro servicemen in Asia find the primary question on their minds to be what treatment can they expect when they return.[14] Thus the black radical is likely to find his demands for increased militancy in the struggle for civil rights reinforced by the very war he denounces. No

[12] This paragraph is based on opinion survey results in William Brink and Louis Harris, *Black and White: A Study of U.S. Racial Attitudes Today*, 162–75.

[13] For the Howard University incident, see *The New York Times*, March 22, 1967.

[14] Brink and Harris, *Black and White*, 175; Whitney M. Young, Jr., "When the Negroes in Vietnam Come Home," *Harper's Magazine*, 234 (June, 1967), 63–69.

less ironical is the position of white society. By structuring a situation whereby the Negro finds his best chance for equal opportunity in the military services, white America has produced a powerful force that is working to destroy the racial barriers it is so reluctant to pull down on its own volition.

Bibliography

A. MANUSCRIPT COLLECTIONS

Army General Staff Papers. National Archives Record Group 319, Washington, D.C.

Oscar Chapman Papers. Harry S Truman Library, Independence, Missouri.

Jonathan Daniels Papers. University of North Carolina Library, Chapel Hill, North Carolina.

James V. Forrestal Papers. Princeton University Library, Princeton, New Jersey.

J. Howard McGrath Papers. Harry S Truman Library, Independence, Missouri.

Charles R. Murphy Papers. Harry S Truman Library, Independence, Missouri.

Philleo Nash Papers. Harry S Truman Library, Independence, Missouri.

Howard W. Odum Papers. University of North Carolina Library, Chapel Hill, North Carolina.

Office of Facts and Figures Papers. National Archives Record Group 208, Washington, D.C.

Office of War Information Papers. National Archives Record Group 44, Washington, D.C.

Personnel Policy Board Papers. National Archives Record Group 330, Washington, D.C.

President's Committee on Equality of Treatment and Opportunity in the Armed Services Papers. Harry S Truman Library, Independence, Missouri.

Franklin D. Roosevelt Papers. Franklin D. Roosevelt Library, Hyde Park, New York.

Rosenwald Fund Papers. Fisk University Library, Nashville, Tennessee.

Secretary of the Army and Assistant Secretary of the Army Papers. National Archives Record Group 335, Washington, D.C.

Secretary of Defense and Assistant Secretary of Defense Papers. National Archives Record Group 330, Washington, D.C.

Secretary of War and Assistant Secretary of War Papers. National Archives Record Group 335, Washington, D.C.

Stephen J. Spingarn Papers. Harry S Truman Library, Independence, Missouri.

Henry L. Stimson Diary. Yale University Library, New Haven, Connecticut.

Harry S Truman Papers. Harry S Truman Library, Independence, Missouri.

B. Public Documents

Appleman, Roy E., *United States Army in the Korean War: South to the Naktong, North to the Yalu.* Washington, D.C., United States Government Printing Office, 1961.

Geis, Margaret L., *Negro Personnel in the European Command: 1 January 1946 to 30 June 1950.* Historical Division, European Command, 1952.

Nelson, Dennis D., *The Integration of the Negro into the United States Navy, 1776–1947.* Washington, D.C., Department of the Navy Publication NAVEXOS-P-526, 1948.

The President's Committee on Civil Rights, *To Secure These Rights.* Washington, D.C., United States Government Printing Office, 1947.

The President's Committee on Equal Opportunity in the Armed Forces, *Initial Report.* Mimeographed. June 13, 1963.

———, *Final Report.* Mimeographed. November, 1964.

The President's Committee on Equality of Treatment and Opportunity in the Armed Services, *Freedom to Serve.* Washington, D.C., United States Government Printing Office, 1950.

Public Papers of the Presidents of the United States, Harry S Truman, 1945, 1946, 1947, 1951. Washington, D.C., United States Government Printing Office, 1961, 1962, 1962, 1965.

Selective Service System, *Special Groups: Special Monograph No. 10.* Washington, D.C., United States Government Printing Office, 1953.

Sher, Ronald, *Integration of Negro and White Personnel in the U.S.*

Army, Europe, 1952–1954. Historical Division, Headquarters, United States Army, Europe, 1956.

United States Commission on Civil Rights, *Employment: 1961 Report.* Washington, D.C., United States Government Printing Office, 1961.

U.S. *Congressional Record*, 76th Congress, 3d Session, 1940.

U.S. *Congressional Record*, 78th Congress, 2d Session, 1944.

U.S. *Congressional Record*, 80th Congress, 2d Session, 1948.

United States Senate, Committee on Armed Services, *Hearings . . . on Universal Military Training.* Washington, D.C., United States Government Printing Office, 1948.

Wiley, Major Bell Irvin, *The Training of Negro Troops.* Washington, D.C., Historical Section, Army Ground Forces, 1946.

C. Newspapers

Baltimore *Afro-American*, 1939–1947.

Pittsburgh *Courier*, 1939–1953.

Chicago *Defender*, 1940–1945.

Norfolk *Journal and Guide*, 1939–1952.

The New York Times, 1940–1953.

D. Personal Correspondence

Oscar R. Ewing to the author, July 22, 1964.

Thomas R. Reid to the author, February 15, 1965; April 1, 1965.

E. Interviews

James C. Evans. July, 1964, Washington, D.C.

Charles Fahy. August 10, 1964, Washington, D.C.

Philleo Nash. August 20, 1964, Washington, D.C.

F. Unpublished Studies

Alexander, Will W., "The Reminiscences of Will W. Alexander." Oral History Research Office, Columbia University.

Berman, William Carl, "The Politics of Civil Rights in the Truman Administration." Ph.D. dissertation, Ohio State University, 1963.

Bush, Charles R., "The Truman Civil Rights Program." Senior Honors thesis, Harvard University, 1964.

Byers, Jean, "A Study of the Negro in Military Service." Washington, D.C., Department of Defense, 1950. (Mimeographed.)

"The Colored Soldier in the U.S. Army: Prepared in the Historical Section, Army War College, May, 1942." Manuscript in the Office of the Chief of Military History.

Granger, Lester, "The Reminiscences of Lester B. Granger." Columbia University Oral History Collection, New York.

Kifer, Allen Francis, "The Negro Under the New Deal, 1933–1941." Ph.D. dissertation, University of Wisconsin, 1961.

Lawrence, Charles Radford, "Negro Organizations in Crisis: Depression, New Deal, World War II." Ph.D. dissertation, Columbia University, 1953.

Memorandum to Lieutenant Colonel Edward J. Barta from Professor Eli Ginzberg. Columbia University, no date.

Parrish, Colonel Noel F., "The Segregation of Negroes in the Army Air Forces." Air University thesis, Maxwell Field, Alabama, 1947.

Paszek, Lawrence J., "Negroes and the Air Force, 1939–1949." Paper read at the Southern Historical Association Meeting, November 12, 1964.

"Report on Gillem Board Policy and Implementation." Study in the records of the President's Committee on Equality of Treatment and Opportunity in the Armed Services, Harry S Truman Library, Independence, Missouri.

Schmidtlein, Eugene Francis, "Truman the Senator." Ph.D. dissertation, University of Missouri, 1962.

"United States Naval Administration in World War II, Bureau of Naval Personnel: The Negro in the Navy." Manuscript in the Bureau of Naval Personnel.

G. BOOKS

Bardolph, Richard, *The Negro Vanguard*. New York, Vintage Books, 1959.

Brink, William, and Louis Harris, *The Negro Revolution in America*. New York, Simon and Schuster, Inc., 1964.

——, *Black and White: A Study of U.S. Racial Attitudes Today*. New York, Simon and Schuster, Inc., 1967.

Brock, Clifton, *Americans for Democratic Action: Its Role in National Politics*. Washington, D.C., Public Affairs Press, 1962.

Broderick, Francis L., *W.E.B. DuBois: Negro Leader in a Time of Crisis*. Stanford, Stanford University Press, 1959.

Broom, Leonard, and Norval D. Glenn, *Transformation of the Negro American*. New York, Harper and Row, Publishers, 1965.

Bullard, General Robert Lee, *Personalities and Reminiscences of the War*. Garden City, N.Y., Doubleday, Page & Co., 1925.

Bush, Noel F., *Adlai E. Stevenson of Illinois: A Portrait*. New York, Farrar, Straus & Young, 1952.

Clark, General Mark W., *Calculated Risk*. New York, Harper & Brothers, 1950.

Cornish, Dudley Taylor, *The Sable Arm: Negro Troops in the Union Army, 1861–1865*. New York, Longmans, Green and Co., 1956.

Coser, Lewis, *The Functions of Social Conflict*. Glencoe, Illinois, The Free Press of Glencoe, Inc., 1956.

Daniels, Jonathan, *The Man of Independence*. Philadelphia, J. B. Lippincott Company, 1950.

Drake, St. Clair, and Horace R. Cayton, *Black Metropolis*. New York, Harcourt, Brace & Co., 1945.

Fehrenbach, T. R., *This Kind of War*. New York, The Macmillan Company, 1963.

Franklin, John Hope, *From Slavery to Freedom: A History of American Negroes*, 2d ed., rev. New York, Alfred A. Knopf, Inc., 1956.

Frazier, E. Franklin, *The Negro in the United States*, rev. ed. New York, The Macmillan Company, 1957.

Freidel, Frank, *F.D.R. and the South*. Baton Rouge, Louisiana State University Press, 1965.

Garfinkel, Herbert, *When Negroes March: The March on Washington Movement in the Organizational Politics of FEPC*. Glencoe, Illinois, The Free Press of Glencoe, Inc., 1959.

Ginzberg, Eli, and Douglas W. Bray, *The Uneducated*. New York, Columbia University Press, 1953.

Greenberg, Jack, *Race Relations and American Law*. New York, Columbia University Press, 1959.

Horton, David S., ed., *Freedom and Equality: Addresses by Harry S Truman*. Columbia, University of Missouri Press, 1960.

Isaacs, Harold R., *The New World of Negro Americans*. New York, Compass Books, 1963.

Johnson, Charles S., *To Stem This Tide: A Survey of Racial Tension Areas in the United States*. Boston, The Pilgrim Press, 1943.

Johnson, Walter, *1600 Pennsylvania Avenue: Presidents and the People Since 1929*. Boston, Little, Brown and Company, 1960.

Kesselman, Louis C., *The Social Politics of FEPC*. Chapel Hill, University of North Carolina Press, 1948.

Killian, Lewis M., and Charles Grigg, *Racial Crisis in America:*

Leadership in Conflict. Englewood Cliffs, N.J., Prentice-Hall, Inc., 1964.

Lee, Alfred McClung, and Norman D. Humphrey, *Race Riot*. New York, The Dryden Press, 1943.

Lee, Ulysses G., Jr., *The United States Army in World War II: Special Studies: The Employment of Negro Troops*. Washington, D.C., U.S. Government Printing Office, 1966.

Little, Arthur W., *From Harlem to the Rhine: The Story of New York's Colored Volunteers*. New York, Covici, Friede, Inc., 1936.

Litwack, Leon F., *North of Slavery: The Free Negro in the Free States, 1790–1860*. Chicago, University of Chicago Press, 1961.

Logan, Rayford W., *The Betrayal of the Negro: From Rutherford B. Hayes to Woodrow Wilson*. New York, Collier Books, 1965.

———, ed. *What the Negro Wants*. Chapel Hill, University of North Carolina Press, 1944.

Lomax, Louis E., *The Negro Revolt*. New York, Harper & Row, Publishers, 1962.

McPherson, James M., *The Negro's Civil War*. New York, Pantheon Books, Inc., 1965.

Meier, August, and Elliott M. Rudwick, *From Plantation to Ghetto: An Interpretative History of American Negroes*. New York, Hill & Wang, Inc., 1966.

Miller, Kelly, *The Everlasting Stain*. Washington, D.C., The Associated Publishers, 1924.

Milton, H.S., ed., *The Utilization of Negro Manpower in the Army*. Chevy Chase, Maryland, Operations Research Office, The Johns Hopkins University, 1955.

Moon, Henry Lee, *Balance of Power: The Negro Vote*. Garden City, N.Y., Doubleday & Company, Inc., 1948.

Murray, Florence, ed., *The Negro Handbook, 1942*. New York, Wendell Malliet and Company, 1942.

———, ed., *The Negro Handbook, 1946–1947*. New York, Current Books, 1947.

———, ed., *The Negro Handbook, 1949*. New York, The Macmillan Company, 1949.

Myrdal, Gunnar, *An American Dilemma: The Negro Problem and Modern Democracy*. New York, Harper & Brothers, 1944.

Nichols, Lee, *Breakthrough on the Color Front*. New York, Random House, Inc., 1954.

Odum, Howard W., *Race and Rumors of Race: Challenge to American Crisis*. Chapel Hill, University of North Carolina Press, 1943.

Ottley, Roi, *New World A-Coming*. Boston, Houghton Mifflin Company, 1943.

Phillips, Cabell, *The Truman Presidency*. New York, The Macmillan Company, 1966.

Powdermaker, Hortense, *After Freedom: A Cultural Study of the Deep South*. New York, The Viking Press, Inc., 1939.

The President's Commission on Higher Education, *Higher Education for American Democracy*. New York, Harper & Brothers, 1947.

Quarles, Benjamin, *The Negro in the American Revolution*. Chapel Hill, University of North Carolina Press, 1961.

——, *The Negro in the Civil War*. Boston, Little, Brown and Company, 1953.

Rose, Arnold M., *The Negro's Morale: Group Identification and Protest*. Minneapolis, University of Minnesota Press, 1949.

Ross, Malcolm, *All Manner of Men*. New York, Reynal & Hitchcock, 1948.

Ruchames, Louis, *Race, Jobs, and Politics*. New York, Columbia University Press, 1953.

Rudwick, Elliott M., *W.E.B. DuBois: A Study in Minority Group Leadership*. Philadelphia, University of Pennsylvania Press, 1960.

Schlesinger, Arthur M., Jr., *The Age of Roosevelt: The Politics of Upheaval*. Boston, Houghton Mifflin Company, 1960.

Scott, Emmett J., *The American Negro in the World War*. Chicago, Homewood Press, 1919.

Silberman, Charles E., *Crisis in Black and White*. New York, Random House, Inc., 1964.

Stallings, Laurence, *The Doughboys: The Story of the A. E. F., 1917–1918*. New York, Harper & Row, Publishers, 1963.

Steinberg, Alfred, *The Man From Missouri: The Life and Times of Harry S Truman*. New York, G. P. Putnam's Sons, 1962.

Stouffer, Samuel A., and others, *The American Soldier*. Princeton, Princeton University Press, 1949. 3 vols.

Tatum, Elbert Lee, *The Changed Political Thought of the Negro 1915–1940*. New York, Exposition Press, 1951.

Truman, Harry S, *Memoirs*. Garden City, N.Y., Doubleday & Company, Inc., 1955–1956. 2 vols.

Tumin, Melvin M., *Desegregation: Resistance and Readiness*. Princeton, Princeton University Press, 1958.

Wedlock, Lunnabelle, *The Reaction of Negro Publications and Organizations to German Anti-Semitism*. Washington, D.C., Howard University Press, 1942.

White, Walter, *A Man Called White.* New York, The Viking Press, Inc., 1948.

Wiley, Bell Irvin, *Southern Negroes: 1861–1865.* New Haven, Yale University Press, 1938.

Yinger, J. Milton, *A Minority Group in American Society.* New York, McGraw-Hill, Inc., 1965.

H. ARTICLES

"The Air Force Goes Interracial." *Ebony,* 4 (September, 1949), 15–18.

"American Nazism." *Opportunity,* 19 (February, 1941), 35.

Aptheker, Herbert, "The Negro in the Union Navy." *Journal of Negro History,* 32 (April, 1947), 169–200.

"Armed Service Jim Crow Policy Ends." *The Crisis,* 56 (May, 1949), 137.

Bernstein, Barton J., "The Truman Administration and the Steel Strike of 1946." *Journal of American History,* 52 (March, 1966), 791–803.

Bethune, Mary McLeod, "My Secret Talks with F.D.R." *Ebony,* 4 (April, 1949), 42–51.

Blumenthal, Henry, "Woodrow Wilson and the Race Question." *Journal of Negro History,* 48 (January, 1963), 1–21.

Bogart, Leo, "The Army and Its Negro Soldiers." *The Reporter,* 11 (December 30, 1954), 8–11.

Bond, Horace Mann, "The Negro in the Armed Forces of the United States Prior to World War I." *Journal of Negro Education,* 12 (Summer, 1943), 268–87.

——, "Should the Negro Care Who Wins the War." *The Annals of the American Academy of Social and Political Science,* 223 (September, 1942), 81–84.

Brearley, H. C., "The Negro's New Belligerency." *Phylon,* 5 (4th Quarter, 1944), 339–45.

Brecher, Ruth, and Edward, "The Military's Limited War Against Segregation." *Harper's Magazine,* 217 (September, 1963), 79–92.

Breckinridge, S. P., "The Winfred Lynn Case Again: Segregation in the Armed Forces." *Social Service Review,* 18 (September, 1944), 369–71.

Brown, Earl, "American Negroes and the War." *Harper's Magazine,* 184 (April, 1942), 545–52.

Brunson, Sergeant Warren T., "What a Negro Soldier Thinks About." *Social Service Review,* 18 (December, 1944), 534–35.

Bunche, Ralph J., "The Negro in the Political Life of the United States." *Journal of Negro Education*, 10 (July, 1941), 567–84.

Cayton, Horace R., "Fighting for White Folks?" *The Nation*, 155 (September 26, 1942), 267–70.

———, "Negro Morale." *Opportunity*, 19 (December, 1941), 371–75.

Clark, Kenneth B., "Morale Among Negroes," in Goodwin Watson, ed., *Civilian Morale*. Boston, Houghton Mifflin Company (1942), 228–48.

———, "Morale of the Negro on the Home Front: World Wars I and II." *Journal of Negro Education*, 12 (Summer, 1943), 417–28.

"Close Ranks." *The Crisis*, 16 (July, 1918), 111.

Collier, John, and Saul K. Padover, "An Institute for Ethnic Democracy." *Common Ground*, 4 (Autumn, 1943), 3–7.

"Colored Troops in Britain." *New Statesman and Nation*, 24 (August 22, 1942), 121.

Cornish, Dudley Taylor, "The Union Army as a School for Negroes." *Journal of Negro History*, 37 (October, 1952), 368–82.

"Crisis in the Making." *Newsweek*, 31 (June 7, 1948), 28–29.

Cushman, Robert E., "Our Civil Rights Become a World Issue." *The New York Times Magazine* (January 11, 1948), 12, 22–24.

Dabney, Virginius, "Nearer and Nearer the Precipice." *The Atlantic Monthly*, 171 (January, 1943), 94–100.

———, "Press and Morale." *Saturday Review of Literature*, 25 (July 4, 1942), 5–6, 24–25.

Dahrendorf, Ralf, "Out of Utopia: Toward a Reorientation of Sociological Analysis." *American Journal of Sociology*, 64 (September, 1958), 115–28.

Davis, John P., "The Negro in the Armed Forces of America," in John P. Davis, ed., *The American Negro Reference Book*. Englewood Cliffs, N.J., Prentice-Hall (1966), 590–661.

Davis, Ralph N., "The Negro Newspaper and the War." *Sociology and Social Research*, 27 (May, 1943), 373–80.

"Documents of the War." *The Crisis*, 18 (May, 1919), 16–21.

Dollard, Charles, and Donald Young, "In the Armed Forces." *Survey Graphic*, 36 (January, 1947), 66–68, 111–16.

DuBois, W.E.B., "The Black Man in the Revolution of 1914–1918." *The Crisis*, 17 (March, 1919), 218–23.

———, "An Essay Toward a History of the Black Man in the Great War." *The Crisis*, 18 (June, 1919), 63–87.

———, "The Negro Soldier in Service Abroad During the First

World War." *Journal of Negro Education*, 12 (Summer, 1943), 324–34.

Dwyer, Robert J., "The Negro in the United States Army: His Changing Role and Status." *Sociology and Social Research*, 38 (November, 1953), 103–12.

Erskine, Hazel, "The Polls: Race Relations." *Public Opinion Quarterly*, 26 (Spring, 1962), 137–48.

"The Fate of Democracy." *Opportunity*, 20 (January, 1942), 2.

"Fighting the Jim Crow Army." *The Crisis*, 55 (May, 1948), 136.

Foreman, Clark, "Race Tension in the South." *New Republic*, 107 (September 21, 1942), 340–42.

Foreman, Paul B., "The Implications of Project Clear." *Phylon*, 16 (September, 1955), 263–74.

Frazier, E. Franklin, "Ethnic and Minority Groups in Wartime." *American Journal of Sociology*, 48 (November, 1942), 369–77.

"Georgia's Vinson: Battling the Pentagon." *U.S. News and World Report*, 55 (September 30, 1963), 16.

Golightly, Cornelius L., "Negro Higher Education and Democratic Negro Morale." *Journal of Negro Education*, 11 (July, 1942), 322–28.

Goodman, George W., "The Englishman Meets the Negro." *Common Ground*, 5 (Autumn, 1944), 3–11.

"Government Blesses Segregation." *The Crisis*, 50 (April, 1943), 105.

Granger, Lester, "Barrier to Negro War Employment." *The Annals of the American Academy of Social and Political Science*, 223 (September, 1942), 72–80.

———, "Racial Democracy — The Navy Way." *Common Ground*, 7 (Winter, 1947), 61–68.

Graves, John Temple, "The Southern Negro and the War Crisis." *Virginia Quarterly Review*, 18 (Autumn, 1942), 500–517.

Greene, Lorenzo J., "Some Observations on the Black Regiment of Rhode Island in the American Revolution." *Journal of Negro History*, 37 (April, 1952), 142–72.

Grove, Gene, "The Army and the Negro." *The New York Times Magazine* (July 24, 1966), 4–5, 49–51.

Hall, E. T., Jr., "Prejudice and Negro-White Relations in the Army." *American Journal of Sociology*, 52 (March, 1947), 401–9.

Hastie, William H., "A Look at the NAACP." *The Crisis*, 46 (September, 1939), 263–64, 274.

———, "The Negro in the Army Today." *The Annals of the American Academy of Political and Social Science*, 223 (September, 1942), 55–59.

———, "Negro Officers in Two World Wars." *Journal of Negro Education*, 12 (Summer, 1943), 316–23.

Hausrath, Alfred H., "Utilization of Negro Manpower in the Army." *Journal of the Operations Research Society of America*, 2 (February, 1954), 17–30.

Henderson, Donald, "Minority Response and the Conflict Model." *Phylon*, 25 (1st Quarter, 1964), 18–26.

High, Stanley, "How the Negro Fights for Freedom." *The Reader's Digest*, 41 (July, 1942), 113–18.

Hoffman, Edwin D., "The Genesis of the Modern Movement for Equal Rights in South Carolina, 1930–1939." *Journal of Negro History*, 44 (October, 1959), 346–69.

Hughes, Everett C., "Race Relations and the Sociological Imagination." *American Sociological Review*, 28 (December, 1963), 879–90.

Jackson, Luther P., "Virginia Negro Soldiers and Seamen in the American Revolution." *Journal of Negro History*, 27 (July, 1942), 247–87.

Johnson, Charles S., "The Negro and the Present Crisis." *Journal of Negro Education*, 10 (July, 1941), 585–95.

Johnson, Guion Griffis, "The Impact of War Upon the Negro." *Journal of Negro Education*, 10 (July, 1941), 596–611.

Jones, Lester M., "The Editorial Policy of the Negro Newspapers of 1917–1918 as Compared with That of 1941–42." *Journal of Negro History*, 29 (January, 1944), 24–31.

Jones, William, "Trade Boycotts." *Opportunity*, 18 (August, 1940), 238–41.

Julian, Joseph, "Jim Crow Goes Abroad." *The Nation*, 155 (December 5, 1942), 610–12.

Kenworthy, E. W., "The Case Against Army Segregation." *The Annals of the American Academy of Political and Social Science*, 275 (May, 1951), 27–33.

———, "Taps for Jim Crow in the Services." *The New York Times Magazine* (June 11, 1950), 12, 24–27.

Lee, Alfred M., "Subversive Individuals of Minority Status." *The Annals of the American Academy of Political and Social Science*, 223 (September, 1942), 167–68.

Leiser, Ernest, "For Negroes It's a New Army Now." *The Saturday Evening Post*, 225 (December 13, 1952), 26–27, 108, 110–12.

Lewis, Roscoe E., "The Role of Pressure Groups in Maintaining Morale Among Negroes." *Journal of Negro Education*, 12 (Summer, 1943), 464–73.

Lockard, Metz T.P., "Negroes and Defense." *The Nation*, 152 (January 4, 1941), 14–16.

Lohman, Joseph D., and Dietrich C. Reitzes, "Note on Race Relations in a Mass Society." *American Journal of Sociology*, 63 (November, 1957), 240–46.

Long, Howard H., "The Negro Soldier in the Army of the United States." *Journal of Negro Education*, 12 (Summer, 1943), 307–15.

MacDonald, Dwight, "The Novel Case of Winfred Lynn." *The Nation*, 156 (February 20, 1943), 263–70.

———, "The Supreme Court's New Moot Suit." *The Nation*, 159 (July 1, 1944), 13–14.

Mack, Raymond W., "The Components of Social Conflict." *Social Problems*, 12 (Spring, 1965), 388–97.

McWhirter, William A., "The National Guard — Awake or Asleep?" *Life*, 63 (October 27, 1967), 85–98.

McWilliams, Carey, "Race Tensions: Second Phase." *Common Ground*, 4 (Autumn, 1943), 7–12.

Martin, Harold H., "How Do Our Negro Troops Measure Up?" *The Saturday Evening Post*, 223 (June 16, 1951), 30–31, 139, 141.

Milner, Lucille B., "Jim Crow in the Army." *New Republic*, 110 (March 13, 1944), 339–42.

Morrow, E. Frederick, "Southern Exposure." *The Crisis*, 46 (July, 1939), 202, 210.

Moskos, Charles C., Jr., "Racial Integration in the Armed Forces." *American Journal of Sociology*, 72 (September, 1966), 132–48.

Mueller, William R., "The Negro in the Navy." *Social Forces*, 24 (October, 1945), 110–15.

"Nazi Plan for Negroes Copies Southern U.S.A." *The Crisis*, 48 (March, 1941), 71.

A Negro Enlisted Man, "Jim Crow in the Army Camps." *The Crisis*, 47 (December, 1940), 385.

"The Negro and Nazism." *Opportunity*, 18 (July, 1940), 194–95.

"The Negro in the United States Army." *The Crisis*, 49 (February, 1942), 47.

"The Negro's War." *Fortune*, 25 (June, 1942), 77–80, 157–58, 160, 162.

Newton, Isham G., "The Negro in the National Guard." *Phylon*, 23 (1st Quarter, 1962), 18–28.

"Now is the Time Not to Be Silent." *The Crisis*, 49 (January, 1942), 7.

Ottley, Roi, "Negro Morale." *New Republic*, 105 (November 10, 1941), 613–15.

————, "A White Folk's War." *Common Ground*, 2 (Spring, 1942), 28–31.

Park, Robert E., "Racial Ideologies," in William F. Ogburn, ed. *American Society During Wartime*. Chicago, University of Chicago Press, 1943 (165–84).

"The Pattern of Race Riots Involving Negro Soldiers." *A Monthly Summary of Events and Trends in Race Relations*, 2 (August–September, 1944), 15–18.

Peck, James L. H., "When Do We Fly?" *The Crisis*, 47 (December, 1940), 376–78, 388.

"The Pentagon Jumps into the Race Fight." *U.S. News and World Report*, 55 (August 19, 1963), 49–50.

Pfautz, Harold W., "The 'New Negro': Emerging American." *Phylon*, 24 (4th Quarter, 1963), 360–68.

"A Philosophy in Time of War." *The Crisis*, 16 (August, 1918), 164.

Powell, Adam Clayton, Jr., "Is This a White Man's War?" *Common Sense*, 11 (April, 1942), 11–113.

Prattis, P.L., "The Morale of the Negro in the Armed Services of the United States." *Journal of Negro Education*, 12 (Summer, 1943), 355–63.

Quarles, Benjamin, "The Colonial Militia and Negro Manpower." *Mississippi Valley Historical Review*, 45 (March, 1959), 643–52.

Reddick, L. D., "The Negro Policy of the American Army Since World War II." *Journal of Negro History*, 38 (April, 1953), 194–215.

————, "The Negro Policy of the United States Army, 1775–1945." *Journal of Negro History*, 34 (January, 1949), 9–29.

Reitzes, Dietrich C., "Institutional Structure and Race Relations." *Phylon*, 20 (1st Quarter, 1959), 48–66.

"Returning Soldiers." *The Crisis*, 18 (May, 1919), 13–14.

Reynolds, Grant, "A Triumph for Civil Disobedience." *The Nation*, 167 (August 28, 1948), 228–29.

"The Roosevelt Record." *The Crisis*, 47 (September, 1940), 343.

Rutherford, William A., "Jim Crow: A Problem in Diplomacy." *The Nation*, 175 (November 8, 1952), 428–29.

Salmond, John A., "The Civilian Conservation Corps and the Negro." *Journal of American History*, 52 (June, 1965), 75–88.

Sancton, Thomas, "Something's Happened to the Negro." *New Republic*, 118 (February 8, 1943), 175–79.

Schuler, Edgar A., "The Houston Race Riot, 1917." *Journal of Negro History*, 24 (July, 1944), 301–38.

240 DESEGREGATION OF THE U.S. ARMED FORCES

Schuyler, George S., "A Long War Will Aid the Negro." *The Crisis*, 50 (November, 1943), 328–29, 344.

Shannon, Fred A., "The Federal Government and the Negro Soldier, 1861–1865." *Journal of Negro History*, 11 (October, 1926), 563–83.

"Snow Cleaners, Cotton Pickers." *The Crisis*, 50 (March, 1943), 72.

Thompson, Charles H., "The American Negro and National Defense." *Journal of Negro Education*, 9 (October, 1940), 547–52.

———, "Negro Morale and World War II." *Journal of Negro Education*, 11 (January, 1942), 1–3.

Thornbrough, Emma Lou, "The Brownsville Episode and the Negro Vote." *Mississippi Valley Historical Review*, 44 (December, 1957), 469–93.

Tindall, George B., "The Significance of Howard W. Odum to Southern History: A Preliminary Estimate." *Journal of Southern History*, 24 (August, 1958), 285–307.

Toppin, Edgar A., "Humbly They Served: The Black Brigade in the Defense of Cincinnati." *Journal of Negro History*, 48 (April, 1963), 75–97.

Tumin, Melvin, "The Functionalist Approach to Social Problems." *Social Problems*, 12 (Spring, 1965), 379–88.

"The Turning of the Tide." *The Crisis*, 15 (December, 1917), 77.

"U.S.A. Needs a Sharp Break With the Past." *The Crisis*, 49 (May, 1942), 151.

"Wallace's Southern Tour." *The Crisis*, 55 (October, 1948), 297.

"We are Accused of Inciting to Riot and Being Traitors." *The Crisis*, 49 (June, 1942), 183.

Weaver, Robert C., "Defense Industries and the Negro." *The Annals of the American Academy of Social and Political Science*, 223 (September, 1942), 60–66.

———, "Racial Employment Trends in National Defense." *Phylon*, 2 (4th Quarter, 1941), 337–58.

Welliver, Warman, "Report on the Negro Soldier." *Harper's Magazine*, 192 (April, 1946), 333–39.

"Where the Negro Stands." *Opportunity*, 19 (April, 1941), 98.

White, Walter, "It's Our Country, Too: The Negro Demands the Right to be Allowed to Fight for It." *The Saturday Evening Post*, 213 (December 14, 1940), 27, 61, 63, 66, 68.

Williams, Robin M., Jr., "Social Change and Social Conflict: Race Relations in the United States, 1944–1964." *Sociological Inquiry*, 35 (Winter, 1965), 8–25.

Wilson, Walter, "Old Jim Crow in Uniform." *The Crisis*, 46 (February, 1939), 42–44; (March, 1939), 71–73, 82, 93.
Wirth, Louis, "Morale and Minority Groups." *American Journal of Sociology*, 47 (November, 1941), 415–33.
Young, Whitney M., Jr., "When the Negroes in Vietnam Come Home." *Harper's Magazine*, 234 (June, 1967), 63–69.

Index

Adkins, Homer M., 49

Advisory Committee on Negro Troop Policies. *See* McCloy Committee

Agriculture, Department of, 36, 143

Afro-Americans. *See* various entries under Negro

Air Force: exclusion of Negroes from, 23, 26, 28–29, 39–40; Negro pilots in, 28–29, 39–40, 47–48, 84, 86, 103; acceptance of Negroes in, 29, 39–41; opposition to integration in, 29, 178–80; segregation in, 30, 45–46, 60, 61, 84–86; assignment policy of, 61, 86; Negro officers in, 65, 67, 84–86; integration of, 159, 175, 177–78, 183, 186, 195, 201–22, 208

Alexander, Will, 40–41, 123*n*70

Allen, George E., 144

Allied Committees on National Defense, 115–16, 117*n*46

Almond, Edward M., 206

American Legion, 50, 78, 133

American Revolution: Negroes' activities in, 5–6

American Sociological Society: and interest in Negro Revolution, 105

Army: segregation in, 1, 3–5, 22–23, 26–27, 30, 37–40, 44–47, 65, 72, 78–79, 81, 104, 160, 162, 165–66, 172, 177, 179–83, 186, 188–95, 199–201, 206, 214, 216–18; relations with Negro civilians, 1, 9–10, 26–28, 37, 45–46, 55, 74–75, 78, 82–83, 85–87, 120, 133, 153; assignment and training of Negro soldiers, 5, 12, 13, 18–19, 23, 28, 37, 39, 41, 44–46, 49–50, 58–59, 60–62, 66, 69–73, 82–83, 85–88, 92–97, 99–104, 150–52, 187–88, 190–98, 203–4, 206–8, 214; racism in, 13, 16, 17, 24, 57, 67–68, 73, 77, 148, 188–89; quota system for enlistment, 23–24, 38, 44–46, 50–53, 59–62, 66, 90–91, 96, 150–51, 187–88, 190-94, 196–98, 202–3, 207, 209; integration in, 46, 48, 61–62, 88–89, 99–101, 197, 200–205, 207–8, 210, 212–15, 218–19. *See also* Fahy Committee; Gillem Board; Korean War; National Guard; Selective Service; Vietnam War; World War I; World War II

Army Air Corps. *See* Air Force

Army General Classification Test: Negro scores on, 56–59, 62, 70, 72, 91, 97, 149

Roosevelt, 87; support of use of Negro Combat Units by, 95; changing attitude toward Negro soldier, 104

McCloy Committee: formation and composition of, 83; ineffectiveness of, 86–88; and Civilian Aide to the Secretary of War, 86, 88, 149; achievements of, 87; and Negro press, 88; support of integration of facilities on military posts by, 88–89; recommendation to use Negro combat units, 93, 95–96; recommendation to study Negro soldier for post-World War II Army, 104

McGrath, J. Howard, 173–74
McKissick, Floyd, 224
McNamara, Robert, 222
McNarney, Joseph T., 149
McNutt, Paul V., 90
Magnuson, Warren G., 208n22
March on Washington Movement (MOWM), 115–23
Marine Corps, 26, 53, 55, 180, 195
Marshall, George C., 46–47, 48, 50, 61, 95
Marshall, S. L. A., 205–6
Marshall, Thurgood, 207
Maybank, Burnet R., 167, 173
Maxwell Field, Alabama, 67
Meier, August, 122
Memphis, Tennessee, 10, 28
Miller, Kelly, 10
Minton, Sherman, 30
Mobile, Alabama, 10
Mollison, Irvin C., 143
Monroe, Georgia, 134, 144
Montgomery, Alabama, 67
Morse, David A., 146
Morse, Wayne, 164
Moton, Robert R., 18, 21
Murphy, Charles G., 146
Muse, Benjamin, 221n3
Myrdal, Gunnar, 106, 115

Nash, Philleo, 134n7, 170, 194
National Association for the Advancement of Colored People (NAACP): during World War I, 8, 11–12, 21; and Franklin D. Roosevelt, 33, 43, 103; during World War II, 48, 74, 82, 86, 109, 123; attitude toward protest movements, 103, 116–17, 123, 125, 165, 169; and Truman, 135, 144, 163, 168; and Korean War, 207
National Guard: exclusion of Negroes from, 28, 62; integration in, 35, 159–62, 223; Negro officers in, 39, 65; relations with Army, 159, 161; segregation in, 220, 222–23; relations with Federal Government, 222–23
National Bar Association, 28
National Colored Democratic Association, 136
National Defense Act of 1940, 30–31
National Defense Establishment, 177
National Emergency Committee Against Mob Violence, 145
National Labor Relations Act, 118
National Military Establishment, 185
National Negro Defense Sunday, 116
National Negro Insurance Association, 28
National Opinion Research Center, 138
National Urban League, 102, 112, 117, 125, 152, 176
National Youth Administration, 35, 37
Naval Academy, 30
Naval war with France: Negroes' service in, 6
Navy: discrimination against Negro sailors, 22, 26, 28, 29–30, 34,